The Bedroom and the State

THE BEDROOM AND THE STATE:
The Changing Practices and Politics of Contraception and Abortion in Canada, 1880-1980

Angus McLaren and Arlene Tigar McLaren

McClelland and Stewart

McClelland and Stewart Limited
The Canadian Publishers
481 University Avenue
Toronto, Ontario
M5G 2E9

Canadian Cataloguing in Publication Data
McLaren, Angus.
    The bedroom and the state

(The Canadian social history series)
Includes bibliographical references and index.
ISBN 0-7710-5532-3

1. Contraception – Canada – History. 2. Birth control
– Canada – History. 3. Abortion – Canada – History.
I. McLaren, Arlene Tigar. II. Title. III. Series.

HQ766.5.C3M24 1986   363.9′6′0971   C86-093392-X

Printed and bound in Canada by Webcom

Contents

Acknowledgements

We would like to thank the following for their comments and suggestions: Margaret Andrews, Paul Bator, David Bercuson, Mary Bishop, Alan Brookes, Suzann Buckley, Terry Chapman, Ramsay Cook, Donna Dippie, Michael Fellman, Anita Claire Fellman, Chad Gaffield, Ellen Gee, Gene Homel, Susan Houston, Debra Ireland, Greg Kealey, Linda Kealey, Jane Lewis, Ian MacPherson, Janice Dickin McGinnis, Wendy Mitchinson, Joy Parr, Alison Prentice, James Reed, Jean-Claude Robert, Joan Sangster, Phyllis Sherrin, Edward Shorter, Ely Silverman, James Snell, Susan Mann Trofimenkoff, Rennie Warburton, and Donald Wilson. Brian Dippie, Lesley Biggs, and Veronica Strong-Boag read the entire manuscript and offered valuable criticisms. We were able to carry out the research for this study as a result of grants from the University of Victoria and the Social Sciences and Humanities Research Council of Canada, for which we are greatly appreciative. Time for writing was made available by the Hannah Institute for the History of Medicine, which generously supported Angus McLaren as a Visiting Professor of the History of Medicine at the University of Toronto. Office space was kindly made available to him by the Institute for the History and Philosophy of Science and Technology at the University of Toronto, and for Arlene Tigar McLaren by the Ontario Institute for Studies in Education.

Enormous help was offered us by the staffs of the Public Archives of Canada, the Provincial Archives of British Columbia, Alberta, Ontario, and Saskatchewan, the City Archives of Vancouver, Edmonton, and Toronto, the Hamilton Public Library, the Archives of the Archbishopric of St. Boniface, the United Church of Canada Archives, the University of Toronto Archives, the Special Collections Library of the University of British Columbia, the Planned Parenthood Associations of Manitoba, Ontario, and Toronto, the Hamilton Birth Control Society, the Sophia Smith Collection of Smith College, the Houghton Library of Harvard University, the Countway Library of Medicine in Boston, Massachusetts, the Contemporary Medical Archives Centre at the Wellcome Institute for the History of Medicine in London, England, the Social Welfare History Archives at the University of Minnesota, the British

Library, and the Library of Congress.

Some of the material contained in this book first appeared in a different form in *Histoire sociale/Social History*, the *Canadian Historical Review*, the *Journal of Canadian Studies*, and *B.C. Studies*; we wish to thank the editors and publishers for permission to reprint this material.

This book has been published with the help of a grant from the Social Science Federation of Canada, using funds provided by the Social Sciences and Humanities Research Council of Canada.

Finally, we wish to acknowledge the indispensable aid of those who typed various versions of the manuscript – Vicky Barath, June Belton, Dinah Dickie, and Gloria Orr.

Introduction

In 1892 John Charlton, MP for North Norfolk, rose in the House of Commons to insist that something be done to prevent Canada from being flooded with birth control material.

> Vile literature is secretly and widely circulated in Canada, literature of a character calculated to undermine the morals of the people, and entail the most disastrous consequences on society. Improper and obscene, or semi-obscene literature is imported into this country and openly sold. Drugs and instruments for procuring abortion and for kindred purposes are advertised secretly and are sold by agents, and this abuse cannot very readily be reached by the law as it now stands.[1]

No one countered Charlton's sensational assertions. Subsection 179c of the 1892 Criminal Code consequently made it an indictable offence to "offer to sell, advertise, publish an advertisement of or have for sale or disposal any medicine, drug or article intended or represented as a means of preventing conception or causing abortion."[2] By defining both contraceptives and abortifacients as obscene, Canada armed itself with a law code less liberal than that of Great Britain and close in spirit to the notorious Comstock laws of the United States. Only in 1969 was the Canadian Criminal Code amended so that the provision of contraceptives ceased to be illegal. The law was also reformed to allow medically approved abortions to be carried out in hospitals. In defending these sections of the 1967 omnibus bill introduced to overhaul the statute books, Pierre Trudeau made what might well remain his best-known assertion: "The state has no business in the bedrooms of the nation."[3] But though the reforms of the 1960's seemed daring at the time, there was reason to wonder whether they made much difference. The Canadian birth rate had, of course, been falling for most of the twentieth century – even in advance of a birth control movement – and the amendments of 1969 thus stand as classic examples of changes in the law tardily following changes in social behaviour.

The lowering of the birth rate was arguably the most important social shift to occur in Canada in this century. The study that follows is the first book-length analysis of this phenomenon. For many, such an account should be a triumphant story of enlightened propagandists beating back the forces of ignorance and winning public acceptance for family planning. That will not be the approach adopted in this study. The working premise of this book is that the decline in Canadian fertility was inextricably entangled in a web of social, sexual, and cultural relationships. To understand why ordinary men and women sought to limit their reproduction and how public figures sought to turn such private concerns to political purposes it is necessary to locate the birth control debate in its social context. In so doing it becomes obvious that the doctors and priests, eugenicists and feminists, politicians and labour leaders who entered the discussion were more concerned by the broader issues of sexual, social, and political power than by the issue of family size. Would birth control, they asked, improve the race? dampen social discontent? emancipate women? strengthen labour? improve marriage? enrich the nation? The questions and answers changed over time.

This book necessarily parallels in a number of ways the pioneering studies of abortion and birth control in America.[4] James Mohr explained how and why nineteenth- and twentieth-century abortion laws came into being. James Reed traced the campaign of feminists, physicians, and philanthropists to make birth control respectable in the United States. Linda Gordon tracked the shifts of the leadership of the birth control movement from American middle-class women at the turn of the century to health professionals in the 1930's and 1940's. Our book differs from theirs, not just because the Canadian experience differed from the American, but because we have attempted to present, in addition to a history of reproductive policies, an intimate portrayal of the reproductive decision-making of ordinary men and women.

Having stated what this book will attempt to do, it is important to make it clear what it will not do. At the outset it must be stressed that although we employ demographic material we are interested primarily in private and public power struggles over control of fertility. We have adopted a qualitative rather than a quantitative approach. Second, the materials we have unearthed pertain mainly to English-speaking, Protestant, urban Canada. Much skilful work has been carried out on Quebec's demographic past, but as we will indicate in Chapter Six the analysis of the fertility debate in francophonia has only just begun. Even less is known about developments in the Maritimes. Because of the limitations of documentation and the variegated nature of Canadian society, each region cannot be given equal treatment. A last caveat has to be made concerning the time period covered. Although we have assumed a thematic rather than a chronological approach, our account deals mainly with the first round in the Canadian birth control debate, which took place between the wars. We could only begin to analyse the second round, which was precipitated by the 1969 reforms and continues to rage today. This study will serve some purpose if, by placing the current discussion in its historical and social context, it indicates the complexities of the issues involved.

The actual raw data on twentieth-century fertility can be given at the outset.[5] Demographers tell us that Canadian fertility had begun its long-term decline by at least the mid-nineteenth century and dropped approximately 30 per cent between 1851 and 1891. The fall was offset to an extent at the turn of the century by the arrival of the prolific immigrants of southern and eastern Europe. This pause in the drop of the birth rate was a unique Canadian phenomenon, but following World War I the country's rapid fertility decline – particularly marked in the 1920's – matched that of other Western nations. Despite the fact that couples were marrying earlier and in slightly higher proportions, completed family size fell from 4.1 children for parents born in 1871 to 2.9 children for parents born in 1911. The crude birth rate (the number of births per 1,000 population) slumped from the high thirties in the nineteenth century to 29.3 in 1921 and to an unprecedented low of 20.3 in 1936. These gross figures masked striking religious, regional, and ethnic fertility differentials. At the start of the century the average family size in rural, French, Catholic Quebec and New Brunswick was twice that in urban, English, Protestant Ontario and British Columbia. But no group, by the 1920's, was immune to falling natality; the population question had forced itself onto the national agenda.

This decline in Canadian fertility, a host of commentators warned, threatened the nation with "race suicide." Doctors who could have been expected to best understand the subject proved, because of their professional caution, among the most vociferous opponents of artificial restriction of family size. Such restriction was condemned by those who took birth control to be both a cause and effect of the modern threats of urbanization, rural depopulation, alien immigration, and feminism. In fact, as we show in Chapters One and Two, contraception and abortion were both being employed early in the nineteenth century. The onset of the reduction of fertility did not have to await the modernization associated with the industrializing world of the 1900's. It is true, however, that the masses did not have access to totally effective and reliable forms of birth control. Limitation of births was often only accomplished at the expense of marital happiness or women's health.

Why were more and more Canadians employing means to restrict fertility? At the turn of the century the extension of compulsory education and the restriction of child labour were no doubt key variables inasmuch as they increased the costs of having children and limited the economic contribution they could make to the household; also important were the rise in non-domestic work for women, the shift in emphasis in the role of the mother from child-bearer to child-rearer, and the transition in the idealized image of the family from the patriarchal to the companionate. The 1920's and 1930's saw a continued reduction of the birth rate explained by those impressed by the myth of the "Roaring Twenties" by reference to sexual licence, affluence, and permissiveness. The actual motives of typical couples attempting to survive the Great Depression appear to have been more mundane. Family limitation was adopted to protect the family, not to undermine it. The first two chapters seek to explain how ordinary people employed contraception and abortion in response to their perceived need to restrict fertility.

The essential "problem" holding back the successful advocacy of birth control in the first decades of the twentieth century was the fact that it was associated in the public mind either with sexual radicals on the far left or with reactionary Malthusians on the far right. Marie Stopes in Britain and Margaret Sanger in America in effect "rescued" birth control from such connections and made it publicly acceptable as a creed. These two dynamic women – feminists inasmuch as they viewed birth control as first and foremost a woman's right – began the process of making contraception morally safe by arguing that it alone permitted the sexual enjoyment and emotional fulfilment that were necessary for stable family life. Many Canadians responded warmly to such an appeal, but as we show in Chapter Three Canada did not produce any feminist birth controller of equal stature. The main women's groups kept their distance from the public campaign for contraception. It was left to a small number of socialists on the West Coast to launch the first Canadian birth control movement of which Stopes and Sanger were in effect the godmothers.

Since conservatives condemned birth control and some prominent socialists defended it, an association of sexual and social radicalism developed in the early twentieth century. In Chapter Four we examine the relationship of the population issue to politics and show how it is necessary to sort out the conflicting motivations and behaviours that Canadian socialists demonstrated when they entered the birth control debate. On the one hand, they were wary of taking the population question too seriously for fear that in so doing they would be capitulating to the hoary old Malthusian argument that social improvement could only be attained by restriction of births. On the other hand, the left was drawn to birth control for the simple reason that it promised some immediate improvement in maternal health and some protection of the fragile, working-class family economy.

Birth control only became respectable and won the support of "financial angels" in the 1930's. The depression and the spectres of working-class unrest and racial degeneration that it conjured up goaded eugenically minded businessmen, club women, academics, and clergymen into supporting a campaign aimed at lowering the fertility of the working class. By the mid-1930's the fertility rate was, as we already noted, at its lowest level in history. The burden of the argument of Chapter Five is that the elaboration by A.R. Kaufman of a uniquely Canadian distribution system of contraceptives and the 1937 legal victory that legitimated his activities marked the successful co-optation of the birth control movement by social conservatives.

The Quebec birth rate fell, we argue in Chapter Six, not as a result of the activities of outside birth controllers such as Kaufman, but in response to social shifts in the province. The decline in francophone fertility in turn permitted the federal government finally to broach the issue of family planning without appearing to favour one region over another. The period from World War II to the creation in 1972 of the Family Planning Division of the Department of Health and Welfare witnessed the shift of responsibility for birth control from voluntary associations to the public sector. Why? Because both the post-war baby boom and the spectre of the "population explosion" in the Third World meant that birth control was now viewed by government as an important instrument of policy. A consumer-oriented society in which women's participation in the work force was required after marriage lent further support to the argument that reliable contraception was a necessity. And, finally, a technological breakthrough was accomplished with the "pill." This meant that doctors would now interest themselves in the subject of contraception because it was scientifically respectable. The fact that "birth control" was now known as "planned parenthood" was a sign that the movement eschewed any early radicalism and sought to present itself as serving family needs. The fertility rate, which had climbed back up from a low of 20.3 per 1,000 in 1936 to a high of 28.0 in 1956, began an unexpected slide and plummeted after 1959 to depths even lower than those reached in the worst years of the depression. In 1976 it was at 15.7 for the nation as a whole; it was even lower in Quebec, where between 1957 and 1971 it had been cut by more than 50 per cent. The old fertility differentials that had so terrorized Anglo-Saxons at the beginning of the century had all but disappeared.

But if the fertility differentials have declined the emotions raised by the discussions of birth control and abortion in Canada have not. In analysing why in past decades some wanted birth control information and others either sought to provide or withhold it, we hope to produce a better understanding of the forces that shaped contemporary attitudes toward abortion and contraception. Birth control is still a vital issue, we believe, because it concerns not simply the number of children born, but the shifting power relationships of the sexes and the classes.

PART I

Women's Struggle To Limit Their Fertility

1

Contraceptive Practices in Canada

In the spring of 1908 the congregation of Toronto's St. James' Cathedral was informed by the Reverend C. Ensor Sharp that the Almighty interested himself directly in the demographic details of Canada's declining birth rate.

> God abhors the spirit so prevalent nowadays which contemns [*sic*] motherhood. How it must grieve Him when He sees what we call race suicide; when He sees the problem of married life approached lightly and wantonly; based on nothing higher and nobler than mere luxury and gratification of passion.[1]

This fear of "race suicide" to which Sharp referred had been popularized in North America by President Theodore Roosevelt, who stated, "The woman who flinches from childbirth stands on a par with the soldier who drops his rifle and runs in battle." This was only the most famous remark to be made by a generation of social observers who attributed the shrinking size of the Anglo-Saxon family to the "selfishness" of women. By the turn of the century Canadians were well acquainted with such concerns. In the Canadian edition of Sylvanus Stall's *What a Young Man Ought to Know* (1897) the author expressed his horrors that many women married, not to bear children, but "for the purpose of practically leading a life of legalized prostitution . . . ."[2] Crown Attorney

J.W. Curry, KC, addressing the city pastors of Toronto in 1901, claimed that employment opportunities permitted women to avoid marriage or to fall back on "crime," which led to a "low birth rate."[3] According to Professor H.E. Armstrong, speaking at the 1909 Winnipeg meeting of the British Association, all attempts to bring women into competition with men were dangerous, "for she will inevitably cease to exercise her specific womanly functions with effect, so delicate is the adjustment of her mechanism."[4] A contributor to the *Canadian Churchman* (1900) went so far as to assert that even the pressures of existing society encouraged, "to put it bluntly, in nine cases out of ten, women to murder their unborn children . . . ."[5]

What exercised the imaginations of these writers was the belief that women were responsible for the fall in marital fertility. In fact, this fall was only a symptom of the major social and economic transformations Canada was undergoing at the turn of the century. Later commentators were to speak of the confidence and optimism of the age, but any examination of the population discussion uncovers many expressions of fear and foreboding. What had been a rural, agrarian society was becoming an urbanized, increasingly industrialized community. These shifts, though only partly understood at the time, were seen as posing major dangers. The population increased from 4.3 million in 1881 to 8.5 million in 1920, yet much of this growth was due to foreign immigration. In 1871, 60 per cent of the population had been of British stock; in 1921, only 40 per cent. Could the new arrivals be Canadianized or would they overwhelm the young nation? The population, moreover, was increasingly drawn to the cities. By 1921 the dividing line was reached when over half of all Canadians were urban dwellers.

It was commonly held that city life was inherently anonymous and immoral and the question was posed if it would succeed in undermining the virtues of rural newcomers. And the virtue of young women was felt to be particularly at risk. By 1921 there were 58,000 more women than men in the cities. The largest contingent of these "surplus" women were in the fifteen-to-twenty-nine age group. This imbalance was due in part to the new employment opportunities offered women in textile mills, tobacco companies, food processing plants, retail stores, and personal service. In 1896 women made up 20 per cent of the active work force; by 1931, 25 per cent.[6] The vast majority of these women would eventually leave their jobs, marry, and raise families, but the anxious expressed their concern that these women would have already formed tastes and habits of independence that would render them unfit to raise the traditionally large family. Middle-class women, on the other hand, were accused of restricting family size simply out of a desire for greater luxury and self-indulgence.

The decline in Canadian fertility was broadly similar to that of other Western nations. This "fertility transition," as demographers call it, entailed the replacement of a society with high birth and death rates by a society with low birth and death rates. Death rates tended to fall sooner, producing the population surge of the nineteenth century. The decline of the birth rate brought the demographic system back into equilibrium. But whereas the lowering of mortality was regarded by most as a natural result of progress, many regarded the lowering of fertility as "unnatural." The same fears of race suicide were voiced in Britain and the United States, but in Canada the anxieties of the middle-class English were exacerbated at the beginning of our period by both the fertility of the Irish and Quebec's successful "revanche des berceaux," and later by the influx of non-British migration. In an article on "The Canadian Immigration Policy," W.S. Wallace, a future editor of the *Canadian Historical Review*, warned,

> The native-born population, in the struggle to keep up appearances in the face of the increasing competition, fails to propagate itself, commits race suicide, in short, whereas the immigrant population, being inferior, and having no appearances to keep up, propagates itself like the fish of the sea.[7]

And turning to the threat of eventual Catholic domination the Anglican *Canadian Churchman* bemoaned the fact that, "As France is to Germany, so seemingly is Ontario to Quebec...." Such attempts by the Protestant churches in Canada to wake the populace to the perils of the situation won the applause of Lydia Kingsmill Commander in *The American Idea, Does the National Tendency Toward a Small Family Point to Race Suicide or Race Degeneration?* (1907). "The French Canadians alone," she informed her readers, "being devout Roman Catholics, primitive and simple-minded, and given to agricultural pursuits are extremely prolific."[8]

As bizarre as these outbursts might first appear, they are nevertheless noteworthy because they point to one of the major social phenomena of Canadian history that has yet to be carefully examined – the decline of the birth rate. The most dramatic decline took place in Ontario, falling by 44 per cent between 1871 and 1901; from 1881 to 1911, Ontario had the lowest fertility of any province. Even Quebec's general fertility rate dropped by 21 per cent between 1851 and 1921 while that of Canada as a whole fell by 41 per cent.[9] (See Table 1.)

TABLE 1
General Fertility Rates, Canada and Selected Provinces, 1871 to 1931
(annual number of births per 1,000 women aged 15-49 years)

Year	Canada	Nova Scotia	Quebec	Ontario	Manitoba	Saskat-chewan	B.C.
1871	189	174	180	191	–	–	–
1881	160	148	173	149	366	–	202
1891	144	138	163	121	242	–	204
1901	145	132	160	108	209	550	184
1911	144	128	161	112	167	229	149
1921	120	105	155	98	125	135	84
1931	94	98	116	79	81	100	62

SOURCE: Jacques Henripin, *Trends and Factors of Fertility in Canada* (Ottawa, 1972), p. 21.

Despite relatively stable marriage rates and improving fecundity, the birth rate of English-speaking families fell; hence, some form of birth control must have been used. Discovering exactly what form is a problem.[10] Traditional histories of birth control assume that the decline of fertility in the late nineteenth century in Europe and North America was due to the diffusion of some new knowledge or technique. It has to be recalled, however, that there were several traditional methods already available. To space births Canadian families had long relied on simple continence and the margin of safety from conception provided when a woman was nursing.[11] In addition, two major methods of family restriction were to be used well into the twentieth century – coitus interruptus and self-induced abortion.

Abortion was to be of special importance. At a time when withdrawal was the most widely used method of contraception – and all studies show that this was the case in Europe and North America until at least the 1930's – numerous couples would discover that a "mistake" had been made.[12] What then? Clearly, those who were intent on limiting family size would have to contemplate the option of abortion as a second line of defence against an unwanted pregnancy. An examination of the history of abortion is moreover of special interest to the historian since more references were made to it by medical and legal observers than to employment of contraceptives. In Chapter Two we will demonstrate how a study of this back-up method of birth control allows one to cast a fresh light on the general question of family limitation. In this chapter we will compare the methods of contraception available to Canadians in the 1890's with those of the 1930's and seek to determine why they were increasingly employed.

How would young Canadian couples of the 1890's seek to control their family size? The information available to them in published form was limited. Section 179c of the 1892 Criminal Code (substituted with Section 207 in 1900) restricted writing on the subject.

> Everyone is guilty of an indictable offense and liable to two years' imprisonment who knowingly, without lawful excuse or justification, offers to sell, advertises, publishes an advertisement of or has for sale or disposal any medicine, drug or article intended or represented as a means of preventing conception or causing abortion.

The English draft code on which the Canadian law was based had only a general section on "obscene libel": in making the sale or advertisement of contraceptives and abortifacients a specific indictable offence the Canadian government was following the more stringent line of the American Comstock laws.[13] Partly as a result of the law there was no organized birth control movement in Canada until the 1930's, by which time the birth rate had already reached a low level and indeed was about to turn upwards.

Discussion of family limitation was restricted but it did take place. From the mass-produced medical and self-help literature, mostly of American origin, that circulated widely in Canada, it is clear that doctors and popular practitioners recognized the growing desire of the public to avoid overly large families.[14] Although respectable physicians would not countenance the use of "mechanical" contraceptives they would on occasion advise the use of certain "natural" means of control. The first means were simple continence – Emma F. Angell Drake in *What a Young Wife Ought to Know* (1908) recommended twin beds – and prolonged nursing, which was widely believed to provide protection against a subsequent conception.[15] The second advised natural method was restriction of intercourse to what was thought to be the "safe period" in the woman's ovulation cycle. Unfortunately, the cycle was completely misunderstood and the so-called "safe period" was mistakenly calculated to fall at mid-month. The correct. cycle was not established until the 1920's, but in the meantime several generations of physicians vaunted the reliability of their schedule. Augustus K. Gardner, for example, in *Conjugal Sins Against the Laws of Life and Health* (1874), advised waiting twelve days after the menses.

> This act of continence is healthy, moral and irreproachable. Then there need be no imperfection in the conjugal act, no fears, no shame, no disgust, no drawback to the joys which legitimately belong to a true married life. Thus excess is avoided, diseases diminished, and such a desirable limitation to the number of children, as is consistent with the peculiar nature of the individuals concerned, is effected.[16]

Canadian readers received similar advice in John Cowan, *The Science of the New Life* (1869), George H. Napheys, *The Physical Life of Women* (1873?), and Winfield Scott Hall, *Sexual Knowledge* (1916).[17] The information was not always consistent. H.W. Long in *Sane Sex Life and Sane Sex Living* (1919) claimed that ten days after the period a woman entered her "free time"; B.G. Jefferis and J.L. Nichols in *Searchlights on Health: Light on Dark Corners* (1894) asserted that from mid-month to within three days of the menses one enjoyed "almost absolute safety."[18] For women with short, regular cycles the suggested schedules might have offered some protection but for most they would have been disastrous. A third natural, but not as well supported, method was the practice of coitus reservatus or intercourse without ejaculation. This method met with some success in John Humphrey Noyes's Oneida Community in upstate New York and its benefits were proclaimed by Alice B. Stockham in *Karezza: Ethics of Marriage* (1896) and in *Tokology: A Book for Every Woman* (1916). The former book was so highly regarded by some Canadian women that it was enthusiastically reviewed by the superintendent of the Department of Purity in Literature, Arts and Fashion of the Woman's Christian Temperance Union.[19] The problem with this form of contraception was that although its advocates claimed it raised the sexual relation to a higher spiritual level, it demanded a degree of self-control available to few Canadian males.

But what of the most reliable known forms of contraception in the nineteenth century – the sheath, douche, and pessary?[20] Doctors would not discuss their use because such appliances were associated in their minds with the libertine, the prostitute, and the midwife and were thus outside the realm of respectable medicine. The importance of the rhythm method and the reason why it was greeted by physicians with enthusiasm was that it was not tainted with such associations; it had been "scientifically" determined and so offered a means by which the medical profession could claim to extend its expertise into the most intimate area of human life.

When one looks for references to "mechanical" means of contraception one finds, because of both legal restrictions and medical distaste for the subject, little direct information. Women who did know about the prophylactic benefits of douching would, however, have been able to read between the lines in the advertisements for the "Every Woman Marvel Whirling Spray," which offered, according to its producer, the Windsor Supply Company, the advantages of "vaginal hygiene." The company's advertisements appeared in such diverse publications as the T. Eaton Company catalogue, Jefferis and Nichols, *Searchlights on Health*, the Toronto *Daily Mail and Empire*, and even in the staid pages of the *Dominion Medical Monthly*.[21] Of course, to be fully effective a douche would have to be used in conjunction with a pessary. Recipes for homemade ones concocted of cocoa butter, boric acid, and tannic acid found in private papers suggest that Canadian women were not slow in producing their own protective devices.[22]

For men the most effective contraceptive was the sheath or condom. By the 1890's they were being mass-produced in Britain and the United States and distributed by druggists in Canadian urban centres. A sensational report on their easy availability was made in 1898 by the purity campaigner C.S. Clark in *Of Toronto the Good*.

I saw a druggist's advertisement a short time ago in a Toronto paper with this significant line: *Rubber Goods of ALL KINDS For Sale*. There is not a boy in Toronto, I dare say, who does not know what that means. . . . A young fellow of sixteen once handed me a pasteboard coin, silvered over. When I mentioned to him that I saw nothing in the possession of such a coin, he laughed and told me to tear off the outside layer. I did so, and discovered one of the articles I have endeavoured to describe.[23]

What is noteworthy in Clark's report, however, is that such contraceptives were assumed to be employed not so much to control marital fertility as to permit extra- or premarital liaisons. They were no doubt used by some to control family size but their relatively high price, their association with venereal disease and prostitution, and the claims of doctors that they caused dangerous inflammation all restricted their employment. This, then, left coitus interruptus as the simplest and most widespread form of contraception. Doctors might condemn it as "mutual masturbation" or "conjugal onanism," but until well into the twentieth century it was the main way in which Canadian couples sought to "cheat nature."[24]

It is a commonplace assumption that the "Roaring Twenties" witnessed a great surge in sexual freedom and experimentation. If this did in fact occur – which some historians deny – it took place without the aid of any new form of contraceptive protection. It is true that many servicemen were introduced to the use of the sheath while overseas during World War I and that some women were aware of Marie Stopes's popularization of the cervical cap in England and of Margaret Sanger's defence of the vaginal diaphragm in the United States.[25] It is also true that Drs. Ogino and Knaus's correct determination of the ovulation cycle was made in the late 1920's and, with Roman Catholic approbation, publicized in the 1930's.[26] But when one compares the effective forms of contraception available to the mass of the people in the 1890's to those to which they had access in the 1930's, one can detect no major advance. The birth rate was brought down, not because of any technological breakthrough, but because more couples intent on limiting their fertility conscientiously employed traditional methods.

In response to such demands the "feminine hygiene" industry became a multimillion-dollar business. In the United States it was estimated that in the 1930's $250 million a year was spent on such products; though figures on Canadian purchases are not available they likely were in the $12 million-a-year range.[27] In popular women's magazines such as *Chatelaine* the advertisements for such products as Lysol and Dettol intimated that they could be turned to contraceptive purposes: "It used to be that feminine hygiene was not discussed. It was taboo. But today it is recognized as modern science's safeguard to health . . . very often to happiness."[28] In addition to such douching products, the women's pages of the popular press were dotted with references to a variety of suppositories and soluble pessaries – Rendells, Norforms, Sanitabs, Zonite, and Zonitors.[29] Rendells's suppositories, which were claimed to produce a swift and sure "protective film," were in fact the only proven contraceptives.[30] The others, like the douches, could act as spermicidal agents but were often no more than vaginal deodorants. They were clearly passed off as contraceptives, however, guaranteed to protect "marital happiness" or intended only for "married women."

Those who preferred a barrier method of birth control were assured by the guarded advertisements of the Novelty Rubber Co., the Sanitary Rubber Goods Co., the Paris Specialty Co., the National Specialty Co., the Federal Supply Co., and a host of other businesses that their orders could be filled.[31] Supreme Specialties of Regina, Saskatchewan, for example, sold, in addition to a number of pessaries and abortifacient pills, an extensive range of sheaths with such exotic names as: Canadian Royal Guards, Merry Widow, Japs, Excella-Never-Rips, Pretty Polly, and Ramses.[32]

There is no way of knowing how many contraceptives were sold in Canada during the interwar period, but clearly the demand was great. A representative of Verdun Laboratories, distributor of Sanitary Rubber Goods, wrote Marie Stopes in 1932 in hopes that she would share the knowledge gained from her English birth control work: "we feel that there is a great field here for the sale of these products, which could be handled to our mutual advantage." He went on to inform her that his company had been selling hygienic rubber goods "in a big way for the past eleven years and [we] have many customers all over Canada. There is great competition here in this line and we want to procure a line for Birth Control that are different."[33]

Neither Marie Stopes nor Margaret Sanger – the two leading international birth controllers in the interwar period – would allow their names to be linked to commercial undertakings.[34] Both were outraged that businessmen should turn to their own financial interests the desperation of women seeking to limit their pregnancies. Stopes wrote a Canadian contact that she could not bear "to think of all the commercial interest on the other side of the water involved in this business of helping women to help them-selves."[35] And it was not simply a question of what Stopes referred to as "scoundrelly commercial firms" profiting from the distress of others.[36] For her, the great tragedy was that the expense of birth control devices kept them out of the hands of poor women who most needed them, yet the dubious legality of contraceptives kept them expensive. Retailers would only stock such merchandise when guaranteed a high markup. But even those who could afford to purchase such products did not always acquire the needed protection. Again, because of the questionable nature of the merchandise, until the 1930's there were no brand names or government regulations. As a result the customer had no guarantee of the merchandise purchased.[37]

The census data tell us the extent to which Canadians were limiting their fertility and a short review of the traditional birth control methods tells us how they did it. To understand *why* they were employing contraceptives is a far more difficult issue. Fortunately, we have invaluable evidence on their motivations in the collections of letters written by Canadians to the birth controllers Marie Stopes and Margaret Sanger.[38] Stopes and Sanger received hundreds of letters from Canadians because, until at least the mid-1930's, the general assumption was made that no birth control movement existed in Canada. Both received requests for information on birth control and sexual counselling from doctors, ministers, nurses, and social workers, as well as from private individuals.

For the purpose of this chapter it is only necessary to draw on the Stopes correspondence.[39] Her typical Canadian correspond-ent was the woman who felt she had no one else to turn to. Marie Stopes, though thousands of miles away, was in effect a mother figure. One woman wrote in 1934, "I might say I had no mother to whom I could go for advise [*sic*] hence a great ignorance on this subject."[40] The assumption that mothers should provide their daughters with such information was also made by a Toronto woman, who wanted to know what to tell her eighteen-year-old daughter, and by a Saskatoon writer, who said of her daughter: "She has one Boy she has only be [*sic*] Married 10 months and I hate to think of the future for her."[41]

A frequent complaint was that clearly the better-off and well-informed knew how to avoid conceptions but that they were shrouding their methods in mystery. A number of these women held doctors responsible for not providing the needed information.

A correspondent in Tecumseh, Ontario, informed Stopes that after having two live births and one stillborn,

> . . . the Doctor attending advised us to avoid having any more: promising to give us birth control knowledge. This he did not do, and I did not care to bring the subject up again. But as I do wish to avoid the misery and misunderstandings my other married friends are going through I am asking you to help me.[42]

More outspoken was a woman who exclaimed, "really it seems almost wicked that Doctors are so 'dumb' in both its uses." She attributed their silence and ignorance to concern that a limitation of births would cut into their practices.[43]

Some women were completely ignorant of birth control.[44] Others, such as a Kendall, Ontario, woman, found that some purportedly effective methods did not work: "I have used lysol douches, also Quinine and cocoa butter pessaries. They were either unreliable or I did something incorrectly."[45] Still others had heard of newer methods like the cap or pessary but wanted more information: did the pessary cause injury, would the condom lower sexual sensitivity, should a quinine pessary be used with the cap?[46]

As might be expected, the main reason Stopes's correspondents wanted birth control information was to limit the size of their families. A Prince Edward Island woman married nine years, with four children and one on the way, wrote: "It seems that all my married life is spent either in having children or nursing them and it does pale on one no matter how much they like children."[47] A Dartmouth, Nova Scotia, mother, who after four years of marriage had two boys, pathetically begged:

> I am writing to you as a very ignorant married women to find out if I too may share your secret. . . . I am taking a great liberty I know but when one worries so from month to month to find a way out would be wonderful.[48]

After having given birth to eight children, an Oshawa woman informed Stopes, one could rationally appraise the moral issues raised by birth control.

> I am thirty-seven years of age and I feel that I have had enough children, indeed I think it is a bigger sin to bring children into the world when you haven't enough to keep them than it is to try to prevent them.[49]

But though most of the women who wrote Stopes already had large families whose size they wished to limit, some had only just begun their child-bearing careers and wanted birth control information so they could plan their families in a purposeful manner. A young married woman in Winnipeg simply wanted information on how to best assure a conception; a Welland, Ontario, mother who had one child and intended to postpone the birth of the second for some time asked: "Could I get information on the best way to conceive a perfect child?"[50] Contraception was employed to plan, space, and limit births.

Although the opponents of birth control depicted the women who employed it as being indifferent to the importance of children and the family, the letters to Stopes tell a very different story. It was because these women took so seriously the roles of wife and mother that they were turning to professional counsellors like Stopes to tell them how to respond to the new challenges of the twentieth century.[51] For example, a young Ontario woman wrote, "I am about to be married and I am anxious that my married life will be as perfect as I can make it, and my fiancee is as anxious as I am that we enter into marriage intelligently."[52] A Toronto woman, fearing that the unexpected arrival of her first child had damaged her marriage and that a second might destroy it, sent Stopes the plea, "Can't you help me save our romance?"[53]

What is especially striking in these letters is their writers' conviction that birth control, by ending the terrible anxiety of becoming pregnant, would restore sexual pleasure to their marriages and strengthen the marital bond. In a ten-page letter an Ontario woman told her tragic story of a life plagued by pregnancies and miscarriages. She faced each conception with anger and fear, her doctors told her to avoid pregnancy but did not say how, and, worst of all, "my husband grew almost to fear his desire for me and I to loathe it."[54] A Toronto woman related a similar tale. After the first birth she and her husband "knew that we must be *careful* (horrible word in marriage)." They used condoms, douches, and coitus interruptus, but all proved unsatisfactory and a second child arrived. The third pregnancy miscarried, because, as the woman admitted, "Yes, I did try to bring it on. I was afraid."[55]

She was afraid, as other correspondents were, that without being able to limit her fertility she would not be able to fill the demanding twentieth-century role of romantic wife and conscientious mother and possibly would lose her husband.[56] A Port Arthur woman who had three babies in four years lamented: "I am tired and miserable most of the time, and certainly do not make an ideal wife and mother."[57] In the interwar period the Canadian media subjected such women to a barrage of exhortations to become more devoted mothers and more appealing spouses. Never mentioned – but understood all the same – was the fact that only birth control would permit the inherently contradictory implications of the cult of domesticity to be resolved.[58]

Birth control was portrayed in these letters as very much a woman's responsibility. Although the opponents of family limitation frequently associated it with some sort of "revolt" of women against male power, Stopes's correspondents frequently fretted about any inconveniences their husbands might have to suffer. A Toronto woman, while discussing with Stopes the employment by her husband of a condom, asked worriedly, "I'll be frank. Doctor is it fair to him? . . . Will he in time weary of such interference?"[59] Few male correspondents expressed such concerns regarding their wives' contraceptive practices. One husband did tell Stopes of his worries:

> We have used rubber appliances but they seem to be too harsh and mechanical, we have also practised withdrawal which cheats my wife of a perfect "orgasm" and leaves her in a very nervous and exhausted condition for days.[60]

In most cases, however, the old assumption was maintained that since the woman faced the greatest risk she should bear the greater responsibility in birth control.

The letters written to Stopes, as valuable as they are, do not tell us everything about the motivations of those who had recourse to contraceptives. They are necessarily self-serving and make no mention of concerns that the writers may have felt Stopes would have disliked. For example, all the women said they had children or intended to have them; anyone who had read Stopes's work knew she was hostile to the notion of couples remaining childless for life. They tended to describe to Stopes their desire for a fulfilling sexual life in terms that she herself had done much to popularize. They downplayed the more mundane but basic causes for the fertility decline – the end of the economic rationality of the large family as child employment was restricted and education costs soared, the increased availability of employment for women in white-collar work and light industry, and the urgent concern, once the depression hit, to protect the family economy as best one could. Nevertheless, the letters, written principally by urban, English-speaking, middle-class Protestants, do confirm the demographers' argument that the Canadian fertility decline was marked by important class, religious, and ethnic differentials.[61] Most important of all, the letters offer precious insights into the lives of women attempting to exert some control over their reproductive functions.

Canadian women also turned to each other for contraceptive advice. This chapter can best be concluded by reproducing the letter of a prairie woman found in the papers of the Saskatchewan feminist, Mrs. Violet McNaughton.[62] Although undated, it obviously was written in the early years of the 1930's. The entire letter warrants examination because it provides a remarkably thorough account of women's understanding of birth control in the interwar period.

Dear Mamma:
    I received your letter last night, the first for a couple of weeks. I rather thought your call came earlier than expected. Am glad she's all right even if it was a girl. Have the little ones the big eyes like Fanny and Elma? So you wanted some information. Well, I can tell you several different methods. I have the *real* recipe of that cocoa butter. Jessie gave me one years ago but I don't believe she used it and I didn't either because it had alum [a caustic astringent] and I'm scared to death of alum. It's as bad as caustic almost tho there is only 1 teaspoon to a .lb of cocoa butter, but M . . . P . . . , the one who lost her baby in Neb, when I was home, gave me another. Her sister back there got it from her doctor after she'd had four. He charged her $50 for it, but since, she's given it to dozens and it works. It's just 1 .lb cocoa butter and 1 oz of common boric acid and ½ ox [sic] of Tannic Acid. It's a powder like boric acid only yellowish. You put the three in a sauce pan over hot water and the cocoa butter will melt. Then stir it all together and pour ½ inch thick in a pie-pan and cool. When cold cut in ½ inch squares like fudge. It smells good enough to eat. Then before each time put one of these pieces up there and it will melt at body heat in a minute or so. Cocoa butter alone is a preventive and so is tannic acid and these absolutely won't harm. I have my own doctor's word for that. I have some made and will send it by this parcel. I made it after Allan was born

but never used it because when he was born my doctor said she'd give a good preventive; so I figured her's was better or easier, and not so messy, and as she uses it herself I figured it must be good. It's a little rubber cup, called a pessary. It really comes in a set, the cup, jelly and douche tablets but the jelly is called Pro-tex. It's made of cocoa butter, tannic acid and I've forgotten the other ingredient, but I believe it was glycerine. Put a little in the cup and slip it up and it just slips over the uterus and there's such a suction it can't slip out of place; you can't feel it either. Then you douche before and after you take it out. The cup costs three dollars but with anything like decent care it will last 2 years. My doctor said its the best and easiest way she knew of, and its the method they are fighting to get thru for the birth control. They have clinics etc. here and they show you how to use them, tho that is mostly for the poor that the welfare and county have to take care of. Its supposed to be only legal for the doctors to tell those who already have 5 living children. Then, of course, there is the Men's Safes. Here they are 25 cents or $3 a dozen. These [*sic*] are a number of jellys with a long applicator like a douche syringe or enema pipes and to screw on the tube like a tube of tooth paste. There are also suppositories. They are about half as big as my thumb. They melt too. Then there is another recipe Laura gave me. It is: 1 cup baking soda, 1 dram quinine, ½ oz. of tannic acid. You mix it all together and get large capsules about this size ⬭ and fill them and use one each time. She said it originally called for alum but she left it out. Either of the two recipes are simple and don't cost much and go quite a long way. Here the cocoa butter is 50 cents a lb. and boric acid about 5 cents an oz. and tannic acid 10 cents an oz. The cocoa butter comes in cakes just like Baker's chocolate. I gave the two recipes to G . . . M . . . last year but have often wondered how she was now. I haven't heard for so long. Did you ever hear of Hilda's dates? There's a rule that you're safe so many days after menstruation until so many days before it again occurs. That was her safe-guard and she was always rubbing it in to all the others even to the older ones who had children, to do as she did, etc. That's an old one and it's like what I heard a party to say once: 'yes, you can regulate a woman but when it comes to the men it's different,' which is, alas, true. However Hilda didn't last long. I had a hard time getting rid of a book-agent (a lady) who was trying to sell me a $10 doctor's book on time. The book wasn't much but that was in it and she insisted that alone was worth $10 etc. You can give Fanny the little jar; tell her to put the jar in warm water and melt it again to cut in squares. I don't see why it shouldn't be good, even if it has stood. I guess there are any number of ways, I knew a woman in Buffalo who had a dear friend. She had a mean jealous husband. They had two girls and he made his brag that he'd see that his wife never got the chance to run around. Said there would be kids in his house every year. He'd keep his brag. This was 25 years ago and those things weren't so popular so she said she'd fix him. So she took a good sized sponge and soaked it with soap suds and put it up next the uterus. It worked for her and he never knew. As soon as she could do so, without arousing his suspicions she would take it out and douche. The girls were then around 16 and 17. I don't see why it wouldn't do, but use water with a few drops of some antiseptic or even plain vinegar. I also know of several other ways but don't like to encourage anyone without more definite information about them. I know several who have their own pet remedies and there are doctors who do it. I know of one in L.A. who charges $40 and one who charges $50 if married and $75 if single, and another who charges $125. These are all in L.A. It's a common subject now-a-days and everyone seems to have their own ones. It's like my Dr. says (Dr. W . . .) she's a real woman) 'when the birth control information becomes legal it will knock a good deal off the doctor's business, especially the ones who do the illegal operations.

Several conclusions can be drawn from the evidence presented in this chapter. First, Canadian fertility was brought down without the massive aid of any modern form of contraception. Second, women, though often assumed to be passive in relation to their fertility, went to great lengths in order to control it. Third, Canadian couples did succeed in limiting family size by use of traditional fertility control methods, but they were plagued by the fear that the methods might fail. That they had to resort to unpleasant and at times ineffective if not actually dangerous remedies was a consequence of the medical profession's refusal to provide them with adequate information on contraception.

It was a cruel irony that many of the eugenically-minded doctors who opposed the family limitation of the "fit" were clamouring for the forced sterilization of the "unfit." In such works as A.B. Atherton's "The Causes of the Degeneracy of the Human Race," R.W. Bruce Smith's "Mental Sanitation, with Suggestions for the Care of the Degenerate, and Means for Preventing the Propagating of the Species," and James B. Watson's *Who Are the Producers of Human Damaged Goods?* (1913), doctors calmly took it upon themselves to decide who should and who should not be allowed to breed.[63] Though they claimed to be protecting "quality" of race, their own criterion of "fitness," namely high socio-economic status, predisposed them to categorize those of a lower class or different culture as genetically inferior.[64] But this eugenic concern for fit stock was, despite the reactionary premises on which it was based, eventually to provide one rationalization for toleration of family planning. As it was made ever more obvious that women could not be prevented from seeking to control their fertility, the argument began to be voiced that safe contraception might be the lesser of two evils. In the *Canadian Medical Monthly* of 1920, A.T. Bond argued that reliable mechanical means of birth control would have to be accepted if only to lower the abortion rate.[65] In the same year the government demonstrated its preoccupation with the unacceptably high levels of infant and maternal mortality by establishing the Council on Child and Family Welfare.[66] The rates of maternal mortality and morbidity slowly forced upon the state and the medical profession the acknowledgement that if they were seriously concerned with the bearing of healthy children they would have to take some steps in easing the burden of motherhood. The impact that abortion had on maternal death rates is the subject of the chapter that follows.

2

Abortion as Birth Control

Canadian couples had a fairly wide variety of contraceptive measures available to them in the first third of the century, all to a greater or lesser extent lacking in reliability.[1] If contraception failed, those who were adamant in their desire to limit family size would then have to face the serious decision of whether or not to seek an abortion. The necessary linkage of abortion with contraception was recognized by Augustus Gardner, who warned his readers: "You have no right 'to take precautions,' or failing this, to resort to murder."[2] He recognized that the very fact that a couple used other methods could prepare them psychologically to fall back on abortion. As the use of contraceptive measures in general increased at the turn of the century, so, too, would the recourse to inducement of miscarriage.

Abortion is often left out of the histories of birth control, but the issue raises a number of vital questions: women's responses to their physical functions, the medical profession's views of women's health, and male and female attitudes toward sexuality. If women resorted to such dangerous remedies it was largely because legal and medical authorities were withholding from them information necessary for the safe control of their fertility. The fact that significant numbers of women (including working-class women) sought abortions is moreover strong evidence that they were not, as was frequently assumed, passive in relation to their own fertility: they wanted to control it and were willing to go to considerable lengths to do so. And, finally, the issue reveals that the development of new methods of birth control and the controversy over their use took place in the presence of a reality not yet fully perceived by historians – a widespread tradition of abortion based on folk remedies.[3]

The abortion question was brought forcefully to the Canadian public's attention in 1908 by "Kit," the writer of the "Women's Kingdom" column in the Toronto *Daily Mail and Empire*.[4] In an article of March 21 entitled "Race Suicide" she noted that though one was inclined to say hard things "of married women trying by every desperate means to avoid motherhood," the real scoundrels were the doctors. "Some fashionable physician living in a grand house, driving his motor, commits – every time he gets the price – a sordid murder, and goes scot free."[5] On the previous March 16 Dr. A.G. Ashton Fletcher, graduate of the University of Toronto and surgeon to the Queen's Own Regiment, was charged along with Harry Saunders, electrician, with the death of Jessie Helen Gould. Gould, a waitress at the Cadillac Hotel, had, it was later reported in court, paid twenty dollars to Ashton Fletcher to induce a miscarriage and died shortly afterwards of acute septic peritonitis.[6] The inquest sparked a series of articles and letters to the editor. One writer to the *Daily Mail* quoted the coroner to the effect that, "for every physician arrested for the crime there are 50 going 'scot free,' and for every physician there are 500 women guilty without the physician's aid."[7]

The Jessie Gould case was not an isolated affair. A perusal of the newspaper advertisements of the time reveals the widespread advertisement and sale of abortifacients as well as abortionists' offers of aid. Among the pills and potions of quacks surreptitiously claiming to have abortive powers were Radway's Pills for "female irregularities"; The New French Remedy: Therapion; Sir James Clarke's Female Pills; Madame Duvont's French Female Pills; Dr. Cowling's English Periodic Pills; Chichester's English Diamond Brand Pennyroyal Pills; Dr. Davis' Pennyroyal and Steel Pills; Old Dr. Gordon's Pearls of Health, which, according to its producer, the Queen Medical Company of Montreal, "Never fails in curing all suppressions and irregularities . . . used monthly"; the Ladies Safe Remedy: Apioline of Lyman and Sons of Montreal, who asserted that it was superior to such traditional remedies as apiol, tansy, or pennyroyal; Cook's Cotton Root Compound "Is successfully used monthly by over 10,000 ladies," claimed Cooks of Windsor, Ontario;[8] and finally Karn's Celebrated German Female Treatment. We know quite a bit about F.E. Karn of 132 Victoria Street, Toronto, because in 1901 he was tried under section 179c. His advertisements contained such statements as,

Thousands of married ladies are using these tablets monthly.

> Ladies who have reason to suspect pregnancy are cautioned against using these tablets. . . . They will speedily restore the menstrual secretions when all other remedies fail. . . . No name is ever divulged, and your private affairs, your health, are sacred to us.

Did such claims, which accompanied in this case what Karn was advertising as Friar's French Female Regulator, amount to an announcement that the product was an abortifacient? The lower court judge was taken in by the warning against pregnant women using the product; the appeal court justices recognized that this was in fact the best way to vaunt its efficacy.[9]

These advertisements of abortifacients are important for two reasons. First, they reveal that women seeking an abortion could obtain drugs and potions without directly involving themselves with an abortionist. Second, by asserting that these means were superior to traditional methods, these announcements indicate that quacks were competing with and borrowing from traditional medical lore. In the *Physiology of Marriage* (1856) William Alcott wrote:

> True it is that many who find themselves pregnant resort to tradition and household practice for what they call relief. Some field, or swamp, or grove contains the needful poison; and forthwith it is swallowed.[10]

A woman would first seek to "put herself right" by drinking an infusion of one of the traditional abortifacients such as tansy, quinine, pennyroyal, rue, black hellebore, ergot of rye, savin, or cotton root. Ergot of rye was long used by midwives to induce labour and today, in the form of ergometrine, is still employed by obstetricians. Savin, as early as 1879, was "well known as a popular abortive" in Toronto.[11] The effectiveness of these drugs is hard to determine but since they were employed generation after generation it must be assumed that they could on occasion induce miscarriage.[12]

If the drugs failed a woman might try bleedings, hot baths, violent exercises, and consumption of large quantities of gin. After this would come the riskier step of attempting a dilation of the cervix with slippery elm, a sponge tent, or catheter. It would only be as a last resort, and if it were still not beyond the sixteenth week when the quickening of the foetus caused an abandonment of all attempts, that the woman would turn to the abortionist.

How would one find the help required? It was only necessary to glance at the advertisements in the personal and medical columns of the local paper. In the Toronto *Daily Mail* for March 21, 1908, there were five advertisements for "Ladies Home Before and During Confinement" and one for a Mrs. M. Summers, who offered to cure "uterine tumours" and "irregularity" and in addition would send a "Women's Own Medical Adviser."[13] In the *Manitoba Free Press* for 1909 one finds similar announcements: "Ladies Avoid Unnecessary Delay and Disappointment," "Notice to Women – Have You Ever Used our Female Regulator?" with the guarantee that all information provided will remain confidential.[14] And, finally, the papers carried the advertisements of physicians and surgeons who, by referring to their specialization in "sexual disorders," could attract the attention of the desperate.[15]

In 1908 Judge Winchester of Toronto complained that scarcely a week went by without a doctor being named in a criminal abortion and asked that the medical association take some action.[16] In the circumstances, the timid reply made by the medical profession was revealing. The editor of the *Canadian Practitioner and Review* admitted that in Toronto alone there were probably half a dozen doctors practising abortion, but he insisted that they were practically ostracized by their colleagues and at least kept out of the Toronto Academy of Medicine. They should be deprived of their licences, he conceded, but how could that be done?[17] In the following year the *Dominion Medical Monthly* went further in an article entitled, "When doctor is accused of criminal abortion . . . ." The author declared, "All doctors in a great city have probably been approached some time or other in this respect."[18] If some gave in to the temptation of a large fee it was because the "open door policy" in medical education had resulted in an oversupply of poor young doctors. The obvious remedy was to improve the lot of practitioners by restricting entry to the profession. What was good for doctors would eventually be good for society at large.

As far as abortion itself was concerned the medical profession took the illegality of the operation as reason enough to continue to support the notion that it was both medically and morally wrong. There were, of course, individual doctors who in the privacy of their consulting rooms alluded to birth control and even helped induce miscarriages. But in public, doctors would only condone the termination of pregnancy by a surgeon if a mother's life was in grave danger and full medical consultation took place. What was ignored was the fact that many women had to rely on self-induced abortions as a form of fertility control because the profession, though it might advise the restriction of family size, often failed to provide the information on contraception that would make this safely possible. Earlier in the nineteenth century doctors might have opposed abortion because of the dangers it posed to the mother's health, but by 1900 hospital abortions could be performed with relative safety. As early as the 1840's Dr. Alfred A. Andrews of Windsor was successfully carrying out therapeutic abortions.[19] By the 1890's the processes of dilation and curettage were well advanced but such operations were refused to all but a few.[20]

What was most striking in the medical discussion of abortion was the fear voiced by numerous doctors that they could be "victimized" by women seeking help. The medical journals carried numerous articles warning physicians to turn a deaf ear to the pleas of patients. Dr. Andrews estimated in the 1870's that in Windsor there were fifty criminal abortions a year. He called on his colleagues to steel themselves against the heart-rending tales of seduced young girls but assumed that married women could be more easily dealt with.

> As for cases of married women, who, in order to shirk the responsibilities of maternity, seek to make you accomplices of a felony, you can have no difficulty. I have hundreds of such applications. The crime of foeticide is fearfully prevalent, and rapidly increasing, and corrupting and debasing the country both morally and physically.[21]

The same line was followed by an editorial in the 1889 *Canada Lancet*.

> What physician, in practice for any length of time, has not had many applications, often accompanied by a considerable bribe, to relieve the victim of the seducer from the social disgrace attached to her sin, or the selfish and degraded married female from the care and trouble naturally devolving on her?[22]

To spurn such pleas was to put one at the possible mercy of a vengeful woman, the editor warned, to assist her was of course out of the question, but even to see her, if she had already attempted to induce her own miscarriage, could put the physician in a position in which he might be held responsible for the consequences. Under such pressures, claimed the writer, some doctors committed suicide. But who were they? The editor gave no examples and the lack of evidence suggests that such scenes of entrapment occurred only in the fervid imaginations of medical journalists.

When it came to explaining the apparent rise in abortion, physicians attributed the blame to the greater education of women and their declining interest in maternity, the advertisement of abortifacients, and the presence of quacks and popular practitioners.[23] The remedies suggested by the medical press included a call for the closer supervision of druggists, a more thorough registration of births and miscarriages, a restriction of medical advertising, and the reportage of all requests for abortion to "some competent executor of the law."[24]

Doctors saw the usefulness of drugstores and newspapers being kept under surveillance but they did not accept the notion that their own profession, though it, too, contributed to the ranks of the abortionists, should be interfered with. Doctors sought to maintain the privilege of the secrecy of the consulting room, which was as sacred as that of the confessional. In fact, they saw themselves as rivalling priests in upholding the moral values of society against the onslaught of abortion:

> I had for many years noted and wondered at the fact [wrote Dr. Andrews] that of the married women who sought my co-operation, nearly all were Protestants . . . the Roman Catholic priesthood, have in their confessional an opportunity of instructing and warning their flock. Protestant women do not go there, but we, and we only, have the private ear of the whole sex, and it is, I conceive our duty, to lose no opportunity of diffusing the information we possess in this regard.[25]

Similarly, a contributor to the *Canadian Practitioner and Review* asserted in 1908: "It is probable that the two classes who are fighting against the evils of race suicide in all civilized countries are practitioners of medicine and priests in the Roman Catholic Church."[26] Doctors thus turned the abortion issue to their own purposes in advancing their claim to be the counsellors and confessors of Protestant Canada.

What view did the women seeking abortion take of their right to do so? Mrs. Mary Wood-Allen in *What a Young Woman Ought to Know* (1898) cautioned that a woman who married but sought to limit family size inevitably would have to face the question of abortion. "If she proposes deliberately to avoid motherhood she puts herself in a position of moral peril, for such immunity is not often secured except at the risk of criminality."[27] The approach that the woman would make to the doctor was described by Emma F. Angell Drake, herself a physician. To her came many a young wife who asked to be "helped out of her difficulty." "Again they say, 'There is no harm until there is life.' " " 'Doctor I have missed my monthly period and have come in to have you give me something to set me right.' "[28] McFadden referred to such women as having "many ways of hiding the actual facts from themselves."[29] Thus, women did not say they sought an "abortion," but rather they wanted to be "made regular" or to "bring on a period." Doctors accused such patients of using euphemisms and circumlocutions, yet many women clearly did not consider what they were doing to be wrong. This was brought out in all the testimony on the subject. They assumed that abortion was permissable before the third month or quickening and when not induced by another person. It was this absence of guilt that most enraged and confused male physicians. Hugh L. Hodge complained, "And when such individuals are informed of the [illegal] nature of the transaction, there is an expression of real or pretended surprise that any one should deem the act improper – much more guilty . . . ."[30] Dr. E.L. Tompkins expressed the same concern in the *American Journal of Obstetrics* (1896):

> There seems to be no incompatibility between high moral and religious views on other subjects and utter lack of the same in regard to abortion. I have been asked recently by a lady who is a typical Christian and a woman of the highest honor and integrity in all other matters, to produce an abortion for a young married friend whom she thought too poor to raise children.[31]

Women and doctors had different views of antenatal life. Women remained true to the traditional idea that until the mother felt the foetus "quicken" it was permissible to take whatever measures necessary to make herself "regular." Dr. Ballock asserted that "I am not able to recall one who was ever particularly distressed over such an act, especially if it happened in the early months of pregnancy."[32] The thought that women rather than doctors should decide on whether life was present was what raised the ire of men such as Hodge. "What, it may be asked, have the sensations of the mother to do with the vitality of the child? It is not alive because the mother does not feel it?"[33] Many women would have answered it was not.

What one finds in examining the abortion issue is that doctors were seeking to instill in the public a new belief in the vitality of foetal life from the moment of conception. It is important to note how relatively new this concept was. Abortion had not been made a statutory crime in British law until 1803, and even then the concept of quickening was retained, as it was in the revised statute of 1828, and only removed in 1837. In a similar fashion, the Offenses Against the Person Act of 1861 made it a crime for the woman to abort herself whereas the acts of 1803, 1828, and 1837 had all been aimed at the abortionist.[34] In short, the notion that a woman less than three months pregnant who sought to "put herself right" was committing a crime was a recent development and had not yet been fully forced on the public conscience. In 1922, O.A. Cannon could still write in the *Canadian Medical Association Journal*,

> The moral conscience of the public, including that of some physicians, needs educating, and it should be someone's business to make it known that from conception the unborn child is a human creature whose destruction is equivalent to murder.[35]

Doctors were never to be totally successful in convincing women of the immorality of abortion. For many it was to remain an essential method of fertility control. Who were they? They would include single women seeking to avoid an illegitimate pregnancy and the hardships that such a birth would entail. We know more about these women than the married because their names appeared frequently in press reports.[36] There were, for example, Jessie Gould, the waitress at the Cadillac Hotel in Toronto who died of acute septic peritonitis in 1908; Mary Ellen Janes of Victoria, who died of blood poisoning in 1895; Kate Hutchinson Gardener, a chambermaid of the Tecumseh Hotel in London who died of an overdose of chloroform in 1878.[37] Doctors could sympathize with the plight of the seduced young girl who was a victim of male lust. But by the beginning of the twentieth century there were reports that some women were seeking abortion, not because they could not marry, but because they wanted to retain their independence. "As one of this sort pithily put it," reported Dr. Edward A. Ballock, "she was not going to give up a hundred-dollar place for a fifty-dollar man."[38] For whatever reasons single women sought abortion, the odds are that the relative number of their attempts would be exaggerated simply because they would more likely be found out. Dr. J.F. Scott noted that married women who already had borne children recognized the signs of pregnancy earlier than the single and could thus take more effective actions.[39] Moreover, a married woman who miscarried raised few suspicions; with a single woman there was the chance of the doctor, neighbours, or even the police investigating. In a time of trouble, a single woman would have fewer resources at her disposal, she would have fewer people to whom she could turn, and the likelihood of dangerous complications were therefore all the greater.

The evidence suggests that most women seeking abortion were married, but the numbers involved are difficult to determine. The number of arrests for abortion would be of some interest but such figures would bear no necessary relationship to the actual numbers of women seeking to terminate their own pregnancies. An abortion only came to the authorities' attention if something went seriously wrong, and the figures of the police indicate, if they indicate anything at all, only the *unsuccessful* attempts. In a popular self-help medical manual such as J.H. Kellogg's *The Home Hand-Book of Domestic Hygiene and Rational Medicine* (1906), one was told that though abortion was fifteen times more dangerous than birth, only one woman in a thousand was ever punished. Where Kellogg drew his figures is not known but some credence could be given to a report in the *Canadian Practitioner and Review* of 1916 entitled "Race Suicide":

> Mrs. McKerron died in the Toronto General Hospital December 19, 1915, after a short illness. An Inquest was held, and the jury brought in a verdict that death was due to blood poisoning caused by an illegal operation performed by Mrs. Cull. In his address to the jury the coroner, Dr. Millen Cotton, said: "The question of race suicide is growing to alarming proportions in this city." He also said there were between three and four hundred cases in the hospitals last year as a direct result of illegal operations, and in addition to these there were many cases in private houses which were not discovered.[40]

Such claims were further substantiated when the activities of professional abortionists were brought to light. The Toronto *Evening Telegram* reported that the police investigations of the activities of a Dr. Andrews gave some idea of the extent of the practice.

> Inspector Stark took possession of all the correspondence in the house, which consisted of between 200 and 350 letters,

involving beyond doubt a number of criminal operations, performed on both married and single females, all over the country. Some of these letters are couched in the plainest language by educated as well as ignorant women, written confidentially but confessing to the greatest acts of shame and seduction, and offering to pay large sums of money for advice and successful treatment. Some contained grateful acknowledgement of what the doctor had done for them, and begging him to keep their secrets from the world. Others asked for immediate advice, and suggest secret interviews, when the would-be patients would be the least likely observed.[41]

To provide an account of the number and type of abortions that is more reliable than the sensational reports carried in the medical journals and the popular press, we have closely examined a range of sources pertaining to the inducement of miscarriages in British Columbia. Of particular value are a number of medical surveys, British Columbia vital statistics, and the records of the attorney general's office. The first two give some indication of the extent of abortions and abortion-related deaths; the third provides a rich mine of information concerning the interplay of abortionists, doctors, lawyers, and women. Such material allows one to flesh out the dry, quantitative accounts presented by vital statistics and convey some sense of the personal dramas posed by abortion.[42]

Beginning with the attorney general's records it should be first noted that we have found only ninety-eight cases dealing with abortion for the period 1896 to 1937.[43] But this low incidence should occasion no surprise. The legal authorities usually only took action when an abortion resulted in death and when there was a possibility of criminal prosecution. Between 1930 and 1939, as many as thirty-six of the thirty-nine abortion cases drawn to the attention of the attorney general involved deaths. These records thus mainly concern *unsuccessful* abortions and have to be treated with that in mind. Nevertheless, they are of great value in offering an intimate picture of women desperately attempting to control their fertility.

Who were the women discovered by the British Columbia legal authorities turning to abortion? They were not the single, seduced girls beloved by sensational reporters. In eighty-five of the ninety-eight cases the marital state was specified: 56.47 per cent were married, 24.88 per cent single, and 17.64 per cent widowed, separated, or divorced. These figures contrast markedly with those published in 1981, which indicated that of those Canadian women aborting 23 per cent were married, 65.8 per cent single, and 11.3 per cent widowed, separated, or divorced.[44] This suggests that in the interwar period abortion was employed to a far greater extent to regulate marital fertility. This conclusion is confirmed when we look at the ages of the women involved: 16.85 per cent were under 20, 51.85 per cent 20-29, 27.77 per cent 30-39, 3.7 per cent 40 or over. In 1981 the comparable figures were 28.3 per cent under 20, 52.2 per cent 20-29, 17.5 per cent 30-39, and 2 per cent 40 or over.[45] The typical woman in the interwar period having recourse to abortion was the older, married woman who already had children, although the records unfortunately do not always provide a full account of her child-bearing career. At least 10 per cent had previously aborted and one stated she had induced sixteen previous miscarriages.[46]

The motives offered by the women to explain their actions ranged from the desire to avoid a pregnancy resulting from a rape to the hope that a limited family would save the family from economic disaster.[47] "My husband and I want to get it done," asserted a Vancouver woman, "because we were so hard up and we were out of work."[48] Doctors traditionally sympathized with the single girl but expressed shock at the actions of the married. "Well it is surprising," stated one physician, "the number of times it is done by people who have absolutely no reason in the world for doing it, other than the fact that they don't want to have another child."[49] Married women frequently assumed that they did have reason on their side. In justifying to a court his suspicious actions, one doctor confessed, "When a patient comes to us like that you have got to do something for her or they get angry with you . . . ."[50] Juries at times also accepted the logic of the women's argument. In a Nelson case in 1902, the judge was so outraged that the jury refused to convict a woman on the strength of the evidence offered by herself and two doctors that he subjected the twelve to a "wigging" for their failure to appreciate their responsibilities.[51]

How was the abortion carried out? In our ninety-eight cases, twenty-seven were self-induced, fifty-one were carried out by another party, and twenty were ill-defined. In the fifty-one cases where at least one other party was involved, twenty-six were women, of whom nineteen were identified as nurses or midwives, and thirty-eight were men, of whom nineteen were identified as doctors. Several abortionists were charged on more than one occasion and one doctor, though never found guilty, was implicated in three separate abortion deaths.[52] In Vancouver some abortionists, such as nurse Clara Jessup in the 1920's and Mrs. Esther Moore in the 1930's, ran "private maternity hospitals" that they advertised in the local press.[53] Others operated out of paramedical offices offering massage, chiropractic, and steam treatments. Clara Katterman, a Victoria masseuse, was reported as telling one woman that she had helped over a hundred patients at fees of $50 to $100: "You don't have to go to Seattle," she said, "to get rid of your trouble. I am a woman's friend."[54] Some patients did view their abortionists as friends and, even when dying as a result of the operation, refused to give implicating information demanded by the police.[55] For women who wanted greater discretion there were also advertisements in the local papers for doctors across the border in Seattle, Sumas, and Blaine, Washington, who specialized in "women's disorders."[56]

What methods were employed to cause abortion? The records indicate that women would, as their desperation grew, move from mild to drastic measures. It is of interest to note that some discriminated between "natural" and "unnatural" tactics. At an 1898 inquest on his wife, a husband testified: "Up to this time I did not know that she had been taking any medicine to bring on a miscarriage. I knew that she has used natural means to bring on a miscarriage. She has put her feet in hot water."[57] After this would come the irritants and emmenagogues, the quinine, and aloes, and ergot or black pills. Dr. F.C. Curtis complained in 1915: "Anyone can get them, they are patent medicine. . . . It is said in the advertisement that they are used for regulating monthly flow but really and truly they are . . . intended to bring about an abortion."[58] Then, if these failed, one would move on to the use of douches of lysol, turpentine, or carbide and finally to the employment of instruments: catheters, speculums, sounds, lead pencils, needles, bougies, crochet hooks, and slippery elm. Usually a combination of techniques was employed. In the cases we have examined the use of instruments predominated, but this is to be expected given the fact that so many ended in death, of which instruments would be the most likely cause. The causes of death in the sixty-five cases where it was given were: fifty by infection (peritonitis or septicemia), ten by hemorrhage or rupture, four by drug toxicity, and one by embolism.[59]

The danger of abortion is hard to establish. Doctors frequently spoke as though it was inevitably followed by death but their own figures did not bear this out. It is also evident that complications arising from instrument-induced miscarriages declined as women turned to their own purposes the antiseptic lessons of Pasteur.[60] Here would be yet another reason why the number of discovered abortions would have less and less relationship to the number of undiscovered.

It is, of course, impossible to determine exactly the rate of abortion in Canada, but all reports indicated that here, as in the United States, it was to play a major role in lowering the birth rate. In 1896, Scott cited a "Report of the Special Committee on Criminal Abortion" of the Michigan State Board of Health that estimated, on the basis of 100 doctors' reports, that 17 to 34 per cent of all pregnancies were aborted.[61] In 1922, Dr. O.A. Cannon wrote in the *Canadian Medical Association Journal* that of the 314 women he had attended during pregnancy fifty-one had aborted. "Of fifty-one women attended by me during abortion, twenty-two admitted criminal interference. This percentage of forty-three would have been materially increased if all the patients had been equally frank."[62] Cannon placed the abortion rate at somewhere between 7 and 14 per cent of live births, a figure remarkably close to that established once the practice was legalized and reliable statistics were made available.

Some idea of the social significance of abortion can be gained if the figures on abortion deaths are viewed as the "tip of the iceberg" of all attempts at induced miscarriage. One of the most striking improvements in the health of Canadian women was brought about by the lowering of the risk of maternal mortality. Between the 1930's and 1960's the chances of dying in pregnancy fell from about 1 in 150 to 1 in 3,000. Maternal deaths, which in the early 1930s had accounted for 10 to 15 per cent of all deaths among women in the child-bearing years, fell in three decades to 2 to 3 per cent.[63] This dramatic breakthrough was so welcomed that few have asked why it occurred so late. In the early nineteenth century about one-quarter of the deaths of women aged between fifteen and fifty were related to pregnancy and its complications. With the onrush of medical improvements associated with Joseph Lister's discovery of antisepsis in 1867, there was the real possibility of eliminating many of the traditional causes of maternal death.[64] Conditions did improve somewhat, but if one were to judge by the statistical data the gains made in the first decades of the twentieth century were still disappointingly modest. Whereas the infant mortality rate fell from 120 deaths per 1,000 live births at the beginning of the century to sixty-eight per 1,000 by 1936, the maternal mortality rate continued to hover at about five per 1,000 and actually rose to a century high of 5.8 per 1,000 in 1930.[65]

Canadian families were becoming smaller, and as a result a higher percentage of all births were the more dangerous first births, which contributed to sustaining the high maternal mortality rate. But even with the larger percentage of primaparous births, the lower age of mothers and the improvement in medical care should have led to a decline in deaths associated with pregnancy. In a 1934 study of 334 maternal deaths in one year in Ontario, an important finding was unearthed. Researchers found that fifty-nine, or 17 per cent of all maternal deaths, were due to abortion. These abortion deaths were "artificially" inflating the number of deaths attributed to normal pregnancies.[66]

By examining the legal, medical, and vital statistics of British Columbia, we find that what the Ontario researchers discovered was not an isolated phenomenon.[67] It is not easy, however, to pin down the number of abortion deaths. How a maternal death was classified depended ultimately on the differing judgements and conflicting concerns of doctors, coroners, and magistrates. There are indications that only two of every three abortion deaths were reported by vital statistics and presumably even a lower ratio of deaths known to medical authorities may have come to the attention of legal authorities. Why was this the case? First, for a report of an abortion death to be made by vital statistics, by the judiciary, and perhaps beyond that by the newspaper press, it had to be passed on by medical authorities. Whether intentionally or not, this process was not always carried out. An ante-mortem or deathbed statement might not have been taken, a death certificate might have been inaccurately drawn up, a post-mortem might not have been held. Figure 1 indicates the various stages at which a report of an abortion death might go astray and thereby fail to show up in the classifications of the next reporting agency, be it vital statistics, the judiciary, or the newspaper press.

The second reason for the failure of the medical records to tally with those of vital statistics and the attorney general is that some doctors simply did not want to report abortion deaths. Because of the illegal nature and moral stigma attached to abortions, many doctors may have concealed them to protect the reputations of their colleagues and patients.

That so few abortion deaths reached the notice of the courts is perhaps dramatic witness to the ambivalence the medical

FIGURE 1
Reportage of Abortion Deaths

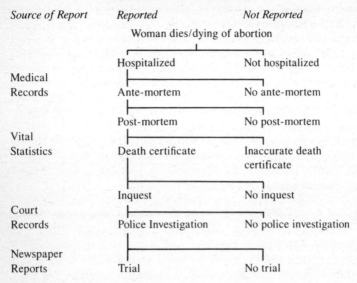

Source of Report   *Reported*   *Not Reported*

Woman dies/dying of abortion

	Hospitalized	Not hospitalized
Medical		
Records	Ante-mortem	No ante-mortem
	Post-mortem	No post-mortem
Vital		
Statistics	Death certificate	Inaccurate death certificate
	Inquest	No inquest
Court		
Records	Police Investigation	No police investigation
Newspaper		
Reports	Trial	No trial

profession felt regarding the status of abortion. British Columbia statistics on abortion were accordingly flawed for the same reasons suggested by an American writer in a 1934 issue of *New Republic*.

It is natural to wonder why, with scores of statistical tables being published year after year, the true state of affairs has not been revealed before. But it is not hard to understand when you know how the statistics are obtained. For example, Anna J. Brown comes into a hospital with a high temperature, and a story of falling down the cellar stairs in the third month of pregnancy. The hospital authorities may or may not believe the cellar-stairs explanation, but their function is to treat her for a dangerous septic condition, not to do police work. If she dies, the death is correctly certified as due to puerperal septicemia, and that's that, so far as the hospital is concerned. This grain of fact is deposited in the county health records. Eventually it is turned over to the federal Census Bureau. And Anna J. Brown, now relegated to the limbo of statistics, becomes one of six thousand infinitely shadowy women who die in this country each year of puerperal septicemia – a disease known to centuries of women as childbed fever.[68]

The result was that enormous discrepancies appeared between what was recorded and what doctors and legal officials knew regarding the numbers having recourse to abortion.

Medical authorities clearly knew better than any other officials the extent of abortion-related deaths; the problem is that we have very little information on the process of classification they employed. It also should be remembered that even doctors missed some cases of abortion – one researcher commented on the "unbelievable gullibility and stupidity of doctors" who misdiagnosed causes of miscarriage-related deaths – and medical statistics have to be presumed to be minimal estimations.[69]

The information concerning abortion deaths reported by British Columbia vital statistics was based on the death certificates completed by doctors.[70] As already indicated, these figures were certainly lower than those known to doctors. Unfortunately, the extent of under-reporting of abortion deaths by vital statistics cannot be determined.[71] This source, therefore, has certain inherent weaknesses. Its great strength is that it allows us to gain an impression of the frequency of *reported* abortion deaths, of changes in their frequency over time, and the extent to which such deaths varied in relation to other causes of maternal mortality.

What was the general twentieth-century pattern of deaths due to abortion in British Columbia? In the vital statistics maternal deaths were classified as due to sepsis (infection), toxemias (eclampsia or poisoning), hemorrhage, abortion without sepsis or toxemias, abortion with sepsis, and other complications. The average number of annual deaths attributed to abortion in the 1930's was 13.3; in the 1940's the number declined to an average of 6.9; and in the 1950's the figure further declined to an average of 4.1. As Figure 2 shows in more detail, the number of annual abortion deaths peaked in 1936 at twenty-one. The decline was very gradual and only in the 1950's did abortion deaths become unusual.

Figure 2 also shows the number of maternal deaths during these four decades. Abortion deaths in almost every year contributed to the level of maternal mortality, but the proportion they contributed varied substantially over time. In the 1920's maternal mortality in British Columbia peaked and then began to decline. In 1924, sixty-nine maternal deaths were reported. By the mid-1930's the figure had dropped to about fifty deaths a year. From 1934 onward the maternal mortality rate began to drop dramatically and consistently. (See Figure 3.)

FIGURE 2
British Columbia Maternal Deaths: 1922-1968

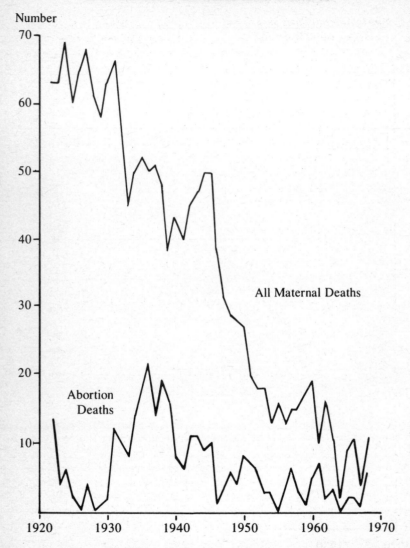

SOURCE: B.C. Vital Statistics.

FIGURE 3
British Columbia Birth and Death Rates, 1920-1970

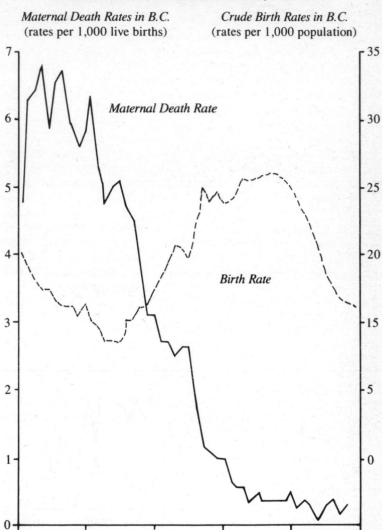

Maternal Death Rates in B.C.
(rates per 1,000 live births)

Crude Birth Rates in B.C.
(rates per 1,000 population)

SOURCE: **B.C. Vital Statistics.**

Ironically, just as maternal mortality rates in the 1930's were reaching ever lower levels, abortion deaths appear to have been reaching unprecedented heights. As Table 2 indicates, from the 1930's to the 1950's abortion deaths continued to claim a large proportion of the maternal deaths. In 1927, according to vital statistics, abortions accounted for only about 6 per cent of all maternal deaths; in 1936 they were responsible for a staggering 42 per cent of all maternal deaths. Even through the 1950's abortion remained a major contributor to the overall maternal death rate.

Why was the rate of abortion deaths, especially during the 1930's and early 1940's, so high? The first reason was that women seeking abortion shared some of the same risks as those bearing children: complications of pregnancy, childbirth, and puerperium or sepsis. But since abortion deaths were rising substantially just as the rate of maternal mortality was declining, other factors besides the risks of childbearing had to be at work. The rate of maternal mortality was, according to medical historians, pulled down by the increased percentage of term deliveries in hospitals, the employment of antibiotics to control infection, the better use of blood and blood substitutes to control hemorrhaging, the identification of high-risk patients, the judicious use of Caesarian section, and more use of prenatal and postpartum care.[72] While hospital practices relating to childbirth improved significantly during the 1930's and 1940's, women who sought the aid of abortionists or attempted to induce their own abortions obviously did not benefit from these developments. Because women were forced to work within an illegal system, they were at a much greater risk of exposure to unsanitary conditions and to methods that were dangerous and undependable. The rate of abortion deaths was high and, in fact, rising through the 1930's relative to other causes of maternal mortality largely because of the illegal nature of the operation, not because of the backwardness of medicine.

But abortion deaths, according to the vital statistics, were not simply increasing relative to the rate of maternal deaths. In the 1930's and 1940's they increased in absolute numbers. Such a rise in abortion deaths suggests that despite the illegality of the procedure more and more women were seeking to terminate their pregnancies. This was the second reason for the high rate of abortion deaths. Certainly, many commentators believed they were witnessing an abortion epidemic. It should be stressed, however, that the rate of abortion deaths as reported by vital statistics is not to be taken as an indicator of the actual number of women who sought abortions. It has been estimated that in industrial countries in the first half of the twentieth century the rate of pregnancies ending in both spontaneous and induced abortions probably rose from 10 to 15 per cent. Despite the obvious risks posed by abortions, its mortality rate was low: it has been deduced that only one-tenth of 1 per cent of all abortions resulted in death.[73] Yet, because so many women were seeking to terminate their pregnancies in the 1930's and the 1940's, the absolute number of abortion deaths was frighteningly high.

We have established that in the three decades between 1920 and 1950 probably close to 500 women in British Columbia died as a result of abortion-related deaths.[74] That would account for approximately 30 per cent of all maternal deaths; Dr. W.D.S. Thomas found that in the 1950's abortion deaths were responsible for 27.5 per cent of maternal deaths.[75] What was the impact of abortion deaths on the national scale? In 1947, Mrs. Strum pointed out to the House of Commons that although every Canadian knew that 41,000 servicemen were killed in World War II, few were aware that since 1926 21,000 women had died in childbirth.[76] But Mrs. Strum was herself unaware – as were all those who thought the answer lay in hospitalization of childbirth – that 4,000 to 6,000 of these women died as a result of bungled abortions.

The conclusions to be drawn are fairly obvious. First, abortion was a traditional form of fertility control. Second, in the interwar period, it was particularly employed as a backup method of birth control by married women who wanted to limit family size. Third, the rise in the number of abortion deaths indicates that many women were trapped between the rising pressures to limit fertility and the implacable opposition of both the government and the medical profession to providing safe and effective means of birth control and abortion. Government legislation deprived the mass of the Canadian population of access to reliable birth control. The population question therefore became a political issue for those concerned by the plight of poor mothers.[77] It is to this subject that we turn in the chapters that follow.

TABLE 2
British Columbia Maternal Deaths: Complications of Pregnancy,
including Abortion

Year	Total Maternal	Abortion Deaths	Percentage of Abortion Deaths
1922	63	13	20.6
1923	63	4	6.3
1924	69	6	8.6
1925	60	2	3.2
1926	65	0	0.0
1927	68	4	6.1
1928	61	0	0.0
1929	58	1	1.8
1930	63	2	2.9
1931	66	12	18.1
1932	54	10	18.5
1933	45	8	17.7
1934	50	14	28.0
1935	52	17	32.7
1936	50	21	42.0
1937	51	14	27.4
1938	48	19	39.5
1939	38	16	42.1
1940	43	8	18.5
1941	40	6	15.0
1942	45	11	24.4
1943	47	11	23.4
1944	50	9	18.0
1945	50	10	20.0
1946	38	1	2.6
1947	32	3	9.3
1948	29	6	20.6
1949	28	4	14.2
1950	27	8	29.6
1951	20	7	35.0
1952	18	6	33.3
1953	18	3	16.6
1954	13	3	23.0

Year	Total Maternal	Abortion Deaths	Percentage of Abortion Deaths
1955	16	0	0.0
1956	13	3	23.0
1957	15	6	40.0
1958	15	3	20.0
1959	17	2	11.7
1960	19	5	26.3
1961	10	7	70.0
1962	17	2	11.7
1963	11	3	27.2
1964	2	0	0.0
1965	9	2	22.2
1966	11	2	18.1
1967	4	1	25.0
1968	11	5	45.4

SOURCE: B.C. Vital Statistics.

PART II

Promises of Sexual and Social Emancipation

3

Socialist Feminists, Maternal Feminists, and Family Limitation

In September of 1924 a recently married woman in Fleming, Saskatchewan, wrote to Marie Stopes in London, England. After congratulating the English author on the great success of her books dealing with birth control and sexual problems – *Married Love* and *Radiant Motherhood* – the writer went on to describe the plight of herself and her husband.

> We are very happy and we wish and hope to have a baby boy one day, but owing to finance, we cannot have that joy just yet; . . . Would you kindly tell me, (I hope I am not taking a liberty) if the theory is correct, that if conception takes place 6 days after the menstrual period, it proves to be a girl – and if conception takes place 7 or 8 days before the menstrual period it proves to be a boy?[1]

Twelve years later a letter requesting information on the prevention, not the determination of the sex, of offspring was written by a young man of Bonnyville, Alberta, to Dr. Matsner of the American Birth Control League first established by Margaret Sanger.

> I am a young man of 24 about to get married (in a Year) and I don't want to go at it knowing as little as I do about

Birth Control. My fiancee and I have already talked about this problem, but we both know very little about methods and their "safety." We wouldn't want a baby the first year for several reasons. M. needs a rest as she has been teaching school for many years, and we couldn't afford it anyway, so we decided we would not indulge in sexual relations at all for one year. When I suggested that it should be easy enough to practice birth-control M. told me that it was almost impossible to get away from a child the first year – "Just look around and see how the newlyweds of recent years made out" she said – and I had to admit they seemed to have failed miserably. Please explain to me why. Is it through ignorance? or is it because they wait until the wedding night to face the problems? or?

He went on to explain why he was writing to an American thousands of miles away: "You see, there are no birth control clinics around here that I know of, I don't know where they are in Canada though."[2]

These two writers were probably typical Canadians inasmuch as when the question of birth control was raised in the 1920's and 1930's they thought first of Marie Stopes, Margaret Sanger, and the organizations they had founded. The popularization of family planning in the twentieth century was very much the work of these two remarkable women. They spread the message of the necessity and the respectability of birth control via tracts and lectures in their own countries and around the world. Both were to act as godmothers for the Canadian campaigns for birth control clinics. Such campaigns, in advancing the rights of women to control their fertility and in changing the methods used, implied potentially important upheavals in the power relationships of men and women. This aspect of the early evolution of Canadian feminism has received little attention. This oversight might be due in part to the fact, as we will demonstrate in what follows, that women on the left – socialist feminists – tended to be more responsive to the issue of birth control than their better-known, socially conservative sisters who have come to be referred to as maternal feminists.

In the United States the anarchist Emma Goldman had begun around 1910 to defend publicly, on libertarian rather than on Malthusian economic grounds, the necessity of birth control. Goldman, in part because of her radical politics, did not create a mass movement, but she helped to win to her views a woman who would – Margaret Sanger.[3] Sanger (1879-1966) was a New York housewife with a vague desire to do something with her life. She had been raised in a progressive atmosphere. Her father – a friend of Henry George – was a socialist and feminist. Her husband, an architect, was active in the Socialist Party. In 1911 Sanger moved to New York City and in her capacities as a nurse began to discover the plight of poor women burdened by series of unwanted pregnancies. At the same time she shifted her support from the Socialist Party to the more radical circles of the Industrial Workers of the World, where birth control was advanced by some as a revolutionary creed. Sanger later dated her own full conversion to birth control, not to the time of her contacts with Goldman, whom she came to see as a rival, but to the occasion of a 1913 trip to France, where she was amazed at the sexual sophistication of ordinary mothers. Back in America, Sanger coined the term "birth control" as a positive description of family limitation to replace the old, gloomily economic label, "neo-Malthusianism." She thus began to try to separate the issue of birth control from some of its old economic and political associations. Her first efforts to win mass support by making the issue less obviously connected to any specific political movement had limited success. Her tract, *Family Limitation*, which described for the benefit of working-class couples the use of simple contraceptives such as douches, condoms, and pessaries, was prosecuted by the federal government.[4] Sanger left America again, via Canada, for England. In the course of this trip she met an Englishwoman also preoccupied by sexual issues and also drifting away from her husband – Marie Stopes. These two brilliant but egocentric women would never recognize the talents of the other but they were in many ways similar. They both, for example, learned to exploit legal battles to spread their doctrines.

The charges against Sanger created unexpected positive publicity, and on her return to the United States in 1916 the government dropped them. Her name had become known across the country, however, and in the future Sanger sought court confrontations. Sanger started out on her first national lecture tour in 1916, turning the defence of birth control into a free-speech issue. Though it was against the law she also established a birth control clinic in Brooklyn and was this time arrested and jailed. In response, she founded the American Birth Control League (ABCL) and began a campaign for legislative reform to permit the opening of medically supervised clinics for the poor. She herself was not to open another until 1923. Meanwhile, Marie Stopes set up her clinic in London in 1921.

Canadians can take some pride in the fact that a fellow countryman bore much of the responsibility for launching Marie Stopes (1880-1958) into her career as a birth control advocate.[5] Stopes was raised in an enlightened upper middle-class family and was the first Englishwoman to receive a doctorate in paleobotany. On a trip to North America in 1911 she met a Canadian botanist, Dr. Reginald Ruggles Gates. He proposed to her almost immediately, and they were soon married in Montreal. But back in London it slowly dawned on Stopes that all was not well in the marriage. It says something about the sexual ignorance of even some of the university-educated women of Edwardian England that Stopes did not realize at first that Gates was impotent and that the marriage had not been consummated. Only in 1914 did she start proceedings for the annulment of the marriage. More important was the fact that, shocked at her own ignorance, she began the serious study of the problems of sexuality. The product of this research was a book entitled *Married Love*. It appeared in 1918 and was a publishing phenomenon, going through seven printings in one year and selling eventually over a million copies.

Stopes's main argument in *Married Love* was that the woman in marriage had as much right to sexual pleasure as the man. Stopes only noted the issue of birth control in passing, but in the huge number of letters she received from her readers she was informed that the inability to limit fertility was the source of much marital misery.[6] In response, she brought out another book at the end of 1918, *Wise Parenthood*. In this second text she directly broached the issue of birth control by providing diagrams of the reproductive organs and descriptions of a variety of contraceptives.[7] She realized only after a year or so that it was not sufficient to describe to poor mothers various forms of fertility control. They had to be made accessible to mothers. Doctors, dispensaries, chemists, and local health officials made it clear that they did not see it as their duty to provide cheap devices for the working class; as a result, in March of 1921 Stopes opened up her Mother's Clinic in Holloway, London. The purpose of the clinic was to show to public officials how such services could be carried out. The birth control clinic was to serve primarily as a model and the chief aim of Stopes's Society for Constructive Birth Control and Racial Progress (SCBCRP), formed in 1921, was to pressure government officials into taking over the responsibility of such institutions.[8]

Stopes and Sanger shared many of the same concerns. They knew that the middle class already restricted births and so they sought to make accessible to lower-class women contraceptives limited as yet to those better off. They both stressed the need for clinics supported by the government and directed by trained personnel to educate the public in contraceptive use. But perhaps most important of all, they downplayed the old economic arguments in favour of birth control usually trotted out by the neo-Malthusians. Stopes and Sanger believed that the problem was to make limitation of family size appear not simply economically necessary but morally respectable. To do this they developed the argument that contraception was not only compatible with pleasure but essential if the woman's passions were to be allowed full expression. In the 1920's and 1930's this emotional defence of fertility control was to prove to be immensely successful. Men and women in Canada as well as in countless other countries wrote to Sanger and Stopes for help and advice. These two women not only aided individuals; they sought to sponsor groups in Canada similar to the ABCL and the SCBCRP for the purposes of lobbying for the reform of the law and the establishment of birth control clinics from Ontario to British Columbia.

British Columbia can claim to be the province in which the birth control movement in Canada was, thanks to Margaret Sanger's initial prodding, first launched. It was not by mere chance that birth control found its original Canadian defenders in the West. British Columbia served, in the early decades of the twentieth century, as a spawning ground for a host of radical movements. The province, in drawing workers from the mines of Scotland and Wales, the mills of Lancashire, the metal works of the Midlands, and the lumber camps of the United States, found itself with an aggressive and sophisticated trade union movement. Labour was led before World War I by the Marxist-oriented Socialist Party of Canada. Following 1918 B.C. Socialists were divided and redivided with the emergence of the Canadian Labour Party, the Communist Party of Canada, the Federated Labour Party, the Independent Labour Party, and, by 1932, the renewed Socialist Party of Canada. These divisions, though they were a manifestation of the electoral weakness of labour, were also evidence of the intensity and liveliness of political debate on the

West Coast. Vancouver, moreover, was home to an active women's movement and to a wide range of other reformist groups – theosophical lodges, the Women's Labour League, the Women's International League for Peace and Freedom, the Anti-Vaccination and Medical Freedom League – all seeking to ensure a better future. It comes as little surprise that within the ranks of such political and social movements, which were necessarily so questioning of received opinions, the issue of family limitation should be raised. In Chapter Four we will examine in more detail the responses of the Canadian left to the issue of family limitation. Here it suffices to say that birth control, as still a very much tabooed subject in the 1920's, had its best chance of finding advocates in a socialist-feminist milieu.[9]

The anarchist Emma Goldman, as we have seen, was the first active public defender of birth control in North America, and was instrumental in drawing to the cause Margaret Sanger, who became the best-known advocate of the movement. Goldman was to remain a radical all her life. Sanger eventually channelled all her efforts into the American Birth Control League and turned her back on her political past. Until the mid-1920's, however, she was still associated in the public mind with her union campaigns in Paterson, New Jersey, alongside such firebrands as "Big Bill" Haywood and with her imprisonment for birth control activities. Accordingly, her attempts to spread her message in the post-World War I world were viewed with sympathy by old leftists. In her public lecture tours Sanger sought to rally local groups made up of feminists, socialists, and progressives to demand birth control clinics. It was just such a trip to Vancouver in 1923 that resulted in the formation of the Canadian Birth Control League.

The American Birth Control League by then had become skilled in organizing Sanger's barnstorming tours. Months ahead of time presumably sympathetic individuals would be contacted and asked to help prepare for Sanger's arrival by renting a hall, informing the press, and arranging publicity. Early in 1923 Anne Kennedy of the ABCL contacted a number of such women from Ottawa to Vancouver.[10] Not all were forthcoming. For example, Sara Heppner of the Sisterhood of the Shaarey Zedek Synagogue in Winnipeg replied that, though she herself was interested in the issue, her institution could not sponsor Sanger's tour because she was too controversial a figure. The older and more conservative members of the synagogue were hostile to such discussions.[11] Cora

Hind, a prominent correspondent for the Winnipeg *Free Press*, sent back an even sharper response. "It is not birth control which needs to be taught to the people at large, whether high or low, but individual self control."[12] The ABCL had assumed that Hind, as an independent journalist and feminist, would sympathize with Sanger's activities, but clearly not all Canadian feminists were responsive.

In Vancouver it appeared at first as though a similar debacle might take place. Kennedy contacted the society woman and poet, Mrs. Isabel Ecclestone Mackay, and through her had been put in touch with Lillie A. Boynston of the Vancouver Women's Canadian Club. In May, the club agreed to sponsor Sanger's talk but soon got cold feet. At this juncture Laura E. Jamieson intervened.[13] She represented the Vancouver branch of the Women's International League for Peace and Freedom, which offered to take over the organization of the B.C. tour. Sanger's talk, consequently, took place at the Women's Building at 752 Thurlow on July 2, 1923.

The event was very much a leftist women's affair. The sponsoring agency, the Women's International League for Peace and Freedom, was led by Laura Jamieson, an active Socialist, and by Helena Gutteridge of the Trades and Labour Council.[14] Advance publicity was offered in the *B.C. Federationist*, which highlighted the political nature of the issue.

> In Canada, as in the United States, it is still a "crime" to teach methods of birth control, because these countries are still in the grip of plutocratic and reactionary forces. [clinics are available in Australia and New Zealand] . . . It is high time that women of this province became equally intelligent.[15]

Three hundred and fifty people came to hear Sanger's talk.[16] The meeting was chaired by Dr. Samuel Petersky, a local physician, and on the platform sat Dr. W.J. Curry, an ardent social democrat, and Dr. Ernest T. Fewster, who was also actively involved in community issues. Sanger's comments were endorsed by two other contributors to the *B.C. Federationist*, Mrs. C. Lorimer and O.J. Mengel.

Dr. Samuel Petersky was an important member of the Vancouver Jewish community, an active Liberal, and a zealous campaigner for improvements in public health. His wife, Amelia Jacoby Petersky, presided over the Vancouver Council of Jewish Women. Petersky was presumably chosen to chair Sanger's meeting because of his respectability. That he was somewhat leery of the discussion of birth control was suggested by Sanger, who wrote afterwards to Alexander Maitland Stephen that "Dr. P . . ." had been "frightened" by the subject and asked her to softpeddle her argument. Dr. Ernest Fewster was a well-known Vancouver physician, theosophist, and poet. His dreamy prose and verse works were similar to those of his friend, Bliss Carman. Dr. W.J. Curry was a frequent contributor to the *B.C. Federationist* and a lecturer and sometimes candidate for the Socialist Party of Canada. O.J. Mengel in the 1920's was a Canadian Labour Party counsellor in South Vancouver. Mrs. C. Lorimer was later to be on the executive of the Socialist Party of Canada and active in the early CCF.[17]

The crux of Sanger's Vancouver talk, as of almost all the others she made across North America, was the depiction of the bright future that lay in store once effective contraception was available to all. Children would be healthy, and motherhood made "glorious." Societies were established to protect children from cruelty but what greater cruelty was there, Sanger asked, than to condemn infants to be born in poverty and ignorance? Similarly, who could say they were in favour of the emancipation of women and fail to support the most basic freedom, the freedom from undesired pregnancies?[18] Sanger's enormous success as a defender of birth control was based on the fact that she presented it as a mystical issue, not as some grubby physiological problem. A sense of her power in spiritualizing the population issue and so drawing into the discussion many who might otherwise have found it repugnant can be gauged by the adoring letter written to her by a Vancouver admirer.

> . . . I have long admired your courage and determination to help restore or bring Spiritual Balance to this earth and its tortured human race . . . I see a beautiful Spiritual Mansion – not made with hands and without sound of hammer or nails – growing for you and your co-workers, eternal in the heavens from which you shall continue to radiate Light and Truth until the suffering millions are redeemed (enlightened).[19]

Unfortunately, once Sanger left British Columbia the basic problem of establishing a birth control clinic – not a Spiritual Mansion – remained and the Vancouver activists had to tackle the mundane task of organizing community support.

The leading advocate of birth control in Vancouver in the 1920's was the poet and politician Alexander Maitland Stephen. He was born in Hanover, Ontario, in 1882 and moved west at the turn of the century to try his luck at punching cattle, homesteading, and prospecting. He lost the use of an arm in World War I and returned to British Columbia to attempt (optimistically) to be both a school teacher and political activist. His push for radical reforms in education soon led to his being fired by the Vancouver School Board. He thus devoted more time to politics and writing. Along with Wallis Lefeaux, Angus MacInnis, Ernest Winch, and Lyle Telford, he was to be active in creating the Socialist Party of Canada. At the same time Stephen was winning a reputation as one of Canada's more interesting poets and novelists.

Active in the Child Welfare Association, the B.C. Art League, and the Vancouver Poetry Society, he produced poetry, novels, anthologies of Canadian verse, and political tracts such as *Marxism: The Basis for a New Social Order* (1933) and *Hitlerism in Canada* (1935). Involved in the Independent Labour Party of the 1920's, the Socialist Party of the early 1930's, and the CCF, he was purged from the latter party in 1937 for his espousal of a common front with the Communist Party. He continued, however, as president of the B.C. League Against War and Fascism and B.C. representative of the Committee to Aid Spanish Democracy. He was a popular speaker: thin, tall, a shock of grey hair, his war-shattered arm hanging by his side, the very image of the poet.[20]

Stephen's efforts in 1923 were to build on the foundations laid by Sanger. Thanks to her the topic of birth control had been broached openly in British Columbia and it was now time, stated Stephen, to make the demand for clinics a part of the socialist program. But, unlike Sanger, he continued to insist on the political nature of the problem:

> The present system of so-called civilization needs unrestricted breeding to make good the normal waste of life through war, disease and famine. Especially does it need a prolific class taught to increase and multiply the teeming millions doomed to servitude and lives of futility.[21]

The church, press, and state all supported the workers' deprivation of both food and sex, asserted Stephen; organized labour could not ignore either issue.

That not everyone within the ranks of labour was drawn to the issue was made clear by the ways in which Stephen, Dr. W.J. Curry, T.A. Barnard, and Mrs. C. Lorimer peppered the columns of the *B.C. Federationist* throughout 1923, 1924, and 1925 with discussions of the radical potential of their campaign.[22] They cited a host of luminaries who dealt with the issue, such as H.G. Wells, Lord Dawson, Herbert Spencer, Grant Allen, and Arthur Brisbane. They portrayed the military as desiring large families for cannon fodder, the church and state as intent on keeping women in ignorance.

Mrs. C. Lorimer provided a specifically feminist defence of family limitation. She argued that doctors and clergymen became aroused by the population issue only when workers limited the size of their families. This was because professionals rightly feared that smaller families could lead to the emancipation of labour. But the real victory was to be eventually won by women. As a result of the slaughter of the war, Lorimer asserted, "a horror of giving birth has taken root in the hearts and minds of millions of women." But, whether or not a woman was to breed or not, the decision had to be hers alone: "woman must become mistress of herself and her first duty shall be to herself." Lorimer accused Dr. J.J. Heagerty of the Department of Health of overlooking the real oppression and poverty caused by large families so that he could lecture women on childbearing and said that he should "shut his mouth."[23]

T.A. Barnard approached the touchy question of whether working-class couples might disagree on the use of contraceptives. Some socialist husbands obviously opposed their wives' attempting to restrict their fertility. Barnard upbraided them for their short-sightedness while admitting that until clinics and good contraceptive information were available such problems were unavoidable.[24]

The main burden of the defence of birth control in the columns of the *B.C. Federationist* was assumed by Stephen. In a series of articles he spelled out the reasons why birth control had to be supported by socialists and socialist feminists. It would improve the health of children and end the slavery of women; it would mean that girls would no longer have to be brought up to salute both the cradle and the flag; it would allow men to perform the duty of protecting their wives from unwanted pregnancies; it would put an end to abortions and the need to have recourse to prostitutes; it would reduce infant and maternal mortality; it would make the working-class home a pleasant place to which the husband would happily return; it would check the reckless breeding of the diseased and the criminal; it would lead to a healthier, stronger labour movement.[25] This curious amalgam of ideas called for the emancipation of women, while assuming that they would remain in the home, and demanded freedom of individuals to determine their own family size, while bemoaning the uncontrolled reproduction of the criminal and the alcoholic. Few of the contradictions were spotted. The very enthusiasm with which birth control was asserted by Stephen to solve almost every social ill was one indication of its growing importance.[26]

In 1924 the spirits of the little band of Vancouver birth controllers were raised once more by a visiting lecturer, this time Anne Kennedy of the ABCL. She stressed the need for a local group to organize itself to tackle the issue of law reform.[27] A conference, she stated, was planned for November. Presumably it took place, because in December Stephen reported in the *B.C. Federationist* that Vancouver was now the home of the Canadian Birth Control League (CBCL).[28] He traced its formation back to Sanger's visit in 1923 and said regular meetings had been held since. The group did not distribute contraceptives but had as its purpose the education of the public. Its basic concerns were, first, good breeding; second, women's health; and third, a woman's right to contraceptive knowledge. The CBCL declared its intention to collect evidence on the relationship of reckless breeding and vice, to establish under law clinics run by physicians where mothers could be instructed, to advocate the sterilization of the unfit, to enlist the support of politicians to change the laws affecting birth control, and to hold annual conferences. In January, 1925, Stephen spelled out the legal problems groups such as his faced. Section 207 of the Criminal Code lumped together abortion, obscenities, and provision of contraceptives as illegal actions. One section of the statute did note, however, that in particular situations if the "public good" were served the law would not be enforced. Stephen stated that the Canadian Birth Control League was not intent on the indiscriminate provision of contraceptives but sought to have doctors and pharmacists, as well as clinics under the direction of doctors, freed from the shackles of the law.[29]

The exact role played by the CBCL is difficult to determine.[30] Whether or not it provided contraceptives and contraceptive information is unclear. Stephen was invited to the Sixth International Neo-Malthusian Conference, which took place in New York in 1925. He could not go but in a written submission reported that though the public in the West was not completely won over the League was progressing.[31] Sanger continued to refer to Stephen Canadians who wrote her requesting birth control information.[32]

In the early 1930's Stephen's colleague in the Socialist Party, Dr. Lyle Telford, appears to have taken over the leadership of the campaign for birth control in British Columbia. A charismatic provincial CCF legislator, though a maverick, he left the legislature to become the first socialist mayor of Vancouver in 1938-39. He shared many of Stephen's concerns, from birth control to support of the Spanish Republic.[33] Stephen's Canadian Birth Control League disappeared but in its place emerged a functioning birth control clinic. In March, 1932, Telford sent to Marie Stopes for her perusal a tract entitled "Birth Control" from the "Birth Control Clinic: Marine Building, Vancouver." No details of the methods of birth control were spelled out but the pamphlet, which was presumably being distributed, did include a defence of family planning. The goal of birth controllers, it asserted, was not childlessness, but *wanted* children, better marriages, freedom for women, and race improvement.[34] In an accompanying letter Telford explained that he and a nurse would run the Vancouver clinic as a private operation; it was not yet possible to have a publicly supported institution. He sought Stopes's advice and assistance in locating publicity material.[35]

Unfortunately, we know nothing of the actual operations of the clinic; through the City Directory, however, we can trace its evolution. Two nurses, Miss F. Morden and Miss Laura Clements, ran the Birth Control Clinic in the Marine Building from 1932 to 1935. From 1936 to 1939 it was directed by Clements, by then Mrs. L.E. Vaughan, from her home at 1050 Gilford, and from 1939 to 1956 from 709 Dunsmuir. The identity and number of its patients remain a mystery.[36]

We do know who the defenders of birth control were. In the 1930's, as in the 1920's, they continued to come mainly from the ranks of the socialist feminists. In February of 1936 the Women's Labour League circulated a petition demanding the establishment of birth control clinics. It began with the statement:

> Whereas: With the widespread unemployment, the burden of caring for the home and children falls principally upon the shoulders of the working class mothers who oftentimes, rather than bring other children into the world, with small prospects of proper food, clothing and attention, resort to the most crude and dangerous means in order to procure abortions, with all its widespread evils, as thousands of women are suffering due to the lack of proper knowledge of Birth Control . . . .[37]

The petition was supported by Mrs. Dorothy Steeves, a provincial

CCF legislator who agreed that birth control information "should be taken out of the realm of privilege." Additional support was given by Miss Mildred Osterhout, a Vancouver school trustee, and Arthur Paskins of the Naturopathic Institute.[38] In the legislative assembly in Victoria the defence of birth control was provided by Steeves, Dr. Telford, and Mrs. Laura E. Jamieson, who sat from 1939 on as CCF MLA for Vancouver.[39]

In the 1920's and 1930's the campaign for birth control in British Columbia, as intermittent as it was, was thus very much the creation of socialists and socialist feminists such as Stephen, Telford, Steeves, and Jamieson. This is not to say that they monopolized the provision of birth control information. Obviously, the doctor and druggist, for those who could pay, were the ones to whom one would turn for contraceptives. As early as 1921 Stopes had been written to by a Vancouver pharmacist. He told her that even in the lightly populated West, family limitation was a problem:

> This is brought home to me daily in my business by the futile yet pitiable requests I get to "give me something to put me right" and again "there's no room for any more at our house – we've got five already and it's more than we can do to look after them as they should be looked after . . . ."[40]

His reason for writing Stopes was to say that, "if I can be of service in the dessemination [sic] of your preventive precepts among the troubled faction of my clientele consider me on command." Once the depression hit many more recognized the possible commercial advantages of dealing with contraceptives. In September of 1929 a man who described himself as a metaphysician, psychologist, and author of a tract entitled "Self-Help" wrote Sanger from Vancouver saying that he would like to participate in the provision of birth control materials.[41] In September of 1934 Sanger received a similar letter from a representative of the Vancouver Bureau of Feminine Hygiene asking if she and her assistant could act as commercial representatives of the ABCL in B.C. Sanger refused to sanction any such links with private enterprisers, but the two women, who were both nurses, apparently did run their Bureau of Feminine Hygiene at least for a year or two out of offices on West Pender and West Georgia.[42] In the early 1940's there were, in addition to the Vancouver Birth Control Clinic of Mrs. Laura E. Vaughan mentioned above, the Birth Control Studio operated by a Mrs.

Duncan and the Birth Control Centre under Mrs. L. Davies.[43] But even with such operations springing up, many people in smaller communities would still be forced to write for assistance to well-known personalities like Stopes and Sanger.[44]

Socialist feminists in British Columbia had established the first birth control league in Canada in the 1920's; in the early 1930's they helped to operate and defend one of the country's first clinics. Given the fact that Stopes and Sanger stressed the enormous importance of contraception in assuring the emancipation of women, this chapter can best be concluded by asking why the mainstream Canadian women's organizations, such as the National Council of Women, did not take the lead in defending birth control.[45]

As we have seen, women who adopted a class analysis seemed to acknowledge fairly readily the importance of family limitation. Women more given to gender politics were less responsive. They tended to avoid making a critique of women's reproductive role because, in the first place, they thought it was unavoidable. The second reason why the leaders of the Canadian movement for women's rights avoided taking up the defence of contraception was out of fear that it might compromise their drive for legal reforms.

Thus, in the 1920's such groups made little mention of birth control. Some women – in particular members of Catholic organizations – were simply opposed on moral grounds, likening contraception to abortion and infanticide. Others took seriously the spectre of race suicide: "Those who marry but voluntarily refuse parenthood are robbing themselves of their greatest joy and are failing to serve the highest interests of their country and generation."[46] Since the war had killed off the finest young men there was an obligation, so the eugenicists asserted, for the fit to reproduce as quickly as possible.[47] Still others took to heart the warnings of doctors that mechanical forms of birth control were dangerous and disreputable. The best-known women's physician in the country – Helen MacMurchy of the Maternal and Child Welfare Division of the Department of Health – stated: "Birth control or contraception is not a normal thing. It should not be undertaken or carried out except for clear, definite and grave reasons of a medical nature and under medical advice."[48] Finally, there were many women who were fearful that contraception would actually decrease the power of women – maternity – while increasing the sexual demands of men.

This latter concern especially preoccupied feminists. In the latter half of the twentieth century it is difficult to appreciate the hopes many women had at the turn of the century for "the pure white life for two." But given their problems with a powerful and abusive patriarchy, their interest in a celibate or near-celibate relationship was not always unreasonable. Just who was going to lose or gain power by the employment of contraceptives?

Most of the members of the Protestant women's groups were not so much opposed to limitation of births as to the specific way in which births were limited. No middle-class woman wanted to be subjected to an endless series of undesired pregnancies. But the fear was that, although in the past women had the right to demand of their husbands conjugal continence, now with artificial methods of contraception women – far from being "freed" – would in effect be stripped of any right to deny their spouses intercourse.[49] The result, warned one writer, would be "frequent stimulation of the racial glands" and accompanying degeneration.[50] For conservative feminists the answer was to limit births by increasing continence. Men were to be raised to the level of self-control enjoyed by women rather than women being dragged down to the lustful depths of men. It was because of this interest in attaining "continent and self-controlled parentage" that Alice Stockham's defence of coitus reservatus drew the attention of the Woman's Christian Temperance Union and Georgina Sackville of Innisville, Alberta, devoted her *Birth Control or Prevention of Conception* to a defence of the rhythm method.[51]

Birth control was also considered ideologically dangerous by that generation of Canadian feminists, including Nellie McClung and Emily Murphy, who regarded motherhood as woman's highest calling.[52] In Canada in the late nineteenth and early twentieth centuries (and in the United States, as Linda Gordon has shown) many women saw their status as dependent on their maternal function. Given the real paucity of alternative roles, their reproductive choices were circumscribed. It was logical enough for many to assume that their best hopes for improved political and social rights lay in the claims they could make as mothers or future mothers. It followed that they might well fear birth control, which appeared to devalue their sacrifice and jeopardize their arguments. In the light of such beliefs it is possible to understand Murphy's assertion that "The chief concern of society lies with nests and birdlings. Any system . . . that interferes with those should be promptly stepped on with a heavy and well-shod shoe."[53]

The dignity of "race motherhood" and "mothercraft" were exalted by maternal feminists prior to World War I as part of their campaign for the vote. After it was attained the various women's groups proceeded in the 1920's to devote themselves to developing programs of interest to mothers and children.[54] Baby welfare centres, better-baby contests, and well-baby clinics proliferated. Club women fought for mothers' pensions and juvenile courts with the same purposes in mind of shoring up the family and winning increased respect for the maternal role.[55] Birth control thus was shunned by the major women's organizations because they feared its espousal in effect would undercut programs centred on the mothering ideal. When in 1922 the National Council of Women of Canada examined Margaret Sanger's *Birth Control Review*, it was in a meeting devoted to "objectionable printed matter and films."[56]

There were a few dissenting voices. Flora MacDonald Denison responded to the race suicide panic with the observation, "Better to look after the children that are here than to fuss too much about the ones that will never exist."[57] Edith Lang, a contributor to *Women's Century*, while hoping that males would eventually accept greater conjugal continence, asked in 1920:

. . . in the meantime, because nothing is more degrading to womanhood, and therefore more immoral, than unwanted motherhood, would it not be advisable for our women to understand the scientific means which are available to save them from that most unsocial act of conceiving an unwanted child, and for those contraceptive means which are endorsed by scientific persons to be legally available in certain drugstores of good repute?[58]

An affirmative answer was only to be made publicly by the major women's organizations after the depression hit. The most responsive were the prairie farm women's organizations. In June, 1929, the women's branch of the Saskatchewan section of the United Farmers of Canada called for the legalization of birth control on the grounds that it was "the only humanitarian way of preventing a mother from being overburdened and broken in health with too numerous progeny."[59] The UFC further called for the setting up of clinics in which trained doctors would disseminate the necessary information. The Seventh Labour Women's Social and Economic Conference, which met in Winnipeg's West End Labour Hall in March of 1930, also debated the issues of sterilization, companionate marriage, and women's employment. The secretary of the organization, Beatrice Brigden, chided those who were slow to recognize the importance of the discussion of family limitation. "We may as well face the facts. There is nothing in the world too private or too sacred to remain closed to investigation.... Today she [the woman] can enjoy the privilege of voluntary motherhood."[60] In Winnipeg, also, in June, 1932, Mrs. Sam Rodin announced that the triennial meeting of the National Council of Jewish Women unanimously endorsed lifting the ban on birth control.[61] Similar resolutions were passed in 1933 by the United Farm Women of Alberta.[62] Even Emily Murphy, a vocal opponent of birth control in the 1920's, had swung round in support by 1932.[63] The leading Canadian women's organizations were slow in publicly defending birth control. They only did so in the 1930's when their moral misgivings were overwhelmed by evidence of the social and economic misery resulting from unwanted pregnancies.

The Canadian women's organizations were not alone in finding it difficult to respond to the issue of fertility control. In British Columbia, as we have seen, contraception was defended by the left. In the following chapter we will place those developments in context by examining in detail the various ways in which Canadian socialists sought to disentangle the political and private interests compounded by the notion of "birth control."

4

Socialism Versus Malthusianism

Writing to the Alberta Department of Public Health in 1937, A.R. Kaufman, later hailed as the "father" of the Canadian birth control movement, asserted that only a reduction in the birth rate could stave off social disorder.

> The writer feels that Canada must choose between birth control and revolution, as some day the funds for relief and the various social services may be lacking and needy people will likely fight and steal before they starve.[1]

Kaufman, a wealthy manufacturer, provided the funds to begin both the widespread diffusion of contraceptive materials in Canada and the establishment of birth control clinics in Toronto and Windsor. No detailed history of the early birth control movement in Canada has as yet been written. The few sketches of the campaign that do exist focus on the activities of the group of middle-class philanthropists headed by Kaufman. In part for conservative social purposes, they laid the basis in the depths of the 1930's depression for what was to become the family planning movement in Canada.[2] As we saw in Chapter Three, however, the discussion of restriction of family size did not have to await the enlightened interest of respectable doctors, social workers, and business leaders. Leftists established in the 1920's the first birth control league in Canada. The purpose of this chapter is to place the British Columbia developments in the context of the response to the population question of the Canadian left as a whole from the 1890's to the 1930's.

From the turn of the century the issues of Malthusian or neo-Malthusian solutions to the economic problems posed by capitalism were hotly debated in the publications of the Canadian left. The discussion of the social and political ramifications of birth control in Canada first found prominence in the pages of reformist periodicals, but this does not mean, of course, that only their restricted readership was interested in the issue. Family size in all segments of Canadian society was declining after World War I and most middle-class Canadians of the 1920's were aware of the propagandizing activities in favour of contraception carried out in Britain by Marie Stopes and in the United States by Margaret Sanger. But to find public defenders of birth control prior to the 1930's *within* Canada one had to turn to the writers of the left. The respectable avoided the question. The availability of American and British literature on the subject, combined with the assumption that Canadian legal statutes outlawed the public defence of artificial restriction of family size, effectively retarded the appearance of a native, middle-class, birth control lobby. Thus the left, *faut de mieux*, assumed the defence of birth control and made it part of a general critique of capitalist society. By locating the beginnings of the birth control discussion in its specific ideological context one can begin to reconstruct an accurate picture of Canadian attitudes toward fertility.

The way the Canadian left responded to the issue of birth control was complex. Few of its statements on the subject were free of ambiguities or outright contradictions. Such confusions were understandable. The idea of the social necessity of restricting fertility to ensure the well-being of the individual family was inextricably linked in nineteenth-century minds with the conservative doctrines of Malthus. As a consequence, European and North American socialists were not unnaturally suspicious of any discussion of birth control that could imply that poverty was a result of personal rather than societal failings. Such suspicions were confirmed when, from the 1870's on, the English Malthusian League – the first public organization to defend the morality of artificial restriction of family size – persisted in parading its hostility to labour. Most leaders of the left continued well into the twentieth century to harbour doubts about the wisdom of even broaching the population question.[3] But by the early 1900's the clear evidence that thousands of working-class families were seeking to limit pregnancies forced some left-wing commentators to take a more discriminating view of the whole question. Sympathy for the working class appeared to require, at the very least, that radicals defend the right of ordinary working people to decide for themselves the size of their families, despite the dictates of neo-Malthusians, who insisted that *only* by the implementation of fertility control could prosperity be attained, and of populationists, who damned all family planning as irreligious, unnatural, and unpatriotic.

The response of the Canadian left to birth control reveals three discreet schools of thought. First, individual libertarians or anarchists defended birth control primarily on the basis of the right of the individual to control his or her own life. Second, various Canadian socialists perceived the emergence of the birth control issue as yet one more symptom of the tensions produced by a society riven by economic and social inequalities. And third, the Communist Party remained truest to the nineteenth-century left's suspicion that even addressing the birth control question might detract from the class struggle. The ensuing analysis, more than simply broadening our knowledge of the early history of the single issue of family limitation in Canada, also casts a fresh light on the history of the Canadian left and its attitudes toward women, family, and the forces of social control.

To outsiders at the turn of the century impressed by an apparently boundless frontier and the legendary fertility of the Québécois, Canada appeared to be the last place where one would expect birth control to become an issue. But well before World War I there was, as we have seen, growing evidence that many Canadians were artificially restricting family size.[4] Respectable commentators bewailed what in the main they took to be a sign of the nation's weakness. To find reasoned apologies for the practice it is necessary to turn to radical publications. Anarchists in Europe and America were among the first on the left to be attracted to the birth control issue. Their interests were kindled for two reasons: first, contraception appeared to offer the individual a way of freeing her or himself from both poverty and the morality inculcated by Christianity; and second, so some argued, it could be employed by the masses as a means to restrict the labour supply and thus formed part of the "General Strike."

Possibly the first written defences of birth control originating from Canada were based on the former libertarian argument and were advanced by R.B. Kerr, a Scottish lawyer active in British Columbia between 1893 and 1922.[5] A free-thinker, Kerr was apparently drawn to birth control because, like many public defenders of the practice, he saw it as a weapon to be turned against the churches. At the turn of the century Kerr and his wife, Dora Forster, both contributed to the American anarchist, anticlerical journal *Lucifer*, edited by Moses Harmon. The scientism and sex radicalism or free love of *Lucifer* spilled over, in the first decade of the twentieth century, into a form of popular eugenics. Indeed, *Lucifer* in 1907 became the *American Journal of Eugenics*.[6] Kerr's career followed a similar pattern. Writing from British Columbia, Kerr devoted himself to criticizing the socially conservative doctrines of the only existing birth control journal in the English-speaking world, the *Malthusian* of London. He defended the working class against the traditional charges levelled against it of disinterest in controlling family size and opposed any plan of attempting to force birth control measures on the public.[7] He upbraided the Malthusian League for its concern to appear respectable and vaunted his own radicalism. His distaste for the Malthusian League, which never in any event enjoyed any influence in Canada, stemmed from his impatience with its concern for preserving respectability, a concern that took the form of a defence of the tenets of laissez-faire capitalism and a dislike for popular birth control propaganda. A more active and open discussion was necessary in Canada. For Kerr such activism manifested itself in discussions of free love and pornography and attacks on imperialism, racism, "all superstitions of an imperial and patriotic nature," and America, the puritan police-state that prosecuted Margaret Sanger.[8] But at times a non-libertarian tone also crept into Kerr's work, as in his use of American eugenic ideas to defend selective breeding and his curious suggestion during World War I that millions of Germans be captured and brainwashed into accepting the benefits of birth control.[9] In 1922 Kerr returned to Britain to edit *New Generation*, which replaced the *Malthusian* as the mouthpiece of the Malthusian League. Kerr's importance in the beginning of the discussion of birth control in Canada was that he was the first to advance the argument of individual interests in defence of family limitation. Setting aside the old Malthusian argument that the workers could, as a *class*, improve their situation by restriction of fertility, Kerr retorted: "It is useless to tell a man that if he and ten million others will have small families, he will gain something. The thing to do is to show him how *he* will gain by *having a small family himself*; no matter what the others do."[10] In 1907 Kerr continued his attack on the academic approach of the *Malthusian* and suggested that attempts be made to have the government provide "preventives." "A knowledge of preventives is an important part of popular education and should be furnished by the State."[11]

This libertarian apology of birth control that Kerr adopted before World War I was also propounded in Canada in the 1920's by the American anarchist Emma Goldman.[12] Speaking in Toronto in 1927, she particularly stressed the right of the individual woman to control her own body. Birth control offered a way to avoid abortions and broken marriages. Indeed, Goldman argued that contraception promised to provide a firmer basis for marriage. With fewer but healthier babies, the relationship of the spouses could be more equal and divorce would decline. And the working classes as a whole would benefit; the struggle against capitalism would be more effective once the labourer was freed from the shackles of the overly large family.[13] In Goldman's statements there was thus an advance made from the individualist anarchism of Kerr to what might be called an anarcho-syndicalist position. This stress on a class analysis was in turn taken up by the socialist left, which likewise viewed birth control from a class vantage point.

In moving from the anarchists' interest in birth control to that of the socialists, we soon discover that it was not so much the rights of the individual as it was the question of the relationship of family limitation to labour's struggle against capitalism that drew their attention. It followed that publications focusing mainly on union matters and not interested in or not recognizing the larger confrontation – papers such as *Canadian Labour Press*, *New Democracy*, *Workers' Weekly*, *Machinist Bulletin*, and *Nova Scotia Miner* – rarely if ever broached the subject. But in the politically oriented publications birth control was frequently alluded to. For the purposes of this chapter the non-Communist left, from the syndicalist One Big Union to the Marxist Socialist Party to the agrarian-socialist CCF, can be lumped together.[14] Their responses to the issue of family limitation largely reflected the same concerns: a suspicion that capitalists were turning the population question to their own purposes, a hostility toward an encroachment on working-class family life, and a growing concern for the needs of working-class women.

The first reason for the defence of birth control by the mainstream Canadian left was a consequence of its suspicion that business, the military, and the churches all sought to maintain the existing status quo by inciting the labourer recklessly to reproduce. This charge was levelled in publications such as the *B.C. Federationist* and the *One Big Union Bulletin*. The discussion of the evils of capitalism was broadened to include, in addition to economic exploitation, the sexual exploitation of the working class manifested in postponed marriages, prostitution, and venereal disease. How, these papers asked, could imperialists such as Kipling and Roosevelt express concern for the fall of the birth rate and the degeneration of the white race when the economic system these men sustained made marriage impossible?[15] The president popularized in North America the fear that birth control would spell the end of Western civilization, especially if adopted by the masses. In a discussion of "Woman and the Social Problem" that took place in 1904, Mrs. B. Merrill Burns, provincial secretary of the Socialist Party of British Columbia, responded to Roosevelt's bogey of race suicide.

> . . . do not Presidents and Bishops complain most bitterly today that women are refusing to fulfill their manifest mission and that the "suicide of the race" is threatened. It may be that under an administration of justice and wisdom it will be worth while perpetuating the race. Who can blame women for feeling that it is no credit to them to supply slaves for a wage market. . . .

Burns was not so much calling for women to lower their fertility as she was defending their right to take whatever actions might be necessary to survive in a capitalist system. Perhaps under socialism, which would provide the right supportive milieu, births would increase, but in the existing society, which had undermined the family, one had to expect this "unconscious revolt against maternity so debased."[16]

As Burns's statement indicated, a central preoccupation of socialists was how the restriction of the birth rate might influence not simply individual families but the actual numbers of the working class. The labour movement was already aroused by the evidence that Canadian business was relying on imported labour – Asians in British Columbia, the child migrants of Dr. Barnardo and the Salvation Army in the East, the eastern Europeans on the Prairies – to weaken the working-class movement by increasing the size of the labour pool. Did not business, asked some socialists, praise the large family for the same reasons that it applauded every sort of migrant labour scheme – because both ensured a supply of cheap manpower? Accordingly, in the same papers that carried articles for restriction of immigration appeared articles in favour of birth control. A contributor to the *One Big Union Bulletin* asserted that it was well known that the upper classes wanted the workers to breed:

> They are anxious that the workers become even more productive in order that the labour market may be well stocked with slaves and also that the heavy family ties may render the workers incapable of real effective resistance to capitalist encroachments. . . . there is no crime in the calendar more serious than the practice of advocacy of birth control among the working class.[17]

The syndicalist press in particular supported the strategy of what in France was referred to as the *grève de ventre* – the birth strike – as part of a direct campaign to cripple capitalism.[18] Birth control was thus defended on the grounds of offering both political and economic benefits. And last but not least, it was presented as a unique tactic inasmuch as it meant that reproduction, which traditionally was viewed as holding women back, could now be seen as a powerful force they alone could employ. Women, argued Florence Rowe, could refuse to provide children as cannon fodder for the army or oil for the industrial machine.

> One of the most efficient weapons in the hands of women is not to produce the raw material. Why should women of the working class spend their lives in bearing and rearing "raw material" that the women of the leisured classes may continue to be leisured?[19]

The socialist defenders of birth control further argued that the establishment wanted large families to man both its factories *and* its armies. Before and after World War I the syndicalist and Marxist press was especially hostile to the military and its purported use of workers as "cannon fodder." Even the Boy Scouts were held up for derision by leftist papers as a paramilitary organization, and in 1923 the *One Big Union Bulletin* made concerted assaults on the Boy Scout movement at the time of Baden Powell's western tour.[20] Just as the "birth strike" was advanced as a response to attempts to dilute labour, birth control was proposed as a means to deprive generals of their recruits. The Women's Labour League, which attacked high school military training in the 1920's, was demanding the provision of birth control information by the government in the 1930's.[21] Indivisibly linking the military and the pronatalists, the *One Big Union Bulletin* headlined a report of a populationist speech: " 'Be Ye Fruitful and Multiply' Japanese Butcher Urges Workers to Raise Large Families For Future Cannon Fodder."[22]

Even the churches, by castigating the restriction of family size, could draw down on themselves the same sorts of criticisms the left doled out to the military. With the exception of elements of the SPC, Canadian socialists were rarely anticlerical, but priestly intrusions into the intimate area of family life were resented. For example, in 1918 the *B.C. Federationist* reported that the local clergy attributed the destruction of the family, symbolized by its reduction in size, to the pernicious influences of socialism – in their words, "internationalism." The paper's response was to reply that whether the worker had a small family or lived in "prolific squalor" was a matter that could only concern himself.[23] Protestant socialists were even more forthcoming in attributing to the Catholic Church the attempt to keep workers in moral subjection. "They have ruled us through our ignorance," asserted Florence Rowe, "but as knowledge grows the power of any superstition dies."[24] In a similarly anti-Catholic vein, in 1931 the *One Big Union Bulletin* reprinted an essay ridiculing the pope's recent encyclical on marriage and the family.

> The worker's family, struggling to give one or two children a decent upbringing, will grin at the notion of having sinned by having prevented a dozen hungry ones from tumbling about its feet. The parents who gave one or two dear sons to be torn to pieces by machine guns and explosives or to be poisoned by torturing gases scarcely can be made to regret that they did not have nine to give . . . unemployed fathers, mothers, brothers, sisters of starving and freezing families can scarcely be expected to beat their breasts in sorrow for the unborn, however prevented.[25]

The working-class family's recourse to birth control was defended by the left as a legitimate right; the opposition of conservatives to such practices was taken to symbolize yet another attempt by the upper classes to meddle in the affairs of the lower. The anger of the left aroused by such interference was increased by the knowledge that the wealthy did have access to contraceptive information that the law denied to the poor. The argument advanced by Dorothy Steeves, in demanding in 1936 that the government provide birth control clinics, was that only in this way could contraceptive information "be taken out of the realm

of privilege."[26] Her colleague, Dr. Lyle Telford, supported her
contention in asserting that the local hospital's provision of such
information was insufficient and inequitable: "but they decide there
who should have the advice and who shouldn't. We haven't the
right to refuse it to any reasonable person."[27] The response of
the Minister of Health was to retreat to the realm of rhetoric
and denounce birth control, in language that had not changed
since the time of Teddy Roosevelt, as "a cancer that is sapping
the very lifeblood of our society."[28] The left could not let this
sort of pontificating on the workers' duty to reproduce pass
unchallenged. When in 1926 the *Survey*, an American middle-
class magazine, commented on the need for a high birth rate,
the *One Big Union Bulletin* retorted typically: "Speaking for the
workers, we ask the *Survey* to kindly mind its own business, but
if it must dabble among the diapers to confine its obstetrical
curiousity [*sic*] to Riverside Drive."[29]

Up to this point, the defence of birth control offered by the
left could be judged to be based primarily on negative arguments.
Since business, the military, and the churches all seemed to want
larger families, birth control, which could disappoint such desires,
had to be supported. There was, of course, also the right of the
individual to live his or her own life as might be seen fit, an
argument that appealed more to the libertarian than to the socialist,
who stressed class solidarity. For more positive statements by
the left, it is necessary to turn to its discussion of women.

Canadian socialist publications were among the first to support
the women's movement, but their backing of the suffrage cause
was not always unhesitating. The more radical periodicals at times
portrayed the suffragettes as middle-class women of leisure who
refused to acknowledge the primacy of class divisions. The
discussion of a propertied woman's vote raised the spectre of
the extension of the franchise being used simply to shore up an
existing social system. And when, during World War I, so many
suffragists threw themselves avidly into the war effort, the suspicions of many socialists of the conservative social views of
"advanced" women were amply confirmed.[30] But if the issue of
the vote was downplayed in many left-wing publications, these
same papers did provide a forum for airing the needs of working
women in the areas of health, employment, and housing. In this
context of the role of birth control in progressive social change,
feminist arguments in favour of family limitation surfaced. The

most persuasive came from the pen of Florence Rowe, writing in the *One Big Union Bulletin* in the 1920's. Even at this date, to judge by her line of attack, she still met opponents within the left.

> You ask me: "What has this to do with working class women?" I answer, "it has much to do with them. Is it not from our children that the ranks of labour are recruited? Is it not our sons who are the rank and file of the army and navy? Is it not our sons who are the great sad army of unemployed, gradually becoming, as the years roll on, the great army of the unemployable, for to be continually 'out of work' and obliged to take the quantity and quality of food decided on by someone else is one of the most demoralizing things I know of. It embitters the spirit and lowers the mentality.
>
> Sister women, mothers who think, turn this matter over in your mind. Refuse the undignified position that either Abraham or Paul or the later creations of man's mind, the prayer book, gave you. Look at life as it really is for us of the working class."
>
> The question of the scientific regulation of human births is not offered as the "complete solution" but it is one that has deep significance. Nothing is unrelated, and when seriously studying the problems of the working class this side of life may well be considered in its relation to the ever-growing, more acute class struggle.[31]

Starting with the classical syndicalist arguments in favour of the "birth strike," Rowe proceeded to provide a domestic rationale for family planning that spoke more directly to the needs of women. No matter what its social effects might be, birth control promised to ease the burden of motherhood by sparing women repeated unwanted pregnancies. The state therefore had an obligation, if it had any concern for the physical and psychological well-being of its citizens, to provide to "those married people with sufficient intelligence and love for each other and their children to desire it, the information as how to limit the family without injuring the health or happiness of either."[32] But having asserted that contraceptive knowledge could make existing marriages happier, Rowe added the feminist insight that the goal of radicals was not simply to shore up the existing family structure but to subject it to scrutiny. It was in this light that she criticized the Mothers Allowance Act. Others on the left sneered at the paltry sums provided by this legislation; what Rowe held up for contempt was the assumption that, given sufficient payment, women would accept the humiliating fate of being relegated to the task of mindlessly breeding.[33]

The feminism espoused by Rowe stressed the need for working women to express their social and sexual solidarity. Wealthy women, she wrote, already restricted their births and it was time for working women to instruct each other in such methods and demand the aid of the state: "the women to prevent their daughters' lives being absorbed in the same dolorous way, will insist that a Department of Birth Control be added to the Department of Public Health."[34] Women should find joy in pregnancy but this could not be expected in capitalist society; it was therefore the duty of mature women to protect the young. Putting her beliefs into practice, Rowe advertised the fact that at the Plebs Hall in Winnipeg she was available each day for consultations "on any matter effecting [sic] the welfare of girls or women."[35]

Such feminist arguments were not restricted to women. Speaking at the Royal Theatre in Vancouver in 1919, J.S. Woodsworth, after defending women's political rights and the concept of companionate marriage in which the wife would be regarded by the husband as a "pal," turned to the question of limitation of family size. He castigated the Catholic defence of marital celibacy as "the most abominable doctrine ever taught"; what was needed in place of such old-fashioned doctrines was more sex education. And birth control would have to find a place in such an education. The reporter of the B.C.. Federationist summarized Woodsworth as follows:

> The speaker in conclusion strongly condemned the position taken by law and custom with regard to birth control. In the new social order he believed that the prospective mother would be allowed to say whether she wished her child to be brought into the world or not.[36]

With the addition of the socialist-feminist argument it was possible by the 1920's to piece together from the writings of the Canadian left a fairly well-developed defence of birth control. The phrase "piece together" is used purposefully because it would be misleading to suggest that the question of family limitation was in itself a central preoccupation of socialists. Social change was their concern; birth control was perceived to be of importance only because some socialists saw it playing a positive role in advancing such change. The support that birth control found on the left was thus in some senses equivocal; the same could be said of that proffered by later generations of professional family planners preoccupied by eugenics, child welfare, and the stability of both the family unit and the nation-state. Traces of all these notions appeared in publications of the left, yet the emphasis was distinctly different. The left had elaborated a radical analysis of birth control that sprang from a critique, not a defence, of the existing social system, an analysis based not on eugenic and Malthusian preoccupations but on a concern for individual rights and social obligations.

The Great Depression placed enormous pressures on working-class families. In 1929 only 5 per cent of the population earned more than $2,500 a year. The average wage was $1,200 at a time when the minimum needs of a family of four were estimated at $1,430. And in the worst years of the economic slump, average male salaries fell to $942 and female salaries to $559 a year. It was only to be expected that the leftist press, at the very least, would tacitly accept the necessity of fertility control. J.S. Woodsworth retorted to those who suggested that recourse to birth control was motivated by selfishness:

> I venture to suggest that the reason for the decrease in the size of families, while in part doubtless due to higher standards and even to the desire for luxuries, is also due to the fact that in the middle and wage earning classes it has simply become impossible for people to attempt to rear families of even a moderate size. They cannot afford to have families.[37]

Nonetheless, the issue continued to elicit ambivalent responses in some sections of the left and especially in the Communist press. Opposition to the advocacy of birth control as a social panacea was more widespread than mere attacks on the individual family's recourse to contraception, but the line separating the two issues was often blurred. Even papers such as the *One Big Union Bulletin*, which carried many of the most articulate defences of family limitation, also included from time to time criticisms of its proponents. Such arguments might be embedded in general essays critical of feminist issues, which could detract from the class struggle. Working-class women were in particular warned to avoid such "will-o-the-wisp" movements.[38] Coming closer to the issue, January Mortimer argued in "The Maternal Instinct" that capitalism was depriving women of their right to be fertile.[39] And it was capitalism, claimed an article from the *Socialist Standard* reprinted by the *One Big Union Bulletin* in 1930, that was using birth control to both control the labour supply and shift the responsibility of poverty on to the worker. The author did not totally condemn recourse to contraception. "There are human problems for which birth control may provide the solution, just as there are good reasons why some people should avoid alcohol . . . ." Capitalists, it was suggested, were using the population issue to transfer to the working class the responsibility for the social system's inadequacies. Nominally sympathetic philanthropists were constantly telling workers not to have sex, not to drink, not to go to movies but rather to spend their leisure time in parks and playing fields so that they would be fresh and productive on Monday morning. Thus, what capitalist apologists presented as a means of improving the life of the working-class family had as its real goal that of lowering the employers' costs while increasing the social subordination of employees. "We are to be born, educated, married, rationed in children and alcohol, our lives carefully supervised . . . ." The advocacy of birth control had to be judged a diversion. "The world is rich enough if the workers would but rid it of the out-of-date capitalist system. But we find our work for Socialism impeded by the muddle-headed enthusiasts who preach salvation through prohibition, birth control, industrial psychology and what not." The "smoke-screen" thrown up by such propagandists, intentionally or not, hid from the worker's gaze the real problems posed by capitalism.[40]

"Ithuriel," writing in the *One Big Union Bulletin* in 1931, repeated the charge that only the existence of capitalism made the artificial restriction of fertility necessary. "Economically, socially, psychologically, and physically the practise is unsound and should be unnecessary." Business once needed labour and so lauded large families; when a large population was no longer required capitalists vaunted recourse to family limitation. The fact that some churchmen had come out in favour of birth control only confirmed Ithuriel's view that the campaign was orchestrated by the upper class. Once more the churches were "down on their bellies grovelling to their money masters."[41]

The argument that the upper classes were seeking to tailor the reproductive habits of labour to fit the needs of capitalism was given some credence when doctors in the 1930's preached the necessity of the sterilization of the "unfit." The decade that saw the passage in Nazi Germany of race laws also witnessed in British Columbia and Alberta the passage of bills permitting the forcible sterilization of the mentally ill and retarded. The general trend of the argument in favour of such extreme measures to attain social control was recognized by the left as a growing menace. When C.F. Neelands of the Ontario Reformatory at Guelph called in 1931 for the sterilization of the unfit and the anti-social, the *One Big Union Bulletin* linked such measures to "the ways of the savage," yet another means of "appeasing and controlling only the slaves such as we have today."[42] The capitalist declared to be "moral" whatever act he needed to carry out to ensure his continued control. Similarly, William L. Hutton, a leading eugenicist, was quoted at length by the Communist Party paper, the *Canadian Tribune*: "Who are the feeble-minded?" (asked Hutton). "They are people with the mental capacities and abilities of children. In the cities they tend to drift towards the slums. Indeed slums are largely the product of the segregating of the subnormals. . . . For their benefit as well as for our own we should control their reproduction." But to set up the argument in such a fashion, protested the *Tribune*, was to imply poverty had biological, not social, causes and was simply a more sophisticated way in which to assert that the poor were innately inferior.[43]

In the final analysis, however, a basic source of much of the working-class movement's hostility to the advocacy of birth control was the belief held by many males that contraception was an unnatural, modern, middle-class practice that would only deprive the worker of the joys of heading the traditionally large, healthy family. In a perceptive 1929 article entitled "Sex and the Workers," a commentator observed that the popular idea that all workers once enjoyed such a patriarchal existence was a myth, and, in the Wobbly organizer Jim Thompson's words, "the majority of workers are homesick for a home they never had." But if it was a myth it was a powerful one, and it would make many male workers as hostile to those "meddlers" who preached the benefit of birth control as to those who opposed it.[44]

These suspicions that birth control could distract the workers from the central issue of the class struggle were most vehemently voiced by the Communist press. But the Communist Party of Canada's response to the question was the product of a number of conflicting preoccupations that changed over time. During the 1920's and 1930's the CPC stolidly followed the Comintern line and took as its first duty the defence of the Russian socialist experiment.[45] For many Canadians on the Communist and non-Communist left the most dramatic aspect of the U.S.S.R.'s attempt to create a new society was the restructuring of family life, accompanied after 1920 by the legitimation of abortion and the provision of birth control information. These changes were immediately hailed by the Socialist Party's *Western Clarion* in 1920.[46] In 1927 the syndicalist publication, the *One Big Union Bulletin*, ran a long article by Freda Utley on "How Women Live in Russia," which noted the great strides made in providing maternity benefits and advice on birth control. The latter was done in consultation centres as part of the "struggle against abortion," but Utley concluded that the hope harboured by some that socialism could eventually make unnecessary any family limitation "seems a little naive."[47] Similarly, in 1936 *C.C.F. News* carried the reports of Dr. and Mrs. Victor, recent visitors of Russia, who commented on Russian women's concern for the provision of family limitation information.[48]

Given the liberal attitude of the Soviets toward birth control and the lively interest taken in such policies by progressives in the West, one might have expected that the CPC would have looked kindly upon family limitation. It did not because to do so would have run counter to a basic tenet of the party, the avoidance of any issues that could divert attention from the class struggle.[49] It is true that the Women's Labour League, which came under the party's domination in the 1920's, interested itself in birth control and had as its slogans "Protection of Motherhood" and "Care of Motherhood." But when the party's line hardened in 1929 these mottos were attacked as "sentimental bourgeois slogans." The Sixth Convention of the CPC held that,

> . . . no propaganda on Birth Control, as a remedy of economic evils, be permissible and whatever articles written by women proletarians with an incorrect orientation have to be published, an editorial note, correcting the same, must accompany the article.[50]

The late twenties and early thirties were the time of the Communist Party's heroic isolation – in Canada as everywhere else in the West – and its spurning of the birth control issue was but one aspect of its efforts to keep itself undefiled from movements that aimed only at simple social reforms. This course was abandoned in the mid-thirties. With the rise of fascism the Comintern adopted a new tack calling for "Common Fronts" of all progressive elements. The CPC, which in 1935 had labelled the CCF a "social fascist" organization and attacked pacifist and women's groups as diversionary, was in 1936 exhorting its members to win such organizations to an alliance to defend the Soviet Union. In particular, female members were called on "to strive to promote the coming together of all existing women's organizations without distinction against war and reaction."[51] And so birth control was now taken up for discussion by the CPC as just such a movement in which Communists could woo the interests of working, farming, and middle-class women. In 1936 and 1937 the *Daily Clarion* ran a whole series of articles on birth control. The speeches of British birth control advocate Edith How-Martyn were reported, the radical past of Margaret Sanger noted, medical advice on contraceptives provided, and the acquittal of Canadian birth control activist Dorothea Palmer – "staunch progressive and friend of the people" – applauded.[52] In the summer of 1936 the Vancouver chapter of the Women's Labour League launched a petition demanding birth control clinics that began:

> Whereas: With the widespread unemployment, the burden of caring for the home and children falls principally upon the shoulders of the working class mothers who oftentimes [*sic*], rather than bring other children into the world, with small prospects of proper food, clothing and attention, resort to the most crude and dangerous means in order to procure abortions, with all its widespread evils, as thousands of women are suffering due to the lack of proper knowledge of Birth Control . . . [the government is asked to provide such information.][53]

Finally, at the Eighth Dominion Convention of the CPC in 1937 a call was made for "increased health services such as hospitalization, more clinics including birth control clinics, welfare services, etc. . . . "[54]

This proved to be the climax of the CPC's involvement in the birth control campaign. Ironically, the acceptance by the CPC of the legitimacy of the issue of family limitation took place at the very time when the Communist Party of the Soviet Union, in an effort to build Russia's population, was cutting back access to abortion and contraception. Not for the first nor for the last time was the CPC faced with the dilemma of having to provide an apology for a Soviet policy that weakened the party's credibility in Canada. Many Canadian women Communists were shocked by what they regarded as the regressive steps taken by the Soviet

Union in the matter of abortion. That their protests were heard was made clear by a number of articles on the women's page of the *Daily Clarion* in which tortuous arguments were presented to prove that the right to fertility control had to be fought for in a capitalist but not in a socialist state. In July of 1936, Jessica Smith conceded that a "great deal of confusion in Canada" existed concerning the revisions made in Soviet family law. Such problems could be cleared up, she asserted, once one recognized that abortion had been needed in 1920 in Russia but not in 1936 now that Soviet women were "free" and enjoyed child-care, maternity benefits, and freedom from the stigma of bearing illegitimate children. Such benefits were not enjoyed in Canada and so the struggle for birth control and abortion was warranted. In Russia, which was building up its population not in preparation for war but for peace, such campaigns were unnecessary. "Why then," concluded Smith, "should not the Soviet woman be encouraged in the motherhood that most women desire?"[55] A week later the paper carried an article from N. Krupskaya that made many of the same arguments based on women's "natural needs" and in addition advanced the tendentious assertion that the ordinary Russian women themselves sought to curb their own access to abortion.

Acceding to large numbers of requests from working women regarding the harmfulness of abortions, the Government of the U.S.S.R., with the aim of protecting the health of working women, has prepared a draft law on the prohibition of abortions. . . .[56]

Even the pronouncements of Lenin's widow did not still the concerns of Canadian women. In October, 1936, the *Daily Clarion* headed Anne Rivington's essay with the assertion, "Does the New Law Against Abortion Mean That a Woman is Again Nothing But a Breeder of Children? No, Emphatically No!"[57] The most notable part of Rivington's column was not her defence of Soviet law, which was simply a recapitulation of the arguments of earlier commentators; what stood out in the article was the obvious fear that many rank-and-file members were refusing to accept the party line on this intimate issue.

The inability of the leaders of the party to square the growing interest of Canadians in family limitation with the increasing restrictions on such practices in the Soviet Union appears to have been one reason why, from 1938 onwards, the discussion of birth control was dropped from the CPC press. It would appear that a second reason was that the CPC, in an effort to woo the broadest cross section of the public, abandoned a subject that some might consider too sensitive. Strangely enough, as the threat of fascism grew, the content of the women's page of the *Daily Clarion* became ever more frivolous, with more and more articles devoted to food and fashion.[58]

What was in effect a left-wing monopoly of the discussion of birth control was broken in the 1930's by the emergence in Canada of a socially conservative neo-Malthusian movement. The left had been drawn to the discussion of family limitation, at a time when the topic was still taboo, for a variety of reasons: suspicion of the upper classes turning to their own purposes the population issue; hostility to meddling by outsiders in the family life of the working class; concern for the living standards of working-class women; and, particularly in the case of the Communist Party, responsiveness to attitudes taken toward birth control by socialists abroad.

What can be concluded from this attempt to rescue from obscurity certain specific linkages of sex and politics in the Canadian past? The complexity of attitudes of those on the left toward the issue of birth control clearly prevents one from attempting to impose too categorical an interpretation on the data, but some broad generalizations can be drawn. First, and somewhat surprisingly, there is clearly no inherent reason why birth control should have found its first Canadian defenders on the left. Indeed, given that they drew heavily on the optimistic doctrines of such works as Henry George's *Progress and Poverty* (1879), Edward Bellamy's *Looking Backward* (1888), William Morris's *News From Nowhere* (1890), and Robert Blatchford's *Merrie England* (1894), in which degenerate capitalism was condemned for holding back population growth, their initial hostility to neo-Malthusianism was to be expected.[59] The stress on the moral superiority of reformers would prevent many from broaching the tabooed birth control issue and led some to doubt the revolutionary credentials of those who did. Tom Cassidy, for example, an active propagandist for the OBU who included defences of abortion and birth control in his public lectures, found himself and Catherine Rose accused by the executive in 1923 of being "egotistical enough to consider the vindication of their moral standards of greater importance than the development of the movement."[60] But this very moralism, if turned to the purposes of exalting the importance of the bearing and rearing of children, could also lead in a roundabout fashion to an acceptance of the legitimacy of the restriction of fertility. Such was the path taken by Beatrice Brigden and Florence Rowe.

The second point to be drawn from an analysis of the birth control debate is the importance attributed by the left both to the state and to women. There were early libertarian defenders of contraception in Canada, such as the American Emma Goldman and the Scot R.B. Kerr, but what is most striking about the discussion of the population issue in the 1920's and 1930's was the collectivist spirit that so strongly coloured the left's analysis. This explains in part why there were so few concrete proposals for the provision of birth control services by the labour and farming movements themselves. Birth control was but one more area in which the left asserted that the state ultimately had to step in to provide necessary information and material.

The attribution to the state of such responsibilities was in turn a function of the importance women played in leftist organizations. Indeed, the response of individual movements to the issue of birth control served as a sort of litmus test of their cultural radicalism. Socialist feminists like Florence Rowe and groups such as the Women's Labour League sought to make defence of contraception a central plank in the socialist program. "We all know that rich women can buy anything," asserted the WLL in 1935. "This [restriction of birth control] is a law for the rich and against the poor woman."[61] Particularly in the West, progressives argued that though women's lives would not be fully improved until major social reforms were instituted, in the meantime the burdens of working-class families had to be alleviated. That such feminist arguments did not go unopposed is made clear by the above analysis of the Communist Party's stance. The importance of asking how the various sections of the left responded is that it provides the beginnings of a more fully fleshed view of Canadian politics in which the questions of the relationships of the sexes and the bearing of children are included.

Finally, it has to be acknowledged that, on the official level, no leftist movement considered the birth control issue a number-one priority. Some might conclude that by recognizing such ambiguities and contradictions it is pointless to single out the left's position as worthy of analysis. In response, it must be admitted that the attempt to place the birth control issue within the context of a political ideology did pose real problems – problems that could be skirted by those Canadians who did not approach the question from an ideologically committed point of view. Nonetheless, some of the left did assume that the restriction of family size had political consequences, and this led them to be the first Canadian public defenders of the practice. Individual social workers, doctors, and bureaucrats within the Ministry of Health might surreptitiously interest themselves in the issue, but they did not make their views known. The defence of restriction of family size was therefore to be first assumed by the left. Equally important is that in the discussion of birth control all sections of the left were united at least in their defence of voluntarism. Whether leftists condemned or condoned birth control, they did share a common anti-authoritarian, anti-establishment antipathy toward middle-class meddling in the lives of labouring families.

The last question to be asked is if the left-wing discussion of birth control had any appreciable effect on working-class fertility. Clearly, economic pressures were the overriding reasons for restriction of family size, and, consequently, how one might gauge the impact of ideological arguments within the constellation of motivations appears impossible to determine. But to say that it is difficult to determine the importance of ideology is not the same as saying that therefore ideology is not important. Kaufman was the first to recognize this. On December 3, 1935, he wrote Margaret Sanger that he had an agent, a "quiet worker," spreading birth control propaganda among the Toronto organizations of the unemployed. "We find that practically all types of unemployed, whether rabid communists or otherwise, agree about 90% that birth control is necessary."[62] What concerned Kaufman was that many of these same workers also wanted to know the policy of the Soviet Union toward birth control; his reason for writing to Sanger was to ask how he might best respond. Clues that other Canadian workers did not totally divorce their views on the family from their social and political concerns are found in letters to the press. A "Nanaimo Girl" writing the *B.C. Federationist* in 1914 called on the working class to awaken to the fact that repeated pregnancies produce dull, sickly children and a passive labour force. It was the wealthy who wanted a growing population, she asserted, to provide "strike breakers and militia and specials" and "slaves for the labour market."[63] In a less rhetorical tone, "M.N." informed the readers of the *One Big Union Bulletin* in 1928 that as a "wage slave" he could only afford to raise one child. "I don't want more than one, no matter what big business or its supporters may think." He did not want to raise children to be soldiers; he did not believe in the threat of the "Yellow Peril"; he did not accept Canada's need for added population to increase development. And yet, following this litany of socialist arguments in favour of family limitation, "M.N." asserted that his decision was not ideologically based. Voicing what must have been the sentiments of the mass of Canadian workers, he declared, "I am advocating nothing. I just see my own advantage in the struggle for life . . . ."[64]

PART III

Population Control and Reproductive Rights

5

A.R. Kaufman and the Birth Control Campaign in Central Canada

In 1930 no birth control movement existed in central Canada; by 1937 clinics were active in Toronto, Hamilton, and Windsor, and a Parents' Information Bureau existed in Kitchener. More importantly, a newly organized birth control lobby proved powerful enough to win the acquittal of Dorothea Palmer, who for her door-to-door canvassing in favour of birth control in the poorer neighbourhoods of the small Ottawa Valley town of Eastview was charged with violation of Section 207c of the Criminal Code. The Palmer trial was compared by some at the time as being to the birth controllers what the Scopes monkey trial had been to the evolutionists.[1] The presiding judge not only agreed with the defence's argument that Palmer's activities were justified inasmuch as they served "the public good"; he declared that the existing law did not accurately portray the sentiments of most Canadians. This judgement, confirmed by the Ontario appeal court, marked a breakthrough in the legitimation of birth control in Canada.[2] Such a swift victory, as surprising as it might appear, was to be expected. The 1929 depression and the social fears that it kindled, precipitated the entry into the birth control discussion of clergymen, society women, and philanthropic businessmen who had heretofore remained aloof.

It is important, however, not to exaggerate the demographic

impact of this new movement. Its adherents would claim that they helped lower the birth rate. They clearly did play a role in facilitating the attempts of some couples to limit family size, but to determine quantitatively such effects is impossible. In any event, this new birth control movement only emerged in the 1930's when Canada's fertility rate had already dipped to an unprecedented low level. The importance of the Ontario birth controllers was that they in effect made the advocacy of family planning "respectable." Many of the first Canadian defenders of contraception had associated it, as we have seen, with sexual and political radicalism; the new birth controllers succeeded in presenting family planning as a force that would support rather than subvert existing social, political, and sexual relationships.

This chapter examines the birth controllers' accomplishments – the most famous being their 1937 judicial victory – and seeks to determine their motives, particularly the motives of the architect of the Palmer acquittal and the driving force behind the campaign for contraceptive propaganda, A.R. Kaufman. First, however, by analysing the preoccupations of A.H. Tyrer and Mrs. Mary C. Hawkins we can better understand the context in which Kaufman was to operate.

Today, few Canadians are familiar with the name of A.H. Tyrer, but in the 1930's and early 1940's his *Sex, Marriage and Birth Control* enjoyed greater sales than any other Canadian sex education and contraception publication.[3] Tyrer was very much a pioneer, a claim that he was only too eager to make. He wrote Margaret Sanger to inform her that, "So far I have been fighting a lone fight against prejudice and bigotry . . . out of my own shallow pocket."[4] He told Marie Stopes, "It seems to have fallen on my shoulders to be the propagandist of the Birth Control movement in Canada."[5] He later added with typical immodesty, "I am just plugging along here and sometimes wonder where the courage to carry on comes from."[6] Such claims were inevitably accompanied by appeals for financial support. Tyrer asserted in his autobiography, *And A New Earth* (1944), that he had suffered a life of "inexpressible agony," but he proved all too able to express to his correspondents the financial problems posed by his elderly sister, his cataracts, his illnesses, his loss of investments, and a variety of other trials and "vicissitudes of life."[7]

Tyrer, born in Britain in 1870, came to Canada at the age of seventeen.[8] Always a sickly individual, he started his working life as a teacher but in 1895 entered the Anglican ministry. He spent many years in the United States and appears to have returned to Canada to work in the Muskoka region in the 1920's. Nearing sixty, his eyesight failing, and his wife having just died, he determined in 1929 to devote his remaining years to propagandizing in favour of birth control. He had come to the conclusion, so he asserted in his autobiography, that only population planning would get to the roots of the social misery revealed by the depression.

Tyrer was primarily a propagandist who hoped to harness the energies of the Protestant clergy to the birth control cause. By his own account he eventually sent out 7,000 copies of a twelve-page tract entitled *Some Facts About Birth Control* to every Protestant minister in the country.[9] In the tract Tyrer argued that birth control would put an end to war, maternal and infant deaths, abortion, infanticide, prostitution, divorce, and poverty. Ministers who shared his concerns were asked to send back to him on accompanying application forms the names of married and engaged couples who requested contraceptive information. These couples were in turn sent a sixteen-page pamphlet, *Birth Control and Some of its Simplest Methods*. Its readers could similarly pass on to Tyrer the names of others desirous of receiving the same information. The contraceptive methods described by Tyrer as unsatisfactory but very common were withdrawal and douching. He recommended the use of suppositories, sponges, caps, pessaries, and condoms. He explained how sponges could be cut to the appropriate size, why condoms had to be tested before use, and Marie Stopes's method of making soluble pessaries of cocoa butter, borax, salicylic acid, and quinine bi-sulfate.[10]

Tyrer's form of propagandizing by post via a pyramid system of contacts had several advantages; it was a cheap, discreet method of contacting thousands of individuals across an enormous nation. Its major drawback was that it was left to couples to acquire from druggists and commercial outlets the necessary contraceptives. This meant that the poorest – who in Tyrer's view most needed birth control protection – were the least likely to get it. He believed his pamphleteering did provide help, but he came to realize the need to supplement it with the establishment of some sort of more direct service. He wrote Marie Stopes:

> I am of course working for the establishment of travelling clinics or something of that sort and I am sure it will come. I find great interest among influential people and general approval. Of course I realized the great desirability of contraceptive

knowledge being given by professional men but I am not going to hesitate giving it myself when asked.[11]

In 1930 Tyrer had been put in touch with Stopes by Dr. W.E. Blatz of the Psychiatric Department of the University of Toronto, who had visited Stopes's London clinic.[12] Addressing Stopes as "Dear friend of Birth Control," Tyrer asked if she could provide him with $3,000 to set up a similar clinic in Toronto; she replied she could not.[13]

In 1931 Tyrer turned for support to such American birth controllers as Margaret Sanger and Mary Ware Dennett and through them attempted to tap the resources of American philanthropists.[14] He was so eager to win the support of the affluent that he initially avoided the contentious term "birth control."[15] When he informed Sanger that he had founded the Canadian Voluntary Parenthood League she responded that many might not understand what such a name implied. She asked why he did not employ the clear and concise term "birth control," which she had herself coined.[16] "With perhaps a majority prejudiced and possessed of more or less bigotry," replied Tyrer, "it seemed to some of us that 'Voluntary Parenthood' might perhaps be less flaunting of a red flag."[17] In fact, Sanger's argument finally won out; Tyrer called his 1931 organization the Canadian Birth Control League and in 1932 the Birth Control Society of Canada.

In the early 1930's Tyrer's main objective was to raise funds so that his organization could establish a birth control clinic in Toronto's worst slum, the Ward.[18] His attempts to raise support in Britain and America having failed, he finally projected setting up a counselling centre in Toronto with the support of the Rev. Lawrence Skey and Dr. Rowena Hume. Skey already provided the prospective couples of St. Anne's Anglican Church with marital advice and in the summer of 1931 publicly defended the morality of family planning. To the attacks of fellow churchmen, he replied, "Do I have the right to permit women to go to their deaths from bearing too many children because the doctors and government will not inform them?"[19] The police appeared to imply that he could do as he pleased; they made it clear that they would not interfere with his activities unless official complaints were lodged. As a result, Skey received a flood of letters from couples seeking contraceptive information. It was a small step to proceed with the establishment of an office in which Hume could give medical advice and from which Tyrer could send out his birth control pamphlets. The Marriage Welfare Bureau, as it was ultimately

christened, gave general marriage counselling and directed appli-
cants to physicians who were willing to provide detailed contraceptive information and fit diaphragms.

Tyrer did not think it strange that a birth control clinic should
be harboured by a Protestant church. He found that a good portion
of ministers, in theory at least, supported family planning. He
reported, for example, that 100 of the 400 letters sent to churches
in 1932 asking if they wanted his pamphlet on birth control
methods received favourable responses.[20] The Lambeth Conference of 1930 had, of course, given the Anglican Church's tepid
approval to birth control. Tyrer was disappointed, however, that
his Anglican brethren did not go further in Canada in demanding
the full legalization of family planning propaganda.[21] The fact
that in 1936 the United Church of Canada formally endorsed
the morality of birth control was, he claimed, due in part at least
to his own activities.[22] Catholic couples also sought birth control
information, but Tyrer was convinced that their priests would never
relax their opposition. Indeed, Tyrer presented the campaign for
birth control as very much a contest between the churches. At
times he seemed to argue that Protestants had to defend birth
control for no other reason than that Catholics opposed it. "Thank
God," he exulted, "this is still a Protestant country not yet
dominated by the Italian Vatican."[23]

Having few financial resources, Tyrer could only accomplish
a limited amount. In fact, most of his letters from the early 1930's
were pleas for monetary support. Interestingly enough, however,
he later made no mention in his autobiography of the aid he
received from American and British friends. Instead, he presented
himself as being miraculously rescued from distress in the winter
of 1931-1932 by A.R. Kaufman: "My blindness was increasing
and my bank account was decreasing and was close to the
vanishing point and I was wondering what the next step would
be when, one afternoon, a ring came to my door."[24] Prophetically,
Marie Stopes had turned aside one of Tyrer's numerous requests
for support with the suggestion: "If only you would pray hard
and get some nice American millionaire to die and leave me a
few million you should get enough to found your Canadian clinic
from it!"[25] Kaufman was alive and a Canadian, but he promised,
after determining that he and Tyrer shared similar opinions
concerning the importance of family planning, to provide up to
$500 a year for Tyrer's work.

Tyrer and Kaufman were going to influence each other's

thinking in a variety of ways. The most obvious way Tyrer aped his benefactor was in putting increased stress on eugenic considerations in his defence of birth control. As we will see in greater detail in what follows, Kaufman was very much interested in eugenics and his first involvement in birth control consisted of financing sterilizations. Tyrer was aware of the fact that some eugenicists were opposed to birth control on the grounds that it was a cause of the decline of the fertility of the "best stock." To win Kaufman's continued support Tyrer argued from 1932 onward that eugenic sterilization did have a place in the complete birth control arsenal. In asserting that those who lacked character or intelligence had to be sterilized because they could not be relied upon to employ contraceptives, he moved away from the stance adopted by Margaret Sanger and Marie Stopes, on whom he had first relied. Sanger warned him that sterilization should be viewed as a "war measure" only to be defended in the most extreme cases because its espousal could undermine public support for contraception.[26] Tyrer persisted, however, in putting more and more emphasis on eugenic sterilization.

Tyrer's eugenic concerns were candidly expressed in his 1936 book, *Sex, Marriage and Birth Control (Lifting the Blinds on Marriage)*.[27] Here he presented as the main need for birth control propaganda the fact that the "lower fourth" of the population was producing over one-half of the nation's children. If racial degeneration were to be avoided these "generally irresponsible classes" had to be taught to employ the same contraceptive techniques used by the intelligent.[28] At the same time, Tyrer argued that some sort of government policy had to be implemented that would spare the professional classes the heavy costs of raising and educating their children.

> As soon as a social system is evolved that will remedy all this and take away from parents the fear that more children may mean more distress and poverty, we shall find the birth-rate among the best citizens increasing.[29]

Tyrer reiterated his concern for the fertility of "the best citizens" in his 1944 autobiography:

> These classes [the professional and educated] are producing *less than three children to a family* as against anywhere up *to twenty amongst the labouring classes*. This is the great handicap that confronts social progress today.[30]

He acknowledged that he had once thought the poor could be helped by charity or social programs; now he realized that such intervention actually threatened the "welfare of the race":

> It was a futile effort to improve conditions by feeding the hungry and clothing the naked, when there would have been practically no hunger or nakedness had the people not been producing up to twenty children in the family.[31]

Tyrer was so enamoured of this new theory that he ludicrously suggested to a newspaper that was raising Christmas funds for the poor that his birth control pamphlet be included in its offerings; he was so obtuse that he wondered why the newspaper in question never even deigned to respond to his suggestion.[32]

Tyrer omitted from his account of his dawning realization that the "irresponsible, criminal and mentally deficient" were the source of "most of our social liabilities" the influence of A.R. Kaufman.[33] An analysis of Tyrer's correspondence reveals, however, that by 1933 he was totally dependent on Kaufman and was clearly tailoring his pronouncements to fit those of his benefactor. When Marie Stopes suggested in 1935 that Tyrer affiliate his league with hers, he candidly replied:

> Mr. Kaufman is a good deal of an individualist and I suspect that he might not approve a plan that would disrupt the present set-up that is working effectively. . . . Outside of Mr. Kaufman's good-will and support I should be quite unable to carry on.[34]

But if Tyrer was financially dependent on Kaufman, Kaufman in turn was influenced by Tyrer in two important ways. In the first place, Tyrer demonstrated to the ever-cautious Kaufman that birth controllers did not have to worry about police prosecution. Tyrer reported that Kaufman was at first overly nervous of judicial interference,

> . . . but when he found out that I had tested that attitude by disregarding it entirely, and that my work had been going on for some time and that there had been no interference with me, he concluded that the law was not interested in interfering with a work so healthfully beneficial to the public.[35]

Tyrer appears to have also influenced Kaufman in suggesting that a court case fought over the legitimacy of distributing birth control material should in fact be welcomed. As early as 1931 Tyrer had written Marie Stopes that he would not be frightened by any threat of prosecution because of the obvious "public good" loophole in Section 207c of the Criminal Code. He was convinced that no jury in any province save Quebec would find him guilty.[36] A major court case would, of course, entail heavy legal expenses, but these could be easily borne by Kaufman. It was simply a question of choosing the right time and place.

In Toronto the birth control movement was initially promoted by progressive churchmen like Tyrer. In Hamilton, clubwomen, led by Mrs. Mary Hawkins, assumed a similar prominence. Mary Hawkins (1875-1950) was born in Bronxville, New York, the daughter of a wealthy, philanthropic businessman, Frank R. Chambers. After graduating from Vassar she came to Canada as wife of William C. Hawkins, director of Hamilton Light and Power. Mrs. Hawkins, active in establishing local community services such as the Family Services Bureau and the Community Chest, increased such involvements after her husband's death in 1925. As a friend of Margaret Sanger – whom she met while vacationing at Nantucket – and as a prominent Hamilton clubwoman, Hawkins was in an ideal position, once the depression of 1929 forced on public attention the extent of local poverty, to emerge as patron of the Hamilton birth control movement.[37]

Hawkins was won to the birth control cause by Gertrude Burgar, who, while taking a course at the London School of Economics in 1928, appears to have been in touch with Marie Stopes. When Burgar returned to Hamilton in 1929 to begin social work and assist with the Samaritan Club's care of tuberculosis victims, she became convinced that the Canadian poor also needed birth control information. Since the medical profession was reluctant to provide such a service, she concluded that educated women such as herself would have to act. She wrote Marie Stopes in July, 1929: "I realize that any information given to mothers should be given by doctors, but when they refuse to give it, I feel that there is considerable advice which a social worker could give in certain cases."[38] In November she wrote again to say that she had met Hawkins and that they hoped to form a group and open a clinic. A friend had already been sent to Cleveland to see how the birth control clinic in that city functioned. Initial investigation by Burgar also indicated, so she informed Stopes, that the legal obstacles were not as daunting as first feared.

I think with sufficient public opinion back of us, we could avoid difficulty. I know this will sound optimistic to you because of the great struggle you have been through, but you have paved the way and others have already followed your lead and been successful.[39]

In fact, events were to unfold far more slowly than Burgar anticipated.[40] A Hamilton clinic was about to open in the summer of 1931 but had to be shelved at the last moment due to unexpected medical opposition and the absence of Hawkins. In October, Burgar confided to Stopes:

> We are still very much discouraged over our clinic, but we are still hopeful of getting one started before the expiration of the year. All plans were made to open one in June. Mrs. Hawkins who was financing the whole thing, had signed a lease, purchased equipment and everything was ready, when some of the Doctors in the building threatened to vacate if our clinic had rooms there. Mrs. Hawkins had left town for the summer and consequently everything fell through for the time. However she has now returned and is working on other plans. We also have a wealthy man in Kitchener who has been financing some sterilization work there, and together we have high hopes.[41]

With Hawkins back, new efforts were made, an enlarged group was formed in December, and in March of 1932 the Hamilton clinic was finally opened.[42]

The establishment and continuation of the Hamilton clinic was mainly due to Hawkins's success in winning the support of the local legal, social, and medical authorities. Hawkins wrote Stopes that before the clinic had opened its doors she had sought legal advice and found both the crown attorney and the attorney general sympathetic.[43] She reported that unfortunately the provincial Minister of Health was "very misinformed on the subject of birth control" and that the local medical officer had "the courage of a rabbit."[44] To remedy such failings, she asked Stopes to forward information on how the clinics and local authorities in England co-ordinated their activities. Once convinced of the legality of the clinics and of the support of key provincial ministers, Hawkins was confident of meeting no serious judicial opposition.

To shore up the social support of the clinic, Hawkins recruited the leading clubwomen of Hamilton into the Birth Control Society. They included, for example, Mrs. J.A. Newnham, wife of the Anglican bishop of Moosonee, Mrs. A.R. McLachlin, founder of the women's auxiliary to the Board of Health, Mrs. I. Olmsted of the Infants Home, and Mrs. Thompson, president of the Big Sister Association of Hamilton. To assist her recruitment drive, Hawkins asked that Stopes send her a list of prominent British business leaders who supported birth control; the list was to be used to impress the Hamilton elite with the respectability of the movement. And just in case some feared that birth control smacked of American radicalism, she made a point of playing up the society's links with Stopes's English movement rather than with Sanger's American organization.[45] Hawkins's attempts to lure Hamilton's clubwomen into support of birth control quickly proved themselves; within a year the Birth Control Society of Hamilton grew from fifteen to 200 members. Its clinic not only serviced hundreds of patients; it was visited or contacted by clubwomen from across Canada interested in establishing similar centres in their own cities.[46]

Doctors had unexpectedly sidetracked Hawkins's first attempt at opening a clinic; to counter opposition on that front she assiduously courted the medical profession. The Hamilton clinic always had a medical doctor in attendance. Dr. Elizabeth Bagshaw, who was to work at the clinic for the next thirty-one years, and Dr. R.R. Waddell went to New York to observe how Margaret Sanger's clinic functioned.[47] They returned with pamphlets and with spermicidal jellies that were duplicated by local pharmacists. Help was also given the Hamilton clinic by the supporters of a similar establishment in Cleveland.[48] Hawkins listed in the clinic's brochure the names of seven medical consultants and by the end of 1932 could claim the support of forty-four doctors.[49] Some doctors viewed any clinic as a dangerous rival but, as she told Stopes, Hawkins was willing to challenge them.

> The staff doctors of our Municipal Hospital say (privately) that we should be at the Hospital. I am going to silence them by writing a letter and asking them if they will take over the Clinic and conduct it. I know they won't but they will not be able to say that we are rivals or opportunists.[50]

In fact, by 1935 the Hamilton hospital was co-operating with the clinic to the extent that it allowed its representatives to visit the maternity department to speak to patients wishing information on contraception.[51]

Hawkins not only succeeded in presenting the birth control clinic as an institution worthy of the support of Hamilton's middle-class; she also propagated the idea that the only source of opposition came from either Catholic zealots or political sub-versives. She was confident that the attacks of the local Catholic archbishop could only strengthen the resolve of the movement's Protestant supporters and ridiculed the suggestion of socialists that poverty could be best dealt with by state intervention.[52] Gladys Brandt, one of Kaufman's workers, clearly shared her opinions; she reported to Hawkins in 1934 that birth control activities in the Windsor area were kept confidential because there were "a great many communists and Roman Catholics in the Border Cities."[53] Whether or not such enemies really did exist, it obviously served the interest of Hawkins, intent on winning the support of Protestant business leaders, to suggest that they did.

Why should respectable members of Hamilton society have supported a birth control clinic? Hawkins and her group defended contraception for two main reasons. The first was the humanitarian argument that family planning was a particular blessing for women since it promised to spare them unwanted pregnancies and the threats of miscarriages, abortions, and infant and maternal deaths. But Hawkins's movement complemented the first, "feminist" defence of birth control with a second eugenic argument. Birth control, it asserted, would reduce the incidence of venereal disease, tuberculosis, mental deficiency, and, as a result, the tax burden of the middle classes. This second argument must have been considered the more effective because it received the greater prominence in the group's literature. Readers of that literature were informed that whereas it cost $1,500 to provide 500 women with contraceptives, these same women would have cost the community $30,000 if they each had a child. And the costs did not stop there; ". . . each little newly born citizen would immediatley go on city relief."[54] In 1934 the births of families on relief cost the city, according to the Birth Control Society of Hamilton, $58,878.[55] Hawkins's point was that it served the economic self-interest of the middle classes to support institutions that brought down the birth rate of the lower classes.

The clinic also played a political role that its supporters at times explicitly articulated. It sought to impress on the poor that they alone, and not society as a whole, were responsible for their poverty. It sought to drive home the "recognition of the basic necessity to balance family responsibilities and family budget; and also that lacking this balance, the attempt to convert a social liability into a social asset is futile."[56] The point that the clinic was both distributing contraceptives and seeking to impose middle-class standards on its clientele was brought out in its reports, which stressed the "low intelligence," drunkenness, and violence its volunteers encountered. Clients who did not successfully employ the contraceptives they were provided with were portrayed in annual reports as having somehow "failed" the clinic: "The Clinic regretfully reports many failures through lack of cooperation on the part of the patient, but of these fully one-third return, acknowledging their neglect and promising better for the future."[57] The thought that such results could be taken as evidence of the failure of the clinic's methods or motives does not seem to have been entertained by Hawkins.

The Hamilton birth control clinic never serviced more than a small portion of the working-class clientele toward which its appeals were directed. The clinic operated on the pattern set by Marie Stopes's London clinic.[58] Patients were admitted on presentation of a card signed by a physician, but they could also be introduced via a social worker, other patients, or through reading an advertisement or hearing a public lecture. The clinic at first was open only on Fridays, but later it operated on Tuesdays as well. The doctor in attendance would fit diaphragms or provide instruction on the uses of jellies and suppositories; like the nurses, the attending doctor would receive only a nominal fee. Volunteer social workers provided follow-up studies to see if the contraceptives were being successfully employed. Hawkins financed the entire scheme in the early years, with the society's membership slowly assuming financial responsibility.[59] Patients were charged a fee of $3. The charge was waived for those on relief, who in the early 1930's made up half of the clinic's patients.[60] Three hundred and ninety patients were seen in 1932; by 1935, 1,155 women referred by 129 doctors had been helped.[61] In thirty years, 5,000 patients passed through the clinic's doors, an apparently large number but on average less than two hundred a year.

Although the clinic provided in the form of diaphragms a highly reliable form of contraceptive, the small number of clients it reached preoccupied the "wealthy man in Kitchener" to whom Burgar referred in her 1931 letter to Marie Stopes. A.R. Kaufman was as interested in Hawkins's efforts as in Tyrer's. He sent the Hamilton clinic contraceptive materials, which were gratefully received; the women of Hamilton were not as receptive, however, to Kaufman's reiterated arguments that to be truly successful they had to improve their delivery system.[62]

A.R. Kaufman was the most original of the Canadian birth

controllers and deserves to be ranked along with Margaret Sanger and Marie Stopes for his innovative contributions to family planning. Stopes and Sanger both built their birth control movements around the clinic, the physician, and the vaginal diaphragm. They sought thereby first to present contraception as a respectable subject for medical research, which was not to be associated with grubby rubber shops selling condoms; second, they wanted to attract the support of physicians and politicians who would ultimately see the wisdom of having such clinics incorporated in existing welfare and medical institutions; and third, they aimed to provide women with the most advanced and effective forms of protection, which would allow them to enjoy fully the joys of sexuality and the benefits of planned parenthood. In pursuing such strategies both Stopes and Sanger turned their backs on the gloomy old neo-Malthusians who simply harped on the crude economic argument that if working-class fertility were not curbed social disaster would ensue. Both Stopes and Sanger were ultimately successful. In Britain the government informed local authorities in 1930 that they could provide birth control information through their welfare facilities to those mothers whose health might be jeopardized by additional pregnancies. The United States Circuit Court of Appeal found in favour of the open dissemination of birth control information in 1936, and in the following year the American Medical Association approved contraception as a subject for medical research.[63]

The Hamilton birth control clinic was modelled on those of Stopes and Sanger and its founders hoped it would achieve the same breakthroughs. This clinic also shared with its British and American counterparts one major failing: it provided its quality service to only a tiny proportion of its targeted clientele. For a hard-nosed businessman and neo-Malthusian like Kaufman, this indicated that something was inherently wrong with the system; the importance of his work was based on the fact that he set out to produce something better.

Alvin Ratz Kaufman (1885-1983) was a successful Kitchener manufacturer, owner of the Kaufman Rubber Company, which made rainwear and rubber boots.[64] In all his dealings he demonstrated a desire to dominate and a dispassionate interest in adopting whatever policy was required to produce results. He turned his energies to the question of birth control in part because he harboured the antiquated Malthusian fear of population pressures eventually leading to revolution, in part because he obviously revelled in the possibility of shaping the lives of thousands, of doing, in his words, "something more fundamental than contributing to social work that is palliative and not remedial."[65]

In December of 1929, according to the account that he provided to numerous audiences and correspondents, Kaufman began to lay off employees, as he usually did after the winter rush. When the dismissed workers protested that they were the ones most in need of work he sent Anna Weber, his company nurse, to investigate. She reported, as he recalled, that:

. . . conditions were particularly hopeless in families where one or both parents were more or less mentally deficient, the housekeeping consequently very bad, and frequently too much of the meagre income wasted on non-essentials. I also found that the less intelligence the larger the families, and the more hopeless their condition. I cannot meet competition by using inferior help, and decided that employing such help merely enabled them to increase the social problem by raising more unfortunate, handicapped children.[66]

The factory nurse suggested that Kaufman offer the unemployed, instead of jobs, birth control information or free sterilization. Many agreed. Their response was, according to Kaufman, "surprising." His account was viewed with both surprise and suspicion by those who thought it likely that some workers at least were retained on condition that they employ the services offered by Kaufman.[67] Such an interpretation is supported by the fact that his nurse, Anna Weber, had previously been employed in Chicago, where she had referred mothers to birth control clinics between 1926 and 1929. Quite possibly, when Kaufman brought her to Kitchener in January, 1929, it was with the intention of launching the program that he later presented as being forced on him by events.[68]

Kaufman not only had his own employees sterilized or fitted with diaphragms; he was soon responding to requests for similar services from others referred to him by employers and social workers. Activities went so well in Kitchener that he extended his work to London, Guelph, and the surrounding communities. Hearing of the similar interests of Tyrer and Hawkins, he contacted them both in 1931 to compare notes on their progress. At the same time he sent his personal doctor, R.G. Ratz, to Margaret Sanger's Birth Control Clinical Research Bureau in New York to obtain up-to-date information on the most effective forms of contraception.[69] Kaufman co-ordinated the program of his staff from what he christened in 1933 the Parents' Information Bureau.

Kaufman's initial enthusiasm was tempered, however, as he came to appreciate the problems posed by the delivery and use of the best available contraceptive – the pessary diaphragm. He later recalled:

> Our original cases in Kitchener were practically all pessary cases sent to the local doctors for fittings. Only about one-third of the patients contacted went to the doctor for a pessary fitting in spite of the fact that we averaged over three calls on each case, or an average of about ten cases actually fitted. I gave up in disgust as this method was too expensive to recommend when contacting the lower types, about half of whom were on relief, and on the whole were too shiftless to co-operate properly.[70]

Once one cuts through Kaufman's distastefully condescending rhetoric one can see that he had glimpsed the vital difference between the effectiveness of a contraceptive device and its effective acceptance and use.

Different contraceptives posed different problems. Many women apparently disliked the condom because they associated it with protection from venereal disease and prostitution. Some working-class men, according to Kaufman, also did not like to use it. "Judging from the calibre of people we help, I do not think even half of them use the condoms, as we find the type of men in this lower class much too selfish and inconsiderate."[71] The diaphragm, the most effective of contraceptives, had to be fitted by a doctor and not all doctors could do this skilfully. Kaufman informed one correspondent that "I find at our Windsor clinic about fifty percent of the patients cannot be fitted with a pessary for various reasons, some of which apparently are no credit to obstetricians."[72] Only a minority of working-class women could be cajoled into being fitted with a diaphragm; a good proportion of these eventually abandoned its use. Although many of these women wanted to control their fertility, they so disliked both the nature of the preliminary medical examination and the technique of the particular contraceptive that they did not pursue its employment.

Since Kaufman's main desire was to bring down the working-class birth rate he concluded that this could be accomplished most effectively and economically, not by providing a few women with a highly reliable contraceptive, but by providing many women with a less reliable but more acceptable form of protection. Consequently, the Parents' Information Bureau had fewer and fewer diaphragms fitted and sent out more and more packages of contraceptive jelly, plungers with which to apply it, and condoms.

The diaphragm, to be used properly, had to be fitted by a physician and employed regularly by women who ideally had foresight, privacy, and a knowledge of their bodies. Kaufman conceded that if employed by intelligent, middle-class women the diaphragm would always prove superior, but for those whom he called "shiftless people" less effective means such as a simple spermicidal jelly would prove more successful. He boasted to Clarence Gamble, who was carrying out similar experiments in the United States,

> I believe I can prevent at least twice as many babies per dollar in the unfortunate classes by spreading the use of J., N., and C. [jelly, nozzle, and condom]. A pessary has no efficiency at all with patients the pessary never reaches, and this applies to the majority of the people who are too far from a clinic to attend same.[73]

He based his assertion on 1,000 patients who had been sent simply the jelly and nozzle and a further 9,000 sent jelly, nozzle, and condoms.[74] Kaufman was concerned with what gained the best practical results; scientific sophistication was not his interest. He told his nurses that they should not urge patients to abandon any existing method of protection if, in fact, it seemed to work.[75] And in his quest for the simplest type of contraceptive, he described in *Birth Control Methods* how the poor could employ as crude protectives simple household articles such as tampons soaked in oil, vinegar, or lemon juice.[76]

Stopes, Sanger, and Hawkins all organized birth control clinics in order that women could be fitted with diaphragms by trained doctors. Kaufman, having come to disdain the usefulness of the diaphragm, was similarly led to question the importance of the clinic. He did provide funds for the establishment of clinics in Toronto and Windsor but ultimately withdrew this support when he concluded that he could reach a larger clientele by either direct mailing or visiting nurses.[77] He agreed with more traditional birth controllers that clinics served a political function in publicizing the need for contraceptive information; the problem was that they did little to respond to this need. Kaufman informed an American Birth Control League official that the Toronto clinic was "more for educational purposes than clinical services, because I know that many needy mothers within walking distance of the clinic will not attend it for various reasons."[78] Kaufman claimed that working people lacked the clothes, initiative, and courage required to venture into a clinic; clinics, for their part, medicalized and made needlessly expensive what could have been a simple service.[79] Kaufman wrote Gilbert Colgate of the Citizens Committee for Planned Parenthood that he would "approve of Boards of Health and Welfare organizations including contraception as part of their welfare work as this is the logical place for it anyway and the inclusion costs very little extra money."[80] Clinics set up *solely* to provide birth control information he considered doomed to failure.

In seeking to make birth control respectable, Stopes, Sanger, and Hawkins tried to present it as a medical issue far removed from the crass commercial concerns of the purveyors of condoms. The truth was, however, that commercial outlets distributed far more contraceptives than did clinics. Kaufman, as a businessman, was not perturbed by the idea of using modern managerial techniques to increase the distribution of contraceptives. In April, 1933, he wrote Hawkins to ask what she thought about the Winnipeg activities of the Bureau of Feminine Hygiene. This private firm, by employing nurses on a 25 per cent commission basis, had in the space of eighteen months made more than 1,500 contacts. It was retailing the forty-cent Pro-Race Pessary for one to three dollars apiece.[81] Hawkins was horrified by the idea of businessmen turning poor people's desire to control their fertility to monetary gain; Kaufman, thinking of the thousands of unemployed nurses available, was happily inspired by the idea of how such a commission system could revolutionize the delivery of contraceptive material.[82]

The main undertaking of the Parents' Information Bureau became the elaboration of a system of visiting nurses delivering contraceptive information. The system grew out of Anna Weber's first work in the Kitchener area. After the initial successes Kaufman sent organizers to communities further away with the instructions to contact co-operative doctors and then engage local social workers – usually married graduate nurses – for canvassing.[83] Clinics traditionally relied on a good deal of voluntary work.

Kaufman was unashamed of employing monetary incentives. He told Clarence Gamble in 1934,

> . . . organizers visit various districts and engage local workers who are paid $1.00 to $1.50 commission per patient according to the density of the population. People will not do birth control work for free on account of the prejudice against it. I have considerable trouble finding local workers who have the courage to risk the criticisms they at first think is unavoidable.[84]

Kaufman let it be known he was willing to send organizers in his pay to any part of Canada for a few weeks to set up his distribution system.[85] In the summer, when travel was easier, nurses were encouraged to do rural work where the need was greatest. Commissions were highest for each rural applicant, lowest for each urban. By the late 1930's somewhere between fifty and seventy-five local nurses were involved. Their success was such that by the 1940's Kaufman limited them to sending in only 120 applications each per year; two or three in especially needy areas, however, were allowed greater flexibility.[86]

These workers' task was not to canvass indiscriminately. They were to obtain from doctors, Protestant ministers, social workers, and patients the names of couples who needed birth control information. These people then would be called on. Kaufman informed his nurses that they were not to urge birth control information on those who did not want it.[87] Such pressure was not only counterproductive; it could also strip the PIB of the claim that it was working for the public good.[88] Couples who did want contraceptives would be provided by the nurses with an initial supply of jelly and nozzle. They were also given an application form for further supplies, which, after being co-signed by the worker and if possible by the family doctor, would be sent to the PIB headquarters. Contraceptive packages were sent free to the deserving and sold at cost for $2 to those who could pay. If a pessary was to be fitted the PIB would send the necessary material to a co-operative doctor. Form letter number seventeen, establishing similar arrangements, was sent out to prospective patients whom the nurses could not directly reach.[89]

The system produced a voluminous amount of paperwork, but this, as far as Kaufman could see, was inevitable because his nurses were only paid after an application had been received.[90] Since 99 per cent of the patients received their first supply of contraceptives free, the system was also expensive. For later supplies Kaufman charged thirty-five cents for a tube of jelly, twenty-five cents per dozen condoms, and twenty-five to fifty cents per pessary.[91] To those, such as Stopes, who suspected that commercial concerns were behind Kaufman's activities, he protested:

> I find that I am more or less ruining the contraceptive business in Canada for others on account of my prices which permit no profit to me even when I ignore my overhead expenses. . . . My birth control activities net me a loss of $50,000 per year. Some people think my work is not altruistic, but those who are convinced that I am making a profit in my enterprise are not willing to become partners in spite of my offers to accept partners.[92]

The fact that Kaufman did pour hundreds of thousands of dollars of his own money into the system did not allay the fears of all his detractors; many still regretted the mixing of commercial and contraceptive concerns.

Kaufman had no time for detractors. He was convinced that the PIB had produced a delivery system for contraceptives that was far superior to anything yet in existence. It was a system that he was proud to claim as the product of his work alone. He informed one correspondent, "I have found that when I pay the expenses alone I have no societies to argue with and perhaps make more progress."[93] He judged his own progress as quite remarkable, given the fact that he had patients right across the nation and a growing number of supportive doctors. By the mid-1930's he had nurses operating from Newfoundland to Vancouver Island. They, in turn, were assisted by local doctors. In 1937 Kaufman claimed he had the support of about 1,200 doctors; in 1942 the number had risen to 2,300 or about one-quarter of the profession.[94] To those like Sanger who argued that doctors could be best recruited into the birth control movement via clinics, Kaufman retorted that more discreet approaches were more effective.

> We have learned repeatedly that doctors have contacted us on the request and sometimes insistence of the patients, which is an indication that the education has spread to the people who need the help, and it is not merely a matter of choice with the doctors whether they wish to help their patients or neglect them.[95]

In other words, Kaufman was saying that pressure from the bottom up rather than from the top down was the most effective way to gain doctors' co-operation in distributing contraceptive information. They might shy away from publicly supporting a birth control clinic but, argued Kaufman, they would respond to the moral and monetary demands of their patients to provide birth control discreetly. Kaufman considered this "practical service" far more valuable than the "educational work" of birth control propagandists.

Kaufman's greatest pride was in the number of patients the PIB contacted. From 1935 to 1938 approximately 20,000 new patients were contacted each year.[96] That was the same number that sixteen clinics and two consultation offices in Great Britain reached in the ten-year period 1921-30.[97] Although in the late 1930's Kaufman began to limit the numbers of applications his nurses could send in, they continued to average about 6,000 a year in the 1940's and 4,000 a year through the 1950's. By 1942 he had responded to over 120,000 applications (see Table 3).

Kaufman could reach such a large clientele because he replaced the clinic with the travelling nurse and the diaphragm with spermicidal jelly. He did establish a clinic in Toronto in 1933 but closed it in 1938 after concluding that it simply was not efficient.[98] The clinic had helped 9,000 patients but at the same time the PIB had contacted a further 11,000 in the Toronto area. The PIB could provide contraceptives at one-half to one-third the cost of the clinic – $2 as opposed to $5 per patient – and could reach the poorest section of the community, where people were the most reluctant to visit a medical institution.[99] By mail they could be provided with a simple contraceptive pack they could easily employ; at a clinic it was more likely that the woman would be fitted with a diaphragm she would eventually discard. At the Toronto clinic 69 per cent of patients were fitted with a vaginal pessary or diaphragm, 7 per cent with a cervical cap, and 24 per cent given the jelly, nozzle, and condom.[100] Through the PIB only about 5 per cent of the patients were provided with pessaries and the rest supplied with jelly or foam and condoms.

Being a eugenicist, it was not Kaufman's intent to provide birth control information to whomever wanted it. He believed that the birth rate of the middle classes was, if anything, too low. The PIB directed its attention to the poorer sections of the working class, whose fertility Kaufman regarded as a threat. Speaking at the 1935 annual conference of the combined American and Canadian National Conference of Social Work, he went so far as to assert:

TABLE 3
Parent's Information Bureau Patients

Number of New Cases		Recommended by:		
Year	Total	Patients and Others	Doctors	Social Workers
1935	18,057			
1936	24,909			
1937	23,068			
1938	18,284	2,852	1,004	14,428
1939	11,162			
1940	9,455			
1941	7,990			
1942*	6,212			
1946	5,906	1,222	431	4,253
1947	6,164	1,335	414	4,415
1948	5,802	1,483	465	3,854
1949	6,315	1,719	428	4,168
1950	3,349	1,821	345	1,183
1951	4,147	1,912	389	1,846
1952	4,758	1,775	260	2,723
1953	4,937	1,945	259	2,733
1954	4,447	2,077	280	2,090
1955	4,232	1,953	301	1,978
1956	4,274	2,426	325	1,513
1957	3,453	2,034	327	1,092
1958	3,294	2,020	417	857
1959	3,112	1,943	400	769
1960	3,229	2,128	485	616

*Figures for 1943 to 1945 not available.
SOURCE: Clarence Gamble Papers, Countway Library, Boston, Mass., G 946.

Apparently the present depression and heavy taxation brings a decrease in the birth rate amongst the tax paying classes, while the birth rate amongst those on relief apparently increases, not only relatively, but actually. The tax payers' income must be spread amongst the extra allowance for each additional child.[101]

Kaufman's response was to make poor, married couples with several children his targeted clientele. How successful he was in reaching this group was indicated in a summary of patients

TABLE 4

Cases Registered at the Toronto Birth Control Clinic and the PIB

		Toronto, 1933-34	PIB, 1937	PIB, 1942
Reproductive	Number of applicants	2,126	23,068	6,212
History	Average age	29	28.3	27.5
	(% who report) miscarriages or abortion	30%	20%	n.a.
	Average number of living children	2.8	2.6	2.5
	Average number of dead children	.3	.2	n.a.
Religion	Protestant	88%	79.1%	83.4%
	Catholic	7%	19.0%	11.7%
	Other	5%	1.9%	4.9%
Income	Relief recipients	54%	27.8%	n.a.
	Income less than $12.50 a week		34.8%	n.a.
	Income less than $25 a week	24%		n.a.
	Not available	18%	n.a.	n.a.
Contraceptives	Jelly and pessary	69%	3.7%	20%
Supplied	Jelly	0%	96.3%	0%
	Jelly and condom	24%	0%	25%
	Foam	0%	0%	60%
	Cervical cap	7%	0%	0%

SOURCES: Morgan, "An Analysis," *Journal of Contraception*, 3 (1938), pp. 54-55; *Journal of Contraception*, 8 (1943), p. 119.

advised by the PIB in 1937 and in an analysis commissioned by Kaufman and authored by Lucy Ingram Morgan of 2,126 cases dealt with by the Toronto Birth Control Clinic during 1933 and 1934.[102]

The profiles of the 23,068 patients contacted by the PIB in 1937 and of the 2,126 of the Toronto clinic in 1933-34 were very similar (see Table 4). About 80 per cent were Protestant and 7 to 19 per cent Catholic; the average mother's age was twenty-eight to twenty-nine; she had borne over three children and had just under three still living; 20 to 30 per cent had lost pregnancies; 25 to 50 per cent were on relief. The children of such parents, according to Kaufman, were a threat.

> Children have a right to be born with a reasonable chance to legitimately earn a living, but I fear that the percentage of those who can qualify for very little more than the permanently unemployed is rapidly increasing, and will constitute an unbearable relief burden, or become a menace to society.[103]

Kaufman was proud of his ability to reach this clientele and positively gloated over the fact that Catholics made up 10 to 20 per cent of his recipients.

Kaufman was convinced that he had made a major breakthrough in fertility control in discovering the importance of making the contraceptive itself and the delivery system of contraceptives as simple as possible. There was indeed a certain irony that the harshly practical Kaufman, who never hid his contempt for the working classes, should work for a contraceptive method that they could easily understand and employ while others, like Margaret Sanger, who were motivated by a real empathy for the women they sought to help, contributed to the development of the pill, a high-technology contraceptive whose users would eventually view it with concern and confusion.[104] Kaufman was unusual for his time in understanding that technology in contraceptive use had its limits. The effective contraceptive was the one that was used effectively. "The human element," wrote Kaufman, "is the biggest factor in the efficiency, and not the contraceptive used."[105] The less sophisticated or those he called the "careless" would be best protected by a simple contraceptive like spermicidal jelly, which they could and would easily employ.

The performance of different contraceptives was attributed as well by Kaufman more to the way they were used than to their inherent attributes. "Failures," he reported, "are due more to the calibre of the parents concerned than to the contraceptive method."[106] He believed jelly alone was 90 per cent effective as a contraceptive with patients who had had only one or two pregnancies. Efficiency was lost with each additional child; mothers of large families had to be provided with pessaries.[107] In 1937 he cited figures drawn from 1,500 cases collected over two and one-half years of use that indicated only 10 per cent of the cases had been unsuccessful. Ninety per cent of these failures were attributed by Kaufman to either carelessness or lack of supplies. In only 10 per cent of the failures, or 1 per cent of the total sample, was lack of success due to a fault in the contraceptive.[108]

Such figures are suspiciously high and are not verifiable. Moreover, they raise the very complex question of how one judges the long-term "success" or "failure" of a contraceptive. Lucy Ingram Morgan concluded after her analysis of 2,126 cases at the Toronto Birth Control Clinic that, since over half its patients never provided follow-up information, one could not assert that more than 36 per cent were "known successes," by which she meant they had not conceived for three months or more while employing a contraceptive.[109] The PIB produced its own figures in 1942 of a group of 748 patients whose average time of employment of contraceptives was two years.[110] In this sample 55 per cent said they had been successful and avoided pregnancy while 45 per cent had become pregnant. The latter group's failures were attributed as indicated in Table 5.

TABLE 5
Failure of Contraceptives: PIB

	Number of Patients	Percentage
Planned pregnancies	52	15.6
Failed to renew supplies	132	42.6
Supplies used irregularly	86	26.9
Lack of co-operation	46	14.9

SOURCE: "Clinic Reports," *Journal of Contraception*, 8 (1943) p. 119.

Kaufman was certainly correct in concluding that the birth control clinic and the diaphragm would not have a major impact on national fertility rates. But when faced with reports of failure among his own clientele, all he could think of was producing cheaper and simpler contraceptives. He never seemed to appreciate that the middle class had restricted its family size in order to protect its standard of living. What deterred the lower class from following similar strategies was not a lack of contraceptive knowledge but the lack of the incentive of having a decent standard of living worth defending.

By 1936 the birth control movement in central Canada was in full flight. Despite Section 207c of the Criminal Code, which forbade the sale or advertisement of contraceptives, Tyrer, Hawkins, and Kaufman had actively pursued their propaganda work for over five years without legal interference. The arrest in September, 1936, of one of Kaufman's nurses, Dorothea Palmer, appeared momentarily to place all their work in jeopardy.[111] In fact, the trial that stretched over six months and involved over three-quarters of a million words of testimony proved to be the Canadian birth controllers' best publicized triumph. Kaufman, by winning Palmer's acquittal under the *pro bono publico* escape clause, in effect began the struggle – not completely won until 1969 – for the legalization of all birth control activities. A number of extensive accounts of the Palmer trial have been written; there is no need here to provide yet another.[112] What has to be determined is why the trial occurred and what it represented.

The most recent work done on the Palmer trial has suggested that Kaufman, in order to advance the birth control cause, might have actually sought a legal confrontation. There is evidence that supports such a suspicion. In the first place, Kaufman was aware of the success with which Stopes and Sanger had used the courts in Britain and America to focus attention on the need for contraception. Second, Dorothea Palmer, who took over the canvassing of Eastview from Miss Todd, was a pugnacious birth control advocate. She was not worried, as had been Todd, at the idea of going door-to-door to discuss birth control in a largely Catholic, French-Canadian community. After her arrest the police reported that she said she expected trouble and was glad the "show down" had finally occurred.[113] The final reason why one might suspect that Kaufman had set out to pick a fight with the law was that the little town of Eastview was the perfect place in which to prove – to Protestant English-speaking Canada, in any event – that the distribution of birth control material served the public good.

Eastview, on the Ontario-Quebec border, was a town whose

population of 7,000 was about two-thirds French-Canadian Catholic. In the depression years a quarter of the townspeople were on relief and the remaining local taxpayers could only pay less than 5 per cent of the annual welfare costs of $130,000.[114] Tyrer, Hawkins, and Kaufman all wanted to combat Catholicism, but they were convinced they would not receive a fair hearing in Quebec. A battle fought in Eastview gave them the chance to pose as friends of the poor and to challenge the French-Canadian Catholicism in the protective surroundings of an Ontario court.

A good deal of evidence, however, suggests that Kaufman did not purposely seek a legal confrontation. In the first place, such an undertaking went completely counter to his normal practice of avoiding publicity of any kind. He had repeatedly warned his nurses:

> Birth control procedure should be undertaken quietly without newspaper publicity, and also without discussion in any organizations regardless of the extent of their interest or activity in social work. Help from organizations is unlikely and also impractical as opinions differ.[115]

Kaufman always put his money into the provision of birth control materials, not into birth control propaganda. Indeed, he went so far, despite the pleadings of Margaret Sanger, as to deny aid to *New Generation*, the English neo-Malthusian journal.[116] The second reason why it seems unlikely that Kaufman precipitated the 1936 legal confrontation is that Dorothea Palmer was not the sort of person he wanted to represent the Parents' Information Bureau publicly. Unlike most of his workers, she was neither a registered nurse nor was she married. Indeed, her marriage status was somewhat of a puzzle.[117] Hawkins wrote Sanger in September, 1936: "Unfortunately – for us – the nurse is not a desirable character (recommended to Kaufman by a former worker who did not look up Miss Palmer's credentials)."[118] Kaufman was so worried that Palmer's past history might jeopardize the success of the case that he did not have her called as a witness (and so protected her from cross-examination), forbade her to talk to reporters, and fired her once the trial was concluded.[119] In short, it appears that Kaufman was telling the truth when he asserted that the Palmer arrest came as a surprise and that he suspected it resulted from a trap laid by the police and Catholic authorities.[120]

Upon being notified of the arrest, Kaufman, who had been telling his nurses that their activities were not illegal, decided to launch a major legal campaign. He assigned Palmer's defence to his own lawyer. F.W. Wegenast. The choice of this Brampton attorney best known for his civil work was not as unusual as it might have first appeared. As an adherent of the PIB, a member of the Eugenics Society of Canada, and a supporter of the Orange Lodge, Wegenast was well situated to organize a strong defence based on medical and moral arguments. His task was made all the easier when the magistrate named to hear the case turned out to be Judge Lester Clayton, a progressive and a Protestant.

The crown attorney, Raoul Mercier, was obviously unfamiliar with the birth control debate and never established a consistent attack. Since the charges of the sale and disposal of contraceptives were immediately dropped, the outcome of the trial hinged on whether or not Palmer's door-to-door canvassing on behalf of the PIB served the public good. Mercier, to establish that it did not, called on a number of French-Canadian Catholic obstetricians and gynecologists to testify to the harmfulness of birth control.[121] Under Wegenast's cross-examinations, however, they either admitted their ignorance of modern contraceptive techniques or confessed that their views were dictated more by their religious convictions than by their medical findings.

Wegenast's tactic was to swamp the court with dozens of expert witnesses willing and able to testify at exhaustive length to the morality and necessity of contraceptive use. He first called for the defence the twenty-one women Palmer had visited. All except two gave harrowing accounts of repeated pregnancies, miscarriages, and abortions, and freely testified that they had wanted birth control information.[122] Wegenast then called representatives of the birth control movement, the Eugenics Society of Canada, the medical profession, and the churches.[123] Kaufman was asked to explain how the PIB operated, but the clear purpose of the testimony of other birth controllers, including Anna Weber, Gladys Brandt, Mary Hawkins, and Dr. Margaret Batt, was to portray the particular importance of contraception to women.[124] Dr. W.L. Hutton, the Brantford medical officer and chairman of the Eugenics Society of Canada, was used by the defence to demonstrate that birth control was necessary, that without it the uncontrolled fertility of the "socially inadequate" would pose a danger to the nation.[125] Wegenast then paraded through the witness stand a long roster of churchmen whose very presence indicated the extent to which birth control now had the support of progressive Protestants. The witnesses included Ernest Simms of the Salvation

Army; C.E. Silcox, general secretary of the Social Services of Canada; Alfred Zeidman, director of the Scott Mission of Toronto; Canon T.F. Summerhayes, secretary of the Toronto Social Service Council; Rev. C.G. Hepburn, rector of All Saints, Ottawa; Rev. Roy Essex of the Toronto Memorial Institute, mission, and settlement house; Rev. Dr. John Coburn, secretary of the United Church Board of Evangelism and Social Services; and Rabbi Samuel Sachs of the University Avenue synagogue and the 1934 Toronto Civic Welfare Survey.[126] The burden of their testimony was that Protestants and Jews agreed that voluntary parenthood, when dictated by social or health requirements, was fully acceptable. Wegenast, to explain how such restrictions of fertility could be safely and easily achieved by use of contraceptives, called eminent medical authorities: William A. Scott of the Toronto General Hospital and Dr. George Brock Chisolm of the University of Toronto.[127]

The trial, begun on October 21, 1936, concluded on February 11, 1937, with judgement reserved until March 17. Whatever the verdict, there was no doubt in the minds of the birth controllers that they had achieved a major breakthrough in demonstrating the enormous amount of public support that could now be rallied in respectable quarters in defence of fertility limitation. Indeed, Kaufman declared that he was indifferent to the final legal outcome; of course, Dorothea Palmer, and not Kaufman, would be the one to face the consequences.[128] In any event, Judge Clayton found in Palmer's favour, agreeing with Wegenast that the rich easily obtained contraceptives but that the poor, without the aid of organizations such as the PIB, were prevented from controlling their fertility. Wegenast had demonstrated to Clayton's satisfaction that the law did not reflect the current state of public opinion. The magistrate concluded that Palmer, in instructing the women of Eastview how they could limit family size, was indeed serving the public good.[129]

The importance of the Eastview trial was not that it changed the law. What it changed was the way the law would be applied. Since Wegenast had proved that public opinion in English-speaking Canada was now very much in favour of birth control, the police in the future would be far more cautious in prosecuting under the terms of Section 207c of the Criminal Code. The absolutely crucial roles in Wegenast's defence were played by ministers and doctors, who, in coming forward to defend contraception when employed by the married to protect the health and well-being of the family, made the birth control movement respectable.

The prominent part played in the trial by Protestant clergymen owed something to Tyrer's activities, although he was not as important a force as he liked to think. The Protestant churches certainly had little original to contribute to the population debate in the twentieth century and tended to follow the lead given by eugenicists and medical men. The 1908 Lambeth Conference of the Anglican Church had condemned artificial limitation of family size largely because of eugenic concerns for depopulation.[130] The clergy tended to have small families themselves, however, and it is clear from the number of letters written by ministers' wives to Marie Stopes and Margaret Sanger that discreet conversations about contraception often occurred in Canadian church rectories. The English Anglican Church had no clear line on birth control; hence, when the British government in 1930 allowed doctors to provide birth control advice, the Lambeth Conference of the same year followed public opinion in accepting contraception when "thoughtfully and conscientiously adopted."[131] Canadian Anglicans drifted along in the same direction. When the Reverend T.F. Summerhayes sought to speed things up by gaining the support of the 1932 Toronto Synod for the legalization of contraceptives, he found he was opposed by those who thought he was going either too far or not far enough.[132]

The other Protestant denominations were goaded into a greater appreciation of the birth control issue in 1931 when the Federal Council of Churches in America gave mild support to the notion of family planning.[133] The United Church of Canada in 1934 set up a commission to examine the pros and cons of birth control.[134] Under the direction of the Reverend Dr. Ernest Thomas, the commission submitted a report approving "voluntary parenthood" clinics; it was accepted by the Seventh General Council of the United Church, meeting in Ottawa in October, 1936, just as the Palmer trial was about to begin.[135] The Protestant clergy's arguments in favour of birth control were always based more on social, economic, or eugenic preoccupations than on theological considerations. Birth control came to be but one more issue that would find a niche in the Social Gospel.[136]

Canadian doctors had been just as reluctant as ministers to discuss birth control. The Eastview trial was therefore important inasmuch as it provided a forum where eminent members of the profession finally testified to the innocuousness of contraception.

Gladys Brandt wrote Marie Stopes to inform her that, because of the success of the trial, the first public medical discussion of contraception took place in June, 1937, at the Dominion Medical Association meeting in Ottawa.[137] As we have seen, many individual doctors were sympathetic to birth control prior to this. When Emma Goldman made her 1927 lecture tour of Canada, Dr. Charles Hastings had bemoaned the fact that the wealthy were provided contraceptives by "promiscuous dispensations" rather than by qualified practitioners, while the "subnormal types" gave no thought to controlling their fertility. The answer, according to Hastings, was, "not a wholesale birth control, but an intelligent birth control which should be under the control of the medical profession, the legal profession, and the clergy."[138] Motivated by similar concerns, many doctors co-operated with Kaufman or wrote to Stopes or Sanger. For example, in 1921 a Saskatchewan doctor asked Stopes to explain how her clinic functioned; in 1922 a member of the Ontario Board of Health requested the names of British firms that produced contraceptive "articles"; in 1924 a Calgary physician ordered cervical caps; and in 1925 a Victoria public health nurse asked for pamphlets on family planning.[139] Sanger received a typical letter in 1928 from a concerned official at the Tranquille TB sanitarium, who asked for similar information: "You will understand that when married women are being discharged from any institution such as this, it is necessary for us to advise them not to have children. It is hardly fair to tell them this, and nothing more."[140]

Unfortunately, many doctors did "nothing more." The birth controllers' intent was to force doctors, first privately and finally publicly, to be candid about contraception. Sanger wrote a British Columbia woman in 1928 that she would be sent the name of a local doctor who would fit her with a diaphragm.

This is by far the safest way to obtain proper information for yourself, because the best methods of prevention are based on a physical examination by the adviser, and the patient instructed accordingly. The medical profession will awaken to its duty when people insist upon proper advice.[141]

Kaufman, as we have seen, also believed that grassroots pressure would finally force doctors to come out in support of birth control.

But why did doctors have to be "forced" into the public discussion of birth control? Some, of course, were morally opposed to contraception, but this vocally hostile group never represented more than a minority of the profession. The majority steered away from the discussion altogether because it did not seem to them to be a medical matter. They were motivated primarily by professional caution. Contraception was traditionally associated with the shadowy world of prostitution and quackery. Doctors, intent on projecting an image of themselves as members of an austere, scientific calling, did not want their reputations tarnished by associations with tawdry tradesmen. Dr. Gordon Bates of the Social Hygiene Council expressed the view of most of his colleagues when in 1927 he declared, "The subject is a very controversial one, one that we are keeping clear of. We are not at all interested in the birth control movement."[142] This nervousness of the doctors when facing the issue of contraception could be attributed in part to the fact that they had little professional understanding of the subject. They demonstrated far more enthusiasm for eugenic discussions because the sterilization of the unfit did entail the sort of medical intervention they were familiar with.

In Britain and America the birth controllers set up clinics in part to lure doctors to the movement. Doctors who shied away from anything that smacked of retail trade felt more at home in an institution that was both a health centre and an experimental bureau. Marie Stopes, to further reassure the medical profession that contraception could be viewed as a subject worthy of serious scientific scrutiny, established in 1922 the Medical Research Committee; Margaret Sanger formed her Birth Control Clinical Research Bureau in 1923. Working along similar lines, the American physician Robert Latou Dickinson obtained Rockefeller money in 1925 to begin the Maternity Research Council.[143] In Canada there were neither many clinics nor any research facilities that would attract doctors – as medical scientists – to the subject of birth control. Kaufman, in fact, was very much opposed to medically sophisticated contraceptives. He did succeed in winning the private support of up to one-quarter of the Canadian medical profession, but until 1936 this was not translated into public support.

The Eastview trial did flush into the open physicians sympathetic to family planning, but Canadian doctors, like the Canadian clergy, were also responding to developments abroad. The *Canadian Medical Association Journal*, once it was secure in the knowledge that in Britain and America birth control had been made a subject fit for respectable scientific research, could assert in 1937 that "properly controlled contraception has become part of preventive medicine."[144] Were doctors forced into an acceptance of birth control by the moral and monetary pressures of their patients or were they drawn to the subject as a result of scientific advances? Kaufman had no doubt that the former predominated. He wrote to Guy Burch of the Washington-based Population Reference Bureau that by 1941 he had little trouble gaining the co-operation of medical men: "Even the Catholic doctors seem to have very little prejudice when their purse is affected."[145]

We began this chapter by noting that in 1930 no birth control movement existed in central Canada. Seven short years later Tyrer was congratulating himself on the emergence of Protestant clergymen as defenders of contraception and Hawkins was exulting in the serious interest doctors were now taking in the subject. Kaufman was convinced that he had the support of the government and judiciary. He responded to Clarence Gamble's letter of congratulations following the Eastview trial with the self-satisfied assertion:

> I guess I have them all tamed in Canada now except in the province of Quebec where the intolerant Catholics prefer to ignore federal law if they conflict with Quebec province laws, which I believe are largely dictated by the Catholic church. However, we will see what the province of Quebec can do for the country when I become active there, which may be next year. If they interfere with my workers they will have the federal laws pushed under their noses whether they like it or not.[146]

Kaufman's boast was based on his belief that the English-speaking Canadian establishment was now willing to accept birth control as a legitimate method by which to defend the existing economic system. In the first decades of the century, birth control had been associated either with feminists calling for women to have the right to control their own bodies or with leftists striving for a democratization of contraception. As a result, the respectable middle classes, though they employed birth control, shied away from a public defence of a practice whose only vocal proponents were radicals. The conservative-minded were only willing to rally to the birth control cause in the depression when Tyrer, Hawkins, and Kaufman played up the idea that contraception would bring down welfare costs. Birth control ideology was embraced by the middle classes once they understood how it could be turned to the control of the reproduction of the lower orders rather than to their liberation.

6

Quebec Fertility and Criminal Law Reform

We began this book by noting that many of the fears engendered by the fall of the birth rate at the turn of the century were sparked by English-Canadian preoccupations with the high fertility of the French Canadians. The latter were also going to restrict family size to a significant degree in the first decades of the century, but the birth of the Dionne quintuplets in 1934 was viewed by many as dramatically symbolizing the fertility differential that still separated the country's two founding peoples. The Toronto *Globe* greeted the babies' birth with the acknowledgement that "these latest arrivals will arouse fresh apprehensions regarding French-Canadian ascendancy in Northern Ontario."[1] C.E. Silcox, who in 1937 served as one of Dorothea Palmer's strongest defence witnesses, asserted that the Dionnes were for the English the "symbol of a great fear":

> Behind and a part of the whole problem is the extraordinary fecundity of the French Canadian and the suspicion that the French are deliberately trying to outbreed the English, even though in doing so it may involve the lowering of the standard of wages and living and all that depends on such standards.[2]

A.R. Kaufman began propaganda work in Quebec in 1935 in order to attack directly the high French-Canadian birth rate. He informed the English birth controller Edith How-Martyn:

> I recently started a birth control worker in the attractive Catholic nest in Montreal, and while my organizer and worker have given a few perfectly good Catholics heart failure, the predictions that birth control work cannot be done in Montreal have not been true up to date.[3]

The Family Welfare Association – a Protestant organization –

passed on to Kaufman's worker the names of families who needed birth control information. After being interviewed by a nurse they were sent supplies directly from Kitchener.[4]

A.H. Tyrer went to rhetorical extremes in attempting to arouse English Canadians to the threat posed them by francophone fertility. He asserted, in a 1938 pamphlet entitled *To the Protestant Ministers of Canada*, that the Catholic Church was keeping the "priest-ridden people of Quebec" cut off from birth control information solely to increase the power of the clergy. He further claimed that Catholics had pressured Macmillan to end the publication of his book, *Sex, Marriage and Birth Control*. Tyrer ended his inflammatory tract with the warning that Catholics were organizing behind Adrian Arcand to fight for "a fascist Canada dominated by an obscurantist and reactionary hierarchy."[5] If Protestant Canadians were to save their country from falling into a civil war like Spain's they would, he warned, have to strike first.

The Quebec birth rate was to fall eventually at an astonishing pace, but the drop that occurred twenty years later had nothing to do with the crusading efforts of Kaufman and his Protestant minions. Between 1959 and 1969 Quebec cut its crude birth rate in half, accomplishing in ten years what had taken the rest of the country over a century. The province entered the 1970's with the lowest birth rate of any province. That lowered francophone fertility effectively and permitted the federal government finally to broach safely the decriminalization of abortion and contraception.

To place developments in Quebec in the larger context, we must examine the national demographic trends at the outset. Ironically, the Canadian birth rate bottomed out and began to rise in the late 1930's just as the birth control movement started to gain respectability.[6] The nation in 1941 had a record 255,317 "now-or-never" births fathered by men leaving for the army and this fertility surge was followed by the post-war "baby boom." The birth rate climbed from 20.3 births per 1,000 population in 1936 to 28.0 in 1956. This unexpected growth was misunderstood by many at the time. The baby boom was not simply due to more women having children. It was caused by some women "catching up" and having babies postponed by the war, and by other women marrying earlier and having their children sooner and closer together.[7] The surge was not experienced to the same extent by all provinces. In Ontario the cohort of women born from 1922 to 1926 had families in the post-war period 30 per cent larger than those of the 1907 to 1911 cohort, who had their families in the depths of the depression. In Quebec, post-war family size increased by only 6 per cent.

In 1959 the post-war crude fertility rate peaked at 28.3 and then headed in another unexpected direction – downward. In 1961 it was at 26.1, in 1966 at 19.4, in 1971 at 16.8, and in 1976 at 15.7.[8] This dramatic decline was "unexpected" inasmuch as the previous low point in the 1930's had been attributed to the pressures of the depression. Simple economic preoccupations could no longer be trotted out to explain fertility swings. Nor could religious or ethnic loyalties. As noted above, the most dramatic drop in fertility occurred in Quebec, where the birth rate was cut in half within the decade of the 1960's. In the 1940's each Quebec woman had on average about four children; in the 1970's, about two. This transformation of the French-Canadian family was the most dramatic evidence of the province's "Quiet Revolution."

The census data of 1971, in revealing that Canada's cultural and religious fertility differentials had all but disappeared, threw into sharper relief differences based on education and income. Fertility followed a U-curve when correlated to income, with low- and high-income groups having slightly larger families than middle-income groups. The labour force participation of women was especially significant. Mothers who worked full-time had half as many children as those who had never worked. Education was inversely related to fertility. Here again, length of education of women was crucial; women in the twenty-five-to-thirty-four-year-old cohort who had less than a grade nine education had on average 2.6 children; university-educated women had 1.3 children.[9] New immigrants, traditionally relied on to inflate the fertility rate, no longer fulfilled this function in the post-war world; preference was given by successive governments to the entry of just those professional and middle-class immigrants who had already lowered their birth rate to that of their new country.

Where did Quebec fit in this fertility transition? By lowering its fertility, one might answer, but in fact the story is a good deal more complicated. Even today it is assumed that French Canadians always had families far larger than the national norm. But demographers have revealed the extent to which this is a myth.[10] The crude birth rate of Quebec was in fact lower than that of Ontario prior to 1881 (see Table 6). Throughout the twentieth century French-Canadian fertility declined, but to

English Canadians it appeared to be frighteningly high because their own fertility had dropped so much sooner. Indeed, in the interwar period, when Kaufman and others were bewailing the high birth rate of Quebec, it was in fact falling faster than that of the country as a whole, dropping 22 per cent as compared to a national average of 9 per cent.

TABLE 6
General Fertility Rates, Canada and Selected Provinces, 1871-1965
(annual number of births per 1,000 women aged 15-49 years)

Year	Canada	Nova Scotia	Quebec	Ontario	Manitoba	Saskat- chewan	B.C.
1871	189	174	180	191	–	–	–
1881	160	148	173	149	366	–	202
1891	144	138	163	121	242	–	204
1901	145	132	160	108	209	550	184
1911	144	128	161	112	167	229	149
1921	120	105	155	98	125	135	84
1931	94	98	116	79	81	100	99
1941	87	98	102	73	77	84	73
1951	109	114	117	100	103	110	99
1956	117	121	120	110	109	120	112
1961	112	119	109	108	111	119	104
1965	91	98	88	90	92	100	82

SOURCE: Jacques Henripin, *Trends and Factors of Fertility in Canada* (Ottawa, 1972), p. 21.

Researchers in women's history have alerted us to other complexities in Quebec's demographic past by pointing out how diverse were the childbearing experiences of the province's women.[11] In the first place, Quebec women were divided between those who married and those who did not. Between 14 and 15 per cent remained celibate, a proportion – part of which was sustained by the convents – that was far higher than that found elsewhere in the country.[12] Second, of those who married, most had children but some did not. As in the rest of the country, something like 10 per cent of married women remained childless. If these women were added to those who remained celibate, one finds that around 25 per cent of Quebec women did not contribute to the birth rate.
A third division separated those who had large families from

those who had small families. A basis for the belief in the universality of large Quebec families was provided by the fact that close to half of the children born to mothers born in 1887 came from families in which there were ten or more children. But upon examination of the 1887 age cohort of mothers, one finds that only one in five had ten or more children; although being raised in a large family was fairly common, the bearing of ten or more children was not.[13]

Thus, while there is no denying that many Quebec mothers had large broods, only a minority fulfilled the mythical role of the extraordinarily prolific matron. The 1887 generation who had their families in the first decades of the twentieth century had on average only 5.5 children. They were divided ethnically, with francophones having slightly more children and others having slightly fewer, and by locale, rural birth rates being higher than the urban. The figure of 5.5 children refers, of course, to number of children born. Completed family size, which would take into account losses after birth – due in particular to Quebec's high infant mortality rate – was lower.[14]

An understanding of the complexities of the different reproductive histories of Quebec women is essential if the progress of fertility control in the province is to be understood. The decline in the birth rate was not simply a result of every family restricting births. Rather, one witnessed in the twentieth century the closing of the gap between one group of women with an extremely high fertility rate and another with a high rate of celibacy and childlessness. The birth rate of the former group fell and the marriage and birth rate of the latter group rose. The drop in the number of large families was most dramatic. Comparison of the mothers born in 1887 to those born in 1913 reveals that the number who bore six or more children was almost cut in half.[15] But the fall in average number of children born per mother was offset to an extent by the increase in the number of women who would bear children. The fertility differentials that separated Quebec from the rest of Canada declined as a result of the disappearance of fertility differentials *within* Quebec.

Why was Quebec's fertility rate sustained at a relatively high rate well into the twentieth century? According to the anglophone birth controllers, it was due to Quebecers' lack of access to birth control information. The Catholic Church, asserted Tyrer and Kaufman, was keeping its flock in ignorance. It is obviously true that one would not find Catholic priests aping the Protestant clergy in distributing birth control information. We do have evidence, however, that in at least one francophone Catholic Church presbytery a woman was instructing her friends between 1901 and 1911 on how to limit family size. An indignant male parishioner, in a letter of protest to the local bishop, catalogued her misdeeds.

> Madame N. teaches the young women the evil art of not having children. Living under the priest's roof, exercising as a result the greatest influence, she abuses the confidence placed in her by making known to innocent young women contraceptive methods. . . . Madame N. told Madame F.G. to douche [*se faire des injections*] in order to prevent conception. . . . Madame N. told Madame R, "You should prevent your husband from having relations with you until ten days after your period. Then there is no longer any danger of having children." . . . Madame H.C. told Madame L., "I will not have any more children now that I know everything."[16]

This letter was found in an archive in St. Boniface, Manitoba, but similar illicit exchanges of information likely occurred in Quebec parishes. In any event, the main point is that in French as in English Canada, family limitation initially would be brought down by traditional methods of fertility control: abstinence, extended lactation, coitus interruptus, douching, and the rhythm method. The Quebec birth rate remained higher than that of English Canada, not because of a lack of birth control methods, but because they were not employed to the same extent.[17]

Quebecers would have large families as long as the economic structure provided incentives for having them. They would be called "ignorant" by anglophones, but with many jobs available for young people in farming and light industry and in the absence until 1943 of compulsory education legislation that restricted child labour, it was economically rational to adopt a family strategy of high fertility. This is not to imply that ideas were not important. In the early twentieth century Quebec feminists, nationalists, physicians, and churchmen all lauded the remarkable fertility of the province that had made French-Canadian cultural survival possible. Economic and cultural concerns nicely complemented each other.[18]

It has been generally assumed that the Catholic Church played a key role in sustaining opposition to birth control in Quebec. It is true that Pius XI's 1930 encyclical, *Casti Connubii*, which was in part a response to the Anglicans' tepid acceptance of contraception as enunciated at the Lambeth Conference, crystallized Catholic opposition to fertility regulation. Yet it has to be recalled that in the late nineteenth century the most vociferous opponents of birth control in Canada were Protestants. Catholics, in lashing out at abortion and birth control in the interwar period, were often taking up positions that had been originally established and only recently vacated by their Protestant brethren.[19]

It is also the case that Catholic opposition to birth control was often more nuanced and sophisticated than its Protestant defenders appreciated. Until the 1930's there was little need in Quebec for Catholics to fear the inroads of actual birth control propagandists. Father Henri Martin, in referring in 1923 to the activities of neo-Malthusians, declared:

> Thanks to God and to the vigilance of our civil and religious authorities, we have been spared this shameful propaganda, but the contacts with the old country and especially with our neighbours are so frequent that we cannot help but be affected by the diffusion of those perverse doctrines and infamous practices.[20]

By 1935, however, priests acknowledged that the defenders of birth control could be found, not just in France or America, but in Montreal itself.[21] To deal with such a pervasive threat, careful thought had to be given to constructing a counter-argument.

Not all the arguments advanced were terribly convincing. Some Catholic physicians continued to trot out sensational but unsupported horror stories of contraceptives causing premature senility, acute morbidity, neurasthenia, heart attacks, and cancer.[22] There were priests who opposed all fertility control no matter what the cost in infant and maternal suffering. Father Ferland, for example, argued that the martyrdom of the mother dying in childbirth could only be welcomed since it won the praise of God and man.[23] Still others adopted the blanket approach in attributing "voluntary sterility" to everything they disliked about the modern world, with special emphasis on ambition, egoism, sensuality, urbanization, de-Christianization, and the masculinization of women. To such Cassandras the increasing employment of birth control heralded the ultimate economic and cultural collapse of society.[24]

A more thoughtful Catholic response was made by those who argued that the issue of birth control could not be treated in isolation. They argued that the campaign for birth control had to be seen as part of a broader eugenic movement launched by upper-class Protestant Canadians that had as its goal the control of the fertility of the Catholics and the lower classes.[25] It was pointed out that the birth controllers spoke about the need of tailoring the family to fit the society, rather than changing society to suit the needs of families.[26] Catholic writers were thus sustaining in Quebec an anti-Malthusian argument that was made by socialists in English-speaking Canada. The Catholics' argument that birth control was part of an anglophone plot organized against Quebec could, of course, be supported by any reference to the openly anti-Catholic diatribes of Kaufman and Tyrer. And the assertion that birth control was a symptom of a broader eugenic movement was substantiated by the fact that many of the birth controllers were actively involved in pushing for legislation in favour of sterilization of the feeble-minded.[27]

On a more positive note, Catholic writers argued that the Church had never been indifferent to the burdens of childbearing. It was a perversion of church doctrine to suggest, as some Protestants did, that Catholics favoured mindless propagation. On the contrary, claimed Father Forest, the Church had always insisted on the care and thoughtfulness needed in parenting: Catholics were to trust in Providence but not tempt it.[28] For this reason, pointed out Father Louis-Marie Lalonde, the Church accepted the legitimacy of the rhythm method of contraception.[29]

By following this line of argument, the Catholic Church in Quebec could slowly bring itself to accept the fact that was made abundantly clear in the post-war world: that more and more of its parishioners, in good faith, were limiting family size. Faced with the dilemma either of losing face by having openly to accept birth control or of losing its parishioners, the Church sought a middle way of finding a birth control method that was somehow legitimate. In the 1930's the Church accepted the rhythm method; in the post-war period it supported the efforts of a grassroots Catholic movement known as SERENA that was popularizing a more sophisticated plotting of the ovulation cycle for the purposes of family planning.[30]

The arrival of the contraceptive pill in the early 1960's offered another way out; some Catholics argued that its chief function was to regularize the ovulation cycle and that it only indirectly prevented births. By the late 1960's the Canadian bishops were facing up to a situation in which it was clear they could not enforce their views on their own flock, let alone members of other faiths. The new Quebec, with its sophisticated economy, consumer society, and budding feminist movement, was inimical to large families. It was not a case of Quebec finally following the lead of English Canada; it was rather a case of a people simply adjusting their fertility to meet their current social and economic situation.

Some bishops were convinced that the Church's opposition to birth control was the main reason for its loss of female parishioners.[31] Pope Paul VI's attempt to restore the old moral code with his 1968 encyclical, *Humanae Vitae*, attacking artificial contraception was in effect repudiated by the Canadian bishops. In responding in a collective letter that the use of birth control was a matter of individual conscience, they thus signalled their acceptance of the legalization of contraception.[32] Their stand probably did more than anything else to explode the myth of a monolithic Catholic block vote poised to destroy any politician favourable to reform of the Criminal Code.

Family planning was so widespread in the 1960's that few Canadians realized that the sale and distribution of contraceptives were still theoretically illegal. To appreciate just how slow the Canadian government was in coming to grips with the birth control issue only requires a glance at its neighbours. In Britain, the Minister of Health had instructed local health centres in 1930 that they were allowed to give birth control information to those women whose health could be endangered by pregnancy. In the United States, Eleanor Roosevelt had the Surgeon-General accept from 1942 on funding requests from states with child-spacing programs. In Canada, politicians avoided the issue, convinced that it would bring down on them the wrath of that 45 per cent of the population that was Catholic; as we have seen, however, by the 1960's such opposition was well eroded.[33]

In this context the government belatedly set about amending the laws that made both birth control and abortion criminal offences. Although these sections of the Criminal Code were rarely enforced, their very existence made a mockery of justice. A Toronto pharmacist was jailed as late as 1960 for selling condoms.[34] This case, according to Barbara Cadbury, so astonished and outraged her and her husband George Cadbury that, for the purposes of amending the Criminal Code, they established in 1961 the Planned Parenthood Association of Toronto.[35]

The Cadburys' interest in birth control was, in fact, not quite so recent. Both were from well-connected, progressive English families and had been active around the world in the International Planned Parenthood Federation.[36] In the mid-1950's they began to search out in Canada those sympathetic to such a movement.[37] Kaufman was continuing his work through the Parents' Information Bureau but showed little interest in entering any new venture. Family planning associations existed in Calgary, Hamilton, and Winnipeg, but these served only a small clientele. It is indicative of how moribund the birth control movement was in the 1950's that George Cadbury found that most of those interested in the cause, like Brock Chisolm, C.E. Silcox, and various United Church clergymen, were the same people active in the 1930's. In 1961 the Cadburys created Planned Parenthood of Toronto and in 1963 were the driving force behind the creation of the Canadian Federation of Societies for Population Planning and of the Planned Parenthood Federation of Canada.[38] This latter organization allowed Canada (until then the last major Western power not included) to be represented in the International Planned Parenthood Federation.[39]

In the 1960's doctors could also be numbered among those lobbying for the removal of references to contraception and abortion from the Criminal Code. In the post-war world more and more came to accept family planning as part of preventive medicine.[40] In the main, however, they were reluctant to venture very far in advance of what they took to be middle-class public opinion. To justify such caution they could point to the venomous attacks launched on Dr. Brock Chisolm. When his 1951 talks on the CBC were interpreted by some MPs as implying a support for contraception, he was subjected in the House of Commons to the ludicrous charge of using his "poisonous mind" to advance the causes of international Zionism, Bolshevism, and atheism.[41]

By the 1960's doctors were willing to come forth to defend fertility control because it was now obviously employed by the majority of the population, because their American and British counterparts were supporting it, and because the invention of the intrauterine device (IUD) and the contraceptive pill had made birth control worthy of scientific interest. The pill had been tested from the late 1950's and was available in Canada from 1961. Its profit potential was so great that even the *Financial Post* ran articles in the early 1960's calling for changes in the law relating to contraception.[42] But if the pill played a key role in luring doctors and businessmen into the population debate, the new contraceptive did not necessarily have the revolutionary impact on the birth rate that was claimed.[43] The birth rate would subsequently fall to unprecedented lows, but the drop began in 1958, three to four years before the general use of the pill in Canada. By the late 1970's tubal ligations and vasectomies were the means of fertility control increasingly used by couples who had already achieved their desired number of children.[44] The pill would play an important role, but especially for the unmarried and for women in the early years of marriage.

Others interested themselves in birth control for more pessimistic reasons. A general assumption made by demographers in the 1940's was that all societies would eventually follow the West through a "demographic transition" and lower both their mortality and fertility rates. In the post-war West there was, as we have seen, the pleasant surprise of a baby boom; but Western analysts discovered in the developing world in the 1950's what they fearfully labelled a "population explosion." In books with titles like *Exploding Humanity* and *Our Crowded Planet*, Canadians were warned by such luminaries as Bertrand Russell, Julian Huxley, Adlai Stevenson, and Arnold Toynbee that the uncontrolled fertility of the Third World posed a greater threat to world stability than the risk of nuclear war.[45]

In the 1930's some conservatives, as we noted, were drawn to birth control as a way of maintaining social peace within Canada. In the 1960's another generation of professionals and businessmen saw birth control as a means of maintaining world order. As a result of population fears, human ecologists and conservatives now found the discussion of fertility control an important and "respectable" topic. They thus formed an uneasy alliance with those on the left who were drawn to birth control by their concern for women's rights and individual freedoms. Cadbury, concerned by the relationship of population to resources, established the Canadian Federation of Societies for Population Planning. Robert Prittie, a New Democratic MP, argued that if Canada was to support the use of contraceptives in overseas programs it had to decriminalize birth control. In 1962 Canada had been put in the embarrassing situation of having to abstain on a United Nations vote concerning the provision of population technical assistance.[46] For Canada to support the use in the Third World of contraceptives that were technically illegal at home, Prittie pointed out, would provide ammunition to those who accused the West of "genocide."

It is difficult to determine how effective the lobbying practices of the family planning associations were. From 1963 on they launched aggressive write-in campaigns and younger politicians like Pierre Trudeau and René Lévesque, who perceived themselves as leaders of a new political generation, rallied to their support.[47] In May, 1963, Robert Prittie submitted a bill calling for reform of the Criminal Code.[48] Though initially sidetracked by Créditiste opposition, the bill was reintroduced in 1965-66 and pro-birth control submissions were made to the 1966 Standing Committee on Health and Welfare. Justice Minister Lucien Cardin asserted that birth control was no longer a tabooed subject – a fairly safe pronouncement given that 50 million contraceptives were purchased annually in Canada. Pierre Trudeau – Cardin's replacement at Justice – made the memorable statement, "The state has no business in the bedrooms of the nation," when defending his 1967 omnibus bill introduced to overhaul the Criminal Code.[49] The bill died on the order paper, but Trudeau's reputation as a daring young politician – based largely on his efforts to reform the Criminal Code – grew. As Prime Minister he was to shepherd successfully through the Commons in 1969 the same sort of omnibus bill originally introduced in 1967. To put the issue in perspective, however, it has to be recalled that in the 1960's the attention given to the question of Canada's new flag far surpassed that given to the decriminalization of contraception.

The tiny birth control lobby obviously did not singlehandedly extort reform from a begrudging Parliament. Such an erosion of old moralistic statutes was spontaneously taking place across the Western world in the 1960's.[50] The liberalism, permissiveness, or flexibility of the age was attributed by some to the practical ethos of a prosperous consumer society that chafed at any restraint, by others to a humanitarian if not libertarian desire to separate at last law and morality. The 1969 revision of the Canadian Criminal Code encompassed a number of conscience issues – abortion, contraception, homosexuality, capital punishment – that politicians hoped had finally been defused.

Despite Trudeau's assertion, the 1969 amendments to the Criminal Code did not eject the state from the nation's bedrooms. Politicians continued to believe that population planning was too important to leave to parents. In 1970 the Family Planning Division of the national Department of Health and Welfare was established to help fund the programs of the Planned Parenthood Federation at the local and provincial levels. Direct action by the federal government was limited. Since health matters were under provincial jurisdiction, federal ministers had to cajole the provinces into supporting birth control services. The provincial authorities were attracted by the assertion that contraception could lower social welfare costs, not by feminist or libertarian arguments. "There is good reason to believe," argued a federal health minister, "that effective programmes for family planning would reduce the incidence of unwanted children, of child neglect, abandonment, desertion, welfare dependency and child abuse."[51]

The 1969 amendments to the Criminal Code did give the federal government greater freedom of movement in international affairs. Canada could now support the United Nations' family planning programs and provide birth control in its own aid programs. The Canadian International Development Agency became a donor to the International Planned Parenthood Federation and after 1971 established bilateral agreements to assist developing countries with their population programs.[52]

The changes in the Criminal Code ended the ban on the advertising and selling of contraceptives. But the 1969 reforms that in effect ended the story of the fight for legal contraception served to open the debate in Canada on the issue of free access to abortion. In the early 1960's lawyers and doctors were complaining of the rigidity of the existing law on abortion.[53] Some doctors were especially perturbed by the fact that women continued to die as a result of back-street abortions. The irony was that these concerns were expressed long after the peaking of abortion-related deaths, which occurred, as we saw, in the 1930's. Other doctors were more concerned that the abortion law allowed the state to meddle in matters they believed should have been left to the discretion of physicians. In 1967 the Canadian Medical Association, the Canadian Bar Association, and the Humanist Fellowship of Montreal all made presentations to the government asking for a liberalization of the law. Two hundred and twenty-six therapeutic abortions were carried out in Canadian hospitals between 1954 and 1965; but it was estimated that anywhere from 50,000 to 100,000 illegal abortions had also been performed.[54] The 1969 amendments to the Criminal Code, by permitting the procedure to take place in hospitals where it was approved by a committee, did end the total ban on abortion. Abortion was not legalized, but was made permissible when done in a hospital and certified by a committee of physicians who determined that the "continuation of the pregnancy . . . would or would be likely to endanger the life or health of the woman."[55]

The liberalization of the abortion law did, at last, provide access to hard figures on the number of pregnancies prematurely terminated. In 1975, 49,300 abortions were carried out in Canadian hospitals and a further 9,700 women went to the United States for the operation.[56] The fact that many had to go abroad for this service pointed out the remaining inequities in the law. In some areas hospitals did not establish abortion committees. This was particularly the case in Quebec, which in 1978 had only twenty-four hospitals with abortion committees compared to 109 in Ontario.[57] Even hospitals with committees interpreted the law in dramatically different fashions. As a consequence of such disparities, British Columbia in 1980 had 32.9 abortions for each 100 live births while P.E.I. had only 1.2.[58]

In response to an early appreciation of such inequities, a campaign for the repeal of the abortion law was launched in 1970.[59] A coalition of women's groups sought to have the question of abortion made simply a private matter between a woman and her physician. They focused particular fire on the hospital abortion committee structure, which was marked by inherently unjust features: it empowered doctors to sit in judgement on the fertility-making decisions of women; it was often so slow in its deliberations as to endanger the health of the woman; the criteria it employed and the ways they were applied varied from case to case.

To draw attention to the safety and efficacy of abortions on demand carried out in clinics, Dr. Henry Morgentaler in 1973 publicized the fact that he had successfully carried out over 5,000 in Montreal. When a jury nevertheless found him not guilty of violating Article 251 of the Criminal Code, the Quebec Court of Appeal in February, 1974, in an unprecedented action, quashed the jury finding and ordered Morgentaler imprisoned. After two more jury trials led to two further acquittals, all further charges were dropped.[60] Nothing could better demonstrate the remarkable transformation that had occurred in Canadian attitudes toward fertility control than the fact that three French-Canadian juries should have accepted Morgentaler's argument that his actions were justified because the existing law denied all women equal access to abortion services.

The abortion reform groups that rallied to Morgentaler's defence opened a new chapter in the Canadian fertility debate. Some of the older supporters of family planning found the feminism and radicalism of the new pro-choice activists disconcerting. Many doctors, though in favour of decriminalization of abortion, were opposed to the slogan of "abortion on demand" because it represented a shifting of power from the physician to the patient. Catholics and fundamentalist Protestants hostile to a whole range of changes associated with new family relationships joined forces as the pro-life movement. They opposed abortion both as a cause and effect of women's refusal to accept the dictates of traditional morality. Politicians, believing that public opinion was pretty well evenly divided by the pro- and anti-abortion camps, quickly came to the conclusion that abortion was too volatile an issue to deal with.

The federal government, in an effort to contain discontent, established in September, 1975, a Committee on the Operation of the Abortion Law under the chairmanship of Robin F. Badgley. Its final report pleased no one. Pro-choice forces were disappointed with the committee's conclusion that, despite the glaring inequities of the existing law, it was the operation of the law rather than the law itself that was at fault. Pro-life supporters were angered that no recommendations were made to restrict access to abortion.[61] Despite the best efforts of the federal government to bury the question, abortion remains in the mid-1980's one of the most divisive issues in Canadian life. The struggle between those who wish to restrict and those who wish to extend access to abortion is fought out at every political level, from the election of hospital boards to the election of members of Parliament.[62]

After having surveyed the history of the discussion of contraception and abortion in Canada from the 1880's to the 1980's it is difficult not to have a sense of *déjà vu* when observing the current conflict. A great deal has changed, of course, but in many ways the essential conflict remains the same. The radically different ways in which the pro-life and pro-choice forces understand abortion make it impossible for them to understand each other: the same act represents emancipation or materialism, rationality or recklessness, freedom or fickleness, virtue or vice. The irony is that in Quebec, where women for so long were purportedly prevented from controlling their fertility, the pro-choice movement has had its greatest success.

Conclusion

Fertility control has not been, as is often assumed, simply a private matter, an unchanging political issue, or an unequivocally feminist cause. Indeed, as this book has shown, birth control and abortion have been important issues in both the private and public domains, and these issues have been profoundly affected by changing political interests and social concerns. These causes were advocated – at least in the case of birth control – by groups often unsympathetic to or incognizant of feminist interests. To understand the significance of contraception in Canadian history, it has been necessary to examine both the private behaviour and attitudes of individuals and couples (for example, by analysis of demographic data and personal letters) and the public responses (as demonstrated by public figures, social reform movements, social policies, and laws). The extent to which contraception was a private or public matter changed over time and often in unexpected ways.

Before the nineteenth century, in most Western countries, neither birth control nor abortion before quickening was illegal. With the help of midwives, kin, and friends, women attempted to exercise control over their fertility. The measures they used were often neither safe nor foolproof, but such measures nevertheless could be effective to space births and limit family size. During the nineteenth century, laws aimed at prohibiting the use of birth control and abortion were introduced to the extent even of prohibiting the spread of information. What was once local and private was made into a public and national issue. Yet, while these practices were officially condemned, many segments of the population continued to exercise their right to control their fertility. Throughout the nineteenth and twentieth centuries, the birth rate in Canada steadily declined. Not until the 1930's was the provision of birth control methods and information recognized by the courts as possibly serving the public good. Not until 1969 was the use of contraceptive devices made legal and abortion, under specific conditions, permitted. Canadian laws allowing easier access to birth control and abortion were slower to emerge and generally more restrictive than those of countries like England and the United States.

Ironically, as legal restrictions on contraception began to decline

139

during the middle of the twentieth century in Canada, childbirth and family planning became increasingly entangled with forces external to the sexual relationship.[1] As more reliable contraceptives such as the pill were made available, women became increasingly dependent on scientific research, pharmaceutical marketing, and medical care. These sectors have gained increasing control over human reproduction, but they have not necessarily helped to advance the ability of individuals to make choices concerning their fertility. Contraception and abortion, if anything, have been taken even further out of the private domain and become more subject to public control.

Second, we have shown in this study that effective fertility control has been largely a cultural and social, not a technological, problem. Before reliable birth control devices such as the pill were introduced, the birth rate in Canada had already dramatically declined. Technological advances in birth control were only important when the social and economic variables, such as employment levels and education opportunities, gave individuals a reason to limit their fertility. Individuals often had to make do by trying all sorts of inadequate methods to achieve a desired family size since reliable methods that had been designed were not made readily available to the general public. Their use was largely suppressed by the practices and policies of the law, medicine, and the church. In World War II, for example, the government undertook a massive campaign to combat venereal disease by distributing condoms to soldiers. Not until several decades later, however, could condoms be legally sold for birth control purposes.

The desire to suppress the employment of contraceptives did not stem, however, from one single political motive. At the turn of the century, many commentators were anxious about "race suicide" and castigated well-educated women who were limiting the size of their families for shirking their duty to the nation. Though the desire to discourage the use of contraceptive methods tended to reflect conservative political positions, socialist commentators, for quite different reasons, also often opposed their use. They argued that the problems facing the working class were economic and not related to family size. With the implementation of a socialist society, many claimed, the environment would be sufficiently supportive to make the use of contraceptives unnecessary.

Advocates of the use of contraceptives, similarly, reflected quite different political interests. Some socialists encouraged their use. In British Columbia in the early twentieth century, many socialist feminists stressed that the working-class family and women in particular required effective contraception to reduce the onerous burden of large families and to aid in the struggle toward socialism and the emancipation of women. In contrast, however, most advocates of contraceptive techniques looked to them to serve conservative purposes. A.R. Kaufman, for example, thought that they had to be provided to the poor to prevent them from irresponsibly reproducing themselves and hence to reduce the threat their poverty posed society.

In the politics of contraception, the class interests were never absent and often quite transparent. Middle-class figures called for an increase in the numbers of their own kind and a decrease in those of the working class. Working-class commentators who had an opinion on contraception defined it as either coercive or liberating, depending on the role they assumed it would play in the class struggle. Interestingly, the concern for gender was usually less visible. Women spoke, in general, on behalf of class rather than gender issues in Canada. Although some feminists, such as Laura Jamieson, were strong advocates of the availability and use of contraceptives, no Canadian woman ever had the same singleness of purpose, radically feminist outlook, or impact of Marie Stopes in England or Margaret Sanger in the United States.[2] The desire to protect women from the power of men and to promote their emancipation was rarely articulated, prior to the 1960's, as a political program in Canada in defence of birth control or abortion.

Whatever political stand was taken in Canada, however, it is clear that contraceptive methods never did have one single implication. They were not neutral tools that necessarily served either liberating or coercive purposes. Their implications depended on who interpreted them, who controlled them, under what conditions they were controlled, and for what ends.

Third, we have argued in this book that throughout the twentieth century, the politics of contraception have undergone several dramatic transformations. The use of contraception, once in many respects a tabooed vice, has become within limits an acceptable practice. Those who have advocated the use of contraception have decreasingly been voluntary agencies and private individuals and have increasingly become government officials, medical professionals, scientists, and pharmaceutical company representatives.

Moreover, the official emphasis of advocates of birth control services has shifted significantly from eugenics – promoting the well-born – to family planning – ensuring that an ideal (that is to say, small) family size be achieved. Such advocates have broadened their interests from the national to the international scene. Increasingly, they have become concerned about the "population explosion" in Third World countries and have incorporated family planning into their international aid programs. To summarize, the major shifts in the politics of contraception in Canada, as in other Western industrial countries since World War II, have, in effect, been toward their greater masculinization, bureaucratization, professionalization, medicalization, and commercialization.

The political implications of these shifts in the provision of contraceptive and abortion services have not always been readily apparent. The consequences of birth control services becoming increasingly bureaucratized, professionalized, and commercialized have been both liberating and coercive. On the one hand, access to safe and effective birth control and abortion has improved a great deal. Not only is information more freely available now but women are far more able than ever before to consider birth control alternatives, including abortion, without having to risk their lives. On the other hand, the birth control services, by ultimately being managed and controlled by the government, scientific community, medical profession, and pharmaceutical industry, have often not increased women's sense of controlling their own fertility. They have often been provided services unequally, coercively, and abusively. Some poor women, for example, unable to afford the travel that may be necessary, have been unable to procure abortions.[3] In marketing birth control products, some pharmaceutical companies have abused their power. For example, before adequate research had been undertaken, a massive marketing campaign was launched in the early 1960's by the pharmaceutical industry that was to profit substantially from the sales of the pill. Only several years later did evidence begin to surface indicating that the pill was associated, under specific conditions, with serious illnesses.[4] Similarly, some IUDs, most infamously the Dalkon Shield, were marketed without adequate testing and resulted for some users in death, sterility, or permanent injury.

In addition, within a patriarchal society, the provision of birth control services can lead to substantial shifts in relations between the sexes, benefiting men at the expense of women. Since the major institutions in Canada, as in most societies, tend to be run by men and to reflect their interests, it is possible that the protection of women from childbearing does, in fact, strip them of some of the power they have had as mothers and reduces them to being merely sexual playthings for the pleasure of men.[5] What many feminists in the 1980's are particularly concerned by is the idea that because birth control services have become increasingly subject to the powerful influence of government, business, science, and medicine, women's ability to control their own fertility may be restricted even further in the future.

Fourth, we have noted that advocates of birth control were often unsympathetic to or incognizant of feminist interests; not until the late 1960's were many feminists in Canada viewing birth control and abortion as central prerequisites for advancing the independence of women. As noted in *Still Ain't Satisfied*, the Abortion Caravan of 1970 brought the nascent Canadian women's liberation movement to its feet.[6] Since the 1969 amended law only allowed abortion under very specific conditions, abortion on demand was a particularly important unifying theme for feminists. In its February, 1970, report, the Royal Commission on the Status of Women recommended abortion on request before twelve weeks without restrictions and abortion on request after twelve weeks if the doctor was convinced that the mother's or child's life was at risk. These recommendations were never implemented, nor was the call by such groups as the Canadian Advisory Council on the Status of Women (which was responsible to the government) to decriminalize abortion.[7] Though Trudeau had claimed that the state had no business in the bedrooms of its citizens, abortion became increasingly a public and political issue. Dr. Morgentaler made some progress in ensuring that abortion was a private matter between a woman and her doctor by setting up clinics in Quebec, Manitoba, and Ontario, but in the mid-1980's his clinics were relatively free from public harassment only in Quebec.

Since the mid-1970's, pro-life groups, in particular, gained political momentum in trying to block women's right to obtain abortions. Though the women's liberation movement in Canada has had an important impact on public consciousness, it has yet to win the basic right to obtain abortions. With modern techniques such as the dilation and curettage and the vacuum aspirator, abortions require little medical expertise and can be easily undertaken at a day clinic. Yet, as abortion has become a safer procedure, it faces the danger once again, due to political opposition, of being driven underground and becoming again a risky undertaking.

For some feminists, the right to obtain an abortion is no longer a central issue. So many other problems, such as poor employment opportunities, pornography, violence, inadequate day care, and pensions, have forced themselves upon their attention. But it is likely in the near future that abortion and the more general notion of a woman's right to control her own body will once again reassert themselves as fundamental and unifying themes for feminists. Why is this likely? First, as already noted, the political opposition, in particular to Dr. Morgentaler's clinics, has become increasingly strident. Second, abortion is linked to the growing problem of reproductive technologies.

During the past decade, research on reproductive technologies (artificial insemination, in vitro fertilization, sex selection, genetic engineering, fetal monitoring, artificial wombs, fetal surgery, embryo transplants, and cloning) has grown dramatically.[8] Though the technology has progressed by leaps and bounds, an understanding of its moral, ethical, and political implications has, in contrast, advanced little. What is particularly worrying for feminists is that those who are developing the reproductive technologies show little concern for the interests of women. Hanmer and Allen stated recently:

> Medical ethics and bioethics are stunted, if not stillborn, when it comes to considering women as subjects, persons, rather than the logical objects of medical and scientific "research." For women to seek to achieve control over their own bodies is to make a profound demand – one that runs counter to our times. As we specify the ways in which control has been and continues to be wrested from us, we expose the continuing threat of objectification and experiment.[9]

In a 1984 meeting on the medical ethics of in vitro fertilization held at Laval University in Quebec City, all the experts who participated, with one exception, were male. According to A. Côté, the discussion on in vitro fertilization raised numerous questions, but the real question at the heart of the debate was not formulated:

> How can these men continue to play demi-gods, experimenting

with and orchestrating human reproduction, destroying and modifying according to their pleasure while at the same time prohibiting women's abortions?[10]

Ironically, though women are not allowed to decide whether or not to have an abortion without the intrusion of the law, the medical profession, and the social services, reproduction research, which has such profound implications, is subject to few guidelines.

It is likely, as McDonnell suggests, that abortion will be increasingly fought for under the banner of "reproductive rights."[11] With such an emphasis, the issue of women's right to control their own bodies is likely to stress not so much "choice" as "control." Women not only need to be able to decide on how to regulate their fertility, as consumers, they also need to participate fully in the services themselves that ultimately control and manage their fertility.

This book will have served some purpose if it places the current debate in historical context. The conflict over control of fertility is not a simple product of the post-war world; evidence of such a struggle can be found as far back in time as one wishes to look and is likely to be met in the future as long as opinions differ on the roles of women, children, and the state.

Notes

Introduction

1. *House of Commons Debates*, 2 (1892), pp. 2458-59.
2. *The Criminal Code, 1892*, 55 and 56 Vict (1892), s 179. The code did permit, however, a defence to be made on the grounds that "the public good was served."
3. George Radwanski, *Trudeau* (Toronto, 1978), p. 90.
4. James Mohr, *Abortion in America: The Origins and Evolution of National Policy* (New York, 1978); James Reed, *From Private Vice to Public Virtue: The Birth Control Movement and American Society Since 1830* (New York, 1978); Linda Gordon, *Woman's Body, Woman's Right: A Social History of Birth Control in America* (New York, 1976).
5. See Jacques Henripin, *Trends and Factors of Fertility in Canada* (Ottawa, 1972); Jacques Légaré, "Demographic Highlights on Fertility Decline in Canadian Marriage Cohorts," *Canadian Review of Sociology and Anthropology*, 9 (1974), pp. 287-307; T.R. Balakrishnan, G.E. Ebanks, and C.F. Grindstaff, *Patterns of Fertility in Canada, 1971* (Ottawa, 1970); Walter Mertens, "Canadian Nuptiality Patterns: 1911-1961," *Canadian Studies in Population*, 3 (1976), pp. 57-71; Réjean Lachapelle, *The Demolinguistic Situation in Canada* (Montreal, 1982); Leroy O. Stone and A.J. Siggner, *The Population of Canada* (Ottawa, 1974); Larry H. Long, "Fertility Patterns Among Religious Groups in Canada," *Demography*, 7 (1970), pp. 135-49; Ellen M.T. Gee, "Fertility and Marriage Patterns in Canada, 1851-1971" (Ph.D. thesis, University of British Columbia, 1978).

Chapter 1

1. Toronto *Evening Telegram*, 26 March 1908, p. 9.
2. *What a Young Man Ought to Know* (Toronto, 1897), p. 198.
3. Toronto *Globe*, 17 December 1901, p. 8.
4. *Manitoba Free Press*, 30 August 1909, p. 3.
5. "Childless Marriages," *Canadian Churchman*, 29 November 1900, p. 724. In 1908, the Lambeth Conference of the Anglican Church officially condemned "the practice of resorting to artificial means for the avoidance or prevention of child bearing." E.R. Norman, *Church and Society in England, 1770-1970* (Oxford, 1976), p. 270; and see *Canadian Churchman*, July-August, 1908.
6. M.C. Urquhart and K.A.H. Buckley, *Historical Statistics of Canada* (Cambridge, 1965), pp. 14-18, 38-42; Terry Copp, *The Anatomy of Poverty: The Condition of the Working Class in Montreal, 1897-1929* (Toronto, 1974), pp. 29, 44-45; Veronica Strong-Boag, "The Girl of the New Day: Canadian Working Women in the 1920s," in Michael Cross and Greg Kealey, eds.,

The Consolidation of Capitalism (Toronto, 1983), pp. 169-210. John Herd Thompson with Allen Seager, *Canada 1922-1939: Decades of Discord* (Toronto, 1985), pp. 2-7, 150-51.

7. "The Canadian Immigration Policy," *Canadian Magazine*, XXX (1907-1908), p. 360.

8. *The American Idea, Does the National Tendency Toward a Small Family Point to Race Suicide or Race Degeneration?* (New York, 1907), cited in O.C. Beall, *Racial Decay. A Compilation of Evidence from World Sources* (London, 1911), p. 89. *Canadian Churchman*, 29 November 1900, p. 724; see also 17 January 1901, p. 37. On French-Canadian pressure in the Eastern Townships, see Robert Sellar, *The Tragedy of Quebec: The Expulsion of its Protestant Farmers* (Toronto, 1907; and 1974 with introduction by Robert Hill); Henri Lemay, "The Future of the French Canadian Race," *Canadian Magazine* XXXVII (1911), pp. 11-17; P. Louis Lalande, "La revanche des berceaux," *Action française*, II (1918), p. 98. For fears expressed by the Québécois about their own birth rate, see R.P. Henri Martin, O.P., "La dépopulation," in *Semaine Sociale du Canada, IVe Session, Montreal 1923*; "La Famille," *Compte rendu des cours et conférences* (Montreal, 1924), pp. 140-61; and Susan Trofimenkoff, *Action Française: French Canadian Nationalism in the Twenties* (Toronto, 1975), pp. 74-75.

9. Henripin, *Trends and Factors*, p. 21; see also John Davidson, "The Census of Canada," *Economic Journal*, XI (1901), pp. 595-602; W.J.A. Donald, "The Growth and Distribution of Canadian Population," *Journal of Political Economy*, XXI (1913), pp. 296-312.

10. On statistical evidence that such controls were employed by the upper middle class from the 1850's, see Michael Katz, *The People of Hamilton, Canada West: Family and Class in a Mid-Nineteenth Century City* (Cambridge, Mass., 1975), p. 35; see also Lorne Tepperman, "Ethnic Variations in Marriage and Fertility: Canada in 1871," *Canadian Review of Sociology and Anthropology*, 9 (1974), pp. 287-307. On the relative impact of delayed marriages, changes in proportion married, and birth control, see W.B. Hurd, "The Decline in the Canadian Birth Rate," *Canadian Journal of Economics and Political Science*, 3 (1937), pp. 43-55.

11. See L.F. Bouvier, "The Spacing of Births Among French Canadian Families: An Historical Approach," *Canadian Review of Sociology and Anthropology*, V (1968), pp. 17-26; Jacques Henripin, *La population canadienne au début du XVIIIe siècle* (Paris, 1954), pp. 86-87.

12. On the prevalence of coitus interruptus, see E. Lewis Faning, *Report on an Enquiry into Family Limitation and Its Influence on Human Fertility During the Past Fifty Years. Papers on the Royal Commission on Population. Volume One* (London, 1949), pp. 7-10; Earl Lomon Koos, "Class Differences in Employment of Contraceptive Measures," *Human Fertility*, XII (1947), pp. 97-101.

13. On the American experience, see Gordon, *Woman's Body, Woman's Right*.

14. See Michael Bliss, "Pure Books on Avoided Subjects: Pre-Freudian Sexual Ideas in Canada," *Historical Papers* (1970), pp. 89-108. For a specific

example of the way in which information on "sex hygiene" was brought from America to Canada, see Beatrice Brigden, "One Woman's Campaign for Social Purity and Social Reform," in Richard Allen, ed., *The Social Gospel in Canada.* National Museum of Man Mercury Series. History Division Paper No. 8 (Ottawa, 1975), pp. 36-62.

15. *What a Young Wife Ought to Know* (Toronto, 1908), pp. 131ff.
16. *Conjugal Sins Against the Law of Life and Health* (New York, 1874), pp. 182-83. An additional reason for doctors' enthusiasm for the "safe period" was the Vatican's tacit acceptance from the 1880's of this "natural" form of control. See John T. Noonan, *Contraception: A History of its Treatment by Catholic Theologians and Canonists* (Cambridge, Mass., 1965), pp. 441-42.
17. Cowan, *The Science of the New Life* (New York, 1869), pp. 110ff.; Napheys, *The Physical Life of Women* (Toronto, n.d.), pp. 92-96; Hall, *Sexual Knowledge* (Toronto, 1916), p. 215.
18. Long, *Sane Sex and Sane Sex Living* (New York, 1919); Jefferis and Nichols, *Searchlights on Health: Light on Dark Corners* (Toronto, 1897), p. 248; see also Anon., *Nature's Secrets Revealed* (Marietta, Ohio, 1917), pp. 197ff.
19. There were Canadian editions of both *Karezza* and *Tokology*. For Stockham, see Bliss, "Pure Books," p. 104, and a letter to Francis Marion Beynon in the *Grain Growers' Guide*, 21 January 1921, p. 22. On coitus reservatus, see also Long, *Sane Sex*, p. 128.
20. For the development of contraceptives in the nineteenth century, see the notes in Angus McLaren, "Contraception and the Working Classes: The Social Ideology of the English Birth Control Movement in Its Early Years," *Comparative Studies in Society and History*, XVIII (1976), pp. 236-51.
21. *T. Eaton Co. Catalogue – Spring and Summer*, no. 46 (Toronto, 1901), p. 1920; *Toronto Daily Mail and Empire*, 21 March 1908, p. 21; *Dominion Medical Monthly*, July, 1916; and see *Woodward Catalogue* (Vancouver, 1912), p. 143.
22. Linda Rasmussen *et al., A Harvest Yet to Reap* (Toronto, 1976), p. 72; see also G. Kolischer, "The Prevention of Conception," *Dominion Medical Monthly*, XIX (1902), pp. 116-19.
23. C.S. Clark, *Of Toronto the Good* (Montreal, 1898), p. 127. As examples of what Clark was talking about, see the advertisements of "rubber goods" placed by F.E. Karn Ltd., "The People's Popular Drug Store," in the Toronto *Daily Star*, and by Cyrus H. Bowes in the Victoria *Daily Colonist* of 1906.
24. For attacks on withdrawal, see Napheys, *Physical Life*, p. 97; Jefferis and Nichols, *Searchlights*, pp. 244ff; J.H. Kellogg, *Man, the Masterpiece* (London, 1903), p. 426. That medical warnings against coitus interruptus were not taken seriously, at least by Canadians of Scottish ancestry, is suggested by the fact that the practice was jocularly referred to as "Getting off at Kilmarnock," that is, the last train stop before Glasgow. (Personal communication.)
25. Angus McLaren, *Birth Control in Nineteenth Century England* (London, 1978), p. 210; *Journal of Social Hygiene*, 5 (1919), pp. 163-84.

26. Leo J. Latz, *The Rhythm of Sterility and Fertility in Women* (Chicago, 1932).
27. James Reed, *From Private Vice to Public Virtue: A History of the Birth Control Movement in America From 1830 to 1970* (New York, 1978), Ch. 30. See also John Peel, "The Manufacturing and Retailing of Contraceptives in England," *Population Studies*, 17 (1963), pp. 113-25; *Fortune* (February, 1938), pp. 83-114.
28. *Grain Growers' Guide*, 1 January 1930, p. 19. See also *Chatelaine*, March, 1928, p. 59. For Dettol, see *Chatelaine*, October, 1939, p. 36.
29. See *Chatelaine* for advertisements for Norforms (May, 1936, p. 56); Sanitabs (January, 1937, p. 38); Zonite (October, 1928, p. 32); Zonitors (January, 1940, p. 22).
30. *Chatelaine*, March, 1936, p. 48.
31. See, for example, *The United Farmer*, 22 June 1934, p. 15; 6 July 1934, p. 15; 5 October 1934, p. 15; 9 November 1934, p. 15; *Grain Growers' Guide*, 1 January 1930, p. 19.
32. See advertisement in Marie Stopes to Supreme Specialties, 19 April 1935, Stopes Papers, Contemporary Medical Archives Centre, Wellcome Institute for the History of Medicine; hereafter Stopes Papers, CMAC.
33. C.P.F. to Stopes, 6 May 1932, Marie Stopes Papers, British Museum; hereafter Stopes Papers, BM.
34. George B. Higgs to Verdun Laboratories, 10 June 1932, Stopes Papers, BM.
35. Stopes to G.B., 15 October 1937, Stopes Papers, CMAC.
36. Stopes to M.M., 28 March 1935, Stopes Papers, CMAC.
37. Information provided by Julius Schmidt of Canada Ltd. See also Elizabeth Mitchell, "Contraceptives and the Patent Law," *Family Planning*, 10, 1, pp. 18-19; *Fortune* (February, 1938), pp. 113-14.
38. On English correspondents, see Ruth Hall, *Dear Dr. Stopes: Sex in the 1920s* (London, 1978); Ellen Holtzman, "The Pursuit of Married Love: Women's Attitudes towards Sexuality and Marriage in Great Britain, 1918-1939," *Journal of Social History*, 16 (1982), pp. 39-51.
39. There are collections of Stopes papers in the British Museum and the Contemporary Medical Archives Centre. The latter contains an especially interesting file of Canadian letters, nearly all written after a story on Stopes had appeared in a November, 1934, issue of the *Star Weekly*. These are the letters referred to in what follows. To protect the anonymity of Stopes' correspondents, we have not given their names.
40. J.D. to Stopes, 23 November 1934, Stopes Papers, CMAC.
41. G.H. to Stopes, 14 November 1934; D.L. to Stopes, 20 November 1934, *ibid.*
42. J.G. to Stopes, 5 June 1935, *ibid.*
43. G.S. to Stopes, 9 November 1934, *ibid.*
44. I.S. to Stopes, 26 January 1935, *ibid.*
45. J.D. to Stopes, 23 November 1934, *ibid.*
46. J.H. to Stopes, 21 November 1934; S.S. to Stopes, 11 March 1935, *ibid.*
47. J.M. to Stopes, 15 January 1935; see also A.G. to Stopes, 14 November

1934, and M.M. to Stopes, 27 November 1934, *ibid.*
48. R.C. to Stopes, n.d. 1934, *ibid.*
49. J.B. to Stopes, 25 November 1934, *ibid.*
50. M.W. to Stopes, 25 September 1934, Stopes Papers, BM; D.L. to Stopes, 27 November 1934, Stopes Papers, CMAC.
51. On the role of the counsellor, see Jacques Donzelot, *The Policing of Families* (New York, 1979); Barbara Ehrenreich and Deidre English, *For Her Own Good* (Garden City, 1978); Michel Foucault, *The History of Sexuality* (New York, 1979); Christopher Lasch, *Haven in a Heartless World* (New York, 1977).
52. I.A. to Stopes, 22 November 1934, Stopes Papers, CMAC.
53. J.D. to Stopes, 12 November 1934, *ibid.*
54. R.R. to Stopes, 15 November 1934, *ibid.*
55. G.H. to Stopes, 14 November 1934, *ibid.*
56. J.K. to Stopes, 10 November 1934, *ibid.* After clinics were established in Canada one doctor would write, "There are birth control clinics where the proper information can be obtained. The domestic relations courts have found this one item to be the source of more marital difficulties than any other trouble that enters into life together." Dr. Anne B. Fisher, "Live with a Man and Love It," *Chatelaine*, September, 1937, p. 34.
57. W.M. to Stopes, 13 November 1934, Stopes Papers, CMAC.
58. See, for example, the Lysol ad in the *Manitoba Free Press*, 15 January 1927, p. 15: ". . . a woman's health and youthfulness need not fade with marriage. Modern science provides a simple protection. Sane habits of living, plus the *proper* protection of feminine hygiene. . . . Preserve your health and youth with Lysol." On the discussion of the role of the "Modern Mother," see *Chatelaine*, March, 1931, pp. 15, 69; December, 1931, pp. 13, 39-40; April, 1933, pp. 18, 74; May, 1933, p. 2; June, 1933, pp. 22, 36, 44; Mary Vipond, "The Image of Women in Mass Circulation Magazines in the 1920s," in Susan Mann Trofimenkoff and Alison Prentice, eds., *The Neglected Majority: Essays in Canadian Women's History* (Toronto, 1977), pp. 116-24; Veronica Strong-Boag, "Intruders in the Nursery: Childcare Professionals Reshape the Years One to Five, 1920-1940," in Joy Parr, ed., *Childhood and Family in Canadian Society* (Toronto, 1982), pp. 160-79.
59. G.H. to Stopes, 14 November 1934; see also G.S. to Stopes, 9 November 1934, Stopes Papers, CMAC.
60. I.S. to Stopes, 27 November 1934, *ibid.*
61. Henripin, *Trends and Factors, passim.*
62. Violet McNaughton Papers, E. 3, Birth Control, Archives of Saskatchewan. Other letters written by Canadian women seeking birth control information were written to the *Western Producer*, 29 September 1927; 10 November 1927; and in the 1940's to Dr. O.C.J. Withrow of Toronto; see Withrow Papers, Provincial Archives of Ontario. On women's support networks in the United States, see Elizabeth Hampsten, *Read This Only to Yourself* (Bloomington, 1982).

63. Atherton, *Canada Lancet*, XLI (1907-08), pp. 97-101; Smith, *Canada Lancet*, XL (1906-07), pp. 969-76; Watson, *Who Are The Producers of Human Damaged Goods?* (Toronto, 1913). See also Zlata Godler, "Doctors and the New Immigrants," *Canadian Ethnic Studies*, IX, 9 (1977), pp. 6-17; Terry L. Chapman, "Early Eugenics Movement in Western Canada," *Alberta History*, XX (1977), pp. 9-17.

64. On the relationship of eugenics to contraception, see McLaren, *Birth Control in Nineteenth Century England*.

65. Bond, "The Birth Rate," *Canadian Medical Monthly*, 1920, p. 258. See also Bernarr McFadden, *Manhood and Marriage* (New York, 1916), pp. 87ff.

66. R.D. Defries, *The Development of Public Health in Canada* (Toronto, 1940), p. 78. The argument that a lower birth rate would reduce infant mortality was not accepted at all. Detecting this line of thought in the report of the City Improvement League of Montreal, a Catholic journalist replied, "Catholic mothers hold that to be born and baptised is a good compared with which the duration of mortal life is insignificant, for it means eternal life in heaven. Of course all wish to see infant mortality reduced as far as possible: but we do not want to see male and female professors of eugenics corrupting the morals of Catholic Canadian women, and we are sure the clergy of Montreal will know how to silence them." *America. A Catholic Review of the Week*, II, February 19, 1910, p. 515.

Chapter 2

1. See C. Tietze, "The Use-Effectiveness of Contraceptive Methods," in C.V. Kiser, ed., *Research in Family Planning* (Princeton, 1962), p. 367.

2. A.K. Gardner, *Conjugal Sins* (New York, 1874), pp. 180-81. The readers of the *Canada Lancet* were informed, "Married men and women are either refusing [to bear children] or limiting their output to two or three. This is the fruitful source of prostitutionism, abortionism, onanism, and mental and moral degeneracy." XXVII (1895), p. 337. See also the warnings in Jefferis and Nichols, *Searchlights on Health*, p. 244.

3. On the practice in England, see Angus McLaren, "Abortion in England, 1890-1914," *Victorian Studies*, XX (1977), pp. 379-400; McLaren, "Women's Work and Regulation of Family Size: The Question of Abortion in the Nineteenth Century," *History Workshop Journal*, IV (1977), pp. 71-80; and for New Zealand, Andrée Levesque, "Grandmother Took Ergot: An Historical Perspective on Abortion in New Zealand (1897-1937)," *Broadsheet*, XLIV (1976), pp. 18-31.

4. In the United States, where the birth rate decline had preceded that of Canada, the first surge of protests against abortion came in the 1860's and 1870's. See Horatio Storer, *On Criminal Abortion* (Boston, 1860); John Todd, *Serpents in the Dove's Nest* (Boston, 1867); R. Sauer, "Attitudes Towards Abortion in America 1800-1973," *Population Studies*, XXVIII (1974), pp. 53-67.

5. Toronto *Daily Mail and Empire*, 21 March 1908, p. 21. "Kit," the pioneer woman journalist Kathleen Blake Watkins, knew more than most about

the medical profession as she was married to a physician, Dr. Theodore Coleman.

6. *Ibid.*, 16 March 1908, p. 4. An equally prominent physician, Dr. Archibald Lawson, lecturer on the Principles and Practices of Medicine at Halifax, had been implicated in a similar affair in 1883. See *Canada Medical and Surgical Journal*, XII (1883-1884), p. 252.

7. Toronto *Daily Mail and Empire*, 4 April 1908, p. 21; and see also the *Evening Telegram*, 18, 20 March 1908.

8. Advertisements taken at random from the Toronto *Globe*, November, 1901; Toronto *Daily Mail and Empire*, October, 1892; Toronto *World*, November, 1900; *Dominion Illustrated Monthly*, September, 1898. Cook's Cotton Root Compound appears to have been the most widely advertised product, being puffed as early as 1892 and as late as 1906 in papers as far apart as the Vancouver *Semi-Weekly World*, December, 1900, and the Halifax *Herald*, January, 1906. On the use of cotton root as a popular abortifacient in the southern United States, see Herbert Gutman, *The Black Family in Slavery and Freedom, 1750-1925* (New York, 1976), pp. 80-82.

9. On the Karn case, see R. vs. Karn (1903) 5 *Ontario Law Reports*, p. 704 (C.A.); R. vs. Karn 5 *Canadian Criminal Cases*, p. 479; R. vs. Karn 6 *Canadian Criminal Cases*, p. 543. On other abortives, see R. vs. Scott (1912) 3 *Ontario Weekly Notes*, p. 1167 (C.A.). Some women might have taken such pills simply to ease menstrual pains, but there is little doubt that the intent of the advertisers was to suggest that their products could be put to less innocent use.

10. *Physiology of Marriage* (Boston, 1856), p. 185. It should also be noted that native women had a variety of herbal remedies by which they sought to control fertility. One report held that, "The women [of the Kwakiutl] also practice abortion and infanticide; among some of the Nationalities the proportion of female children destroyed in this way is probably over 60 per cent." "Report for 1872," *Department of Indian Affairs* (Black Series), 3596, file 1241, p. 12. See also George Devereux, *A Study of Abortion in Primitive Societies* (London, 1960). Michael Chapman, "Infanticide and Fertility Among Eskimos: Computer Simulation," *American Journal of Physical Anthropology*, 53 (1980), pp. 317-27.

11. See R. vs. Stitt (1879), 30 *Upper Canada Common Pleas*, p. 30.

12. Pennyroyal and tansy are irritant drugs with a toxic action; ergot of rye, cotton root, and quinine are oxytocic agents that stimulate the mobility of the uterus. On home remedies, see *Canadian Practitioner and Review*, XXXIX (1914), p. 668; C.J. Polson and R.N. Tattersall, *Clinical Toxicology* (London, 1959), pp. 545-49.

13. Toronto *Daily Mail and Empire*, 21 March 1908. Ethnic women also formed their own self-help networks. According to a recent study of the Finns, " 'Mamma' (Lyyli) Anderson's home for maids took care that there were not many illegitimate children. . . . While 'Mamma' did not perform the abortions herself, she made the necessary arrangements with a 'real doctor' and looked after the girls during their convalescence. This service was not only for single women, but also for all who wished to practice family

planning. According to Tyyne Latva, 'You didn't get a bad reputation if you visited Lyyli, the issue of abortion was quite openly discussed. No one that I knew of was ever hurt, except some who had gone to Cleveland to have it done.' " Varpu Lindstrom-Best, *The Finnish Immigrant Community of Toronto, 1881-1913* (Toronto, 1979), p. 34.

14.   *Manitoba Free Press*, 30 August 1909.

15.   Canadian papers also carried the advertisements of American druggists and physicians, and some Canadian women, to protect their anonymity, sought abortions in nearby American cities such as Chicago, Rochester, and Detroit. See, for example, R. vs. Backrack (1913) 28 *Ontario Law Reports*, p. 32 (C.A.), in which the question was posed if the crime committed by Canadians while in America could be prosecuted in Canadian courts.

16.   Toronto *Daily Mail and Empire*, 6 April 1908, p. 4.

17.   *Canadian Practitioner and Review*, XXXIII (1908), p. 253.

18.   *Dominion Medical Monthly*, XXXII (1909), p. 121.

19.   Alfred A. Andrews, "On Abortion," *Canada Lancet*, VII (1875), p. 289.

20.   On therapeutic abortions, see *Canada Lancet*, XIII (1881), pp. 342-43; XXXII (1899), p. 113; *Canadian Practitioner and Review*, XXV (1900), pp. 331, 334-36, 401.

21.   Andrews, "On Abortion," p. 291.

22.   "Abortionists," *Canada Lancet*, XXI (1889), p. 217. See also "Does Abortion Pay?" *Canada Lancet*, XLII (1908-1909), pp. 648-49; John T. Winter, "Criminal Abortion," *American Journal of Obstetrics*, XXXVIII (1898), pp. 85-92.

23.   See, for example, *Canada Lancet*, XXVI (1894), p. 76; XXXVIII (1905), pp. 88-89. A few sex reformers asserted that men, because of their lack of self-control, so burdened women with pregnancies that their seeking abortion was really the fault of males. See Kellogg, *Man*, p. 423; James C. Jackson, *American Womanhood: Its Peculiarities and Necessities* (Dansville, N.Y., 1870), pp. 89-90.

24.   *Lancet*, XXI (1889), p. 217. On the problem of registration, see R.E. Mill, "Birth Registration and Public Health," *Canadian Journal of Public Health*, VI (1915), pp. 135-36.

25.   Andrews, "On Abortion," p. 291.

26.   *Canadian Practitioner and Review*, XXXIII (1908), p. 253.

27.   *What a Young Woman Ought to Know* (Toronto, 1898), p. 241.

28.   Drake, *Young Wife*, pp. 125, 129, 130.

29.   Bernarr McFadden, *Womanhood and Marriage* (New York, 1918), p. 139.

30.   Hodge, *Foeticide or Criminal Abortion* (Philadelphia, 1869), pp. 32-33; see also Ely van de Warker, *The Detection of Criminal Abortion* (Boston, 1872), p. 42.

31.   *American Journal of Obstetrics*, XXXIII (1896), pp. 130-31.

32.   *Ibid.*, XLV (1902), p. 237.

33.   Hodge, *Foeticide*, pp. 21-22; see also Andrew Nebinger, *Criminal Abortion: Its Extent and Prevention* (Philadelphia, 1870), p. 16; "A Physician," *Satan in Society* (New York, 1872), p. 119.

34.   See L.A. Parry, *Criminal Abortion* (London, 1931).

35. "Septic Abortion," *Canadian Medical Association Journal*, XII (1922), p. 166.
36. See R. vs. Cook (1909) 19 *Ontario Law Reports*, p. 174 (C.A.); R. vs. Garrow and Creech (1896) 5 *British Columbia Reports*, p. 61; R. vs. Pettibone (1918) 2 *Western Weekly Reports*, p. 806.
37. Gardener was in fact purposely murdered by Dr. Thomas Neill Cream, a madman who, claiming to provide abortifacients, administered poison to and killed at least two Canadian and four English women. On the career of this Canadian "Jack the Ripper," see W. Teighnmouth Shore, *The Trial of Thomas Neill* (London, 1923).
38. Ballock, *American Journal of Obstetrics*, p. 238. On the fate of the unmarried who went through with their pregnancies, see W. Peter Ward, "Unwed Motherhood in Nineteenth Century English Canada," *Historical Papers* (1981), pp. 34-56.
39. Scott estimated that 75 to 90 per cent of all abortions were carried out by married women. "Criminal Abortions," *American Journal of Obstetrics*, XXXIII (1896), p. 80.
40. *Canadian Practitioner and Review*, XLI (1916), pp. 120-21; and see Kellogg, *The Home Hand-Book of Domestic Hygiene and Rational Medicine* (London, 1906), pp. 356-57.
41. *Evening Telegram*, cited by Clark, *Of Toronto the Good*, p. 124.
42. See Angus McLaren and Arlene Tigar McLaren, "Discoveries and Dissimulations: The Impact of Abortion Deaths on Maternal Mortality in British Columbia," *B.C. Studies* (1985), 3-26.
43. We examined the files of the British Columbia attorney general for court records, inquisitions, and correspondence (hereafter AG (BC), Court Records; AG (BC), Inquisitions; AG (BC), Correspondence).
44. Statistics Canada, Health Division, *Therapeutic Abortion, 1981* (Ottawa, 1983); see also Robin F. Badgley, *Report of the Committee on the Operation of the Abortion Laws* (Ottawa, 1977).
45. Stats Can, *Therapeutic Abortion.*
46. AG (BC), Inquisitions, 1935:193 (reel 70).
47. *Ibid.*, 1926:316 (reel 49).
48. *Ibid.*, 1914:255 (reel 23).
49. *Ibid.*, 1919:105 (reel 33).
50. *Ibid.*, 1922:108 (reel 39).
51. *Nelson Daily News*, 10 May 1902, p. 1; AG (BC), Court Records, 1902:20 (v. 92).
52. *Vancouver Daily Province*, 3 May 1909, p. 1; AG (BC), Inquisitions, 1919:138 (reel 33); 1926:313 (reel 49).
53. On Jessup, see AG (BC), Court Records, 1923:82 (v.271); AG (BC), Inquisitions, 1927:375 (reel 52); AG (BC), Court Records, 1928:17 (v.329). On Moore, see AG (BC), Court Records, 1931:134 (v.209); *ibid.*, 1935:97 (v.436).
54. AG (BC), Court Records, 1917:31 (v.209).
55. AG (BC), Inquisitions, 1921:249 (reel 38).

56. See, for example, an advertisement in the *Vancouver Sun*, 9 January 1918, p. 11. See also AG (BC), Inquisitions, 1921:55 (reel 37); *ibid.*, 1922: 208 (reel 40); AG (BC), Court Records, 1923:31 (v.266). After 1927 there were few references to women going to the United States, which suggests services were then available in sufficient numbers in B.C.

57. AG (BC), Inquisitions, 1898:122 (reel 6).

58. AG (BC), Court Records, 1915:113 (v.202).

59. Air and soap embolism became more common in the 1950's, which suggests a new method was being employed. Slippery elm only appears to have been used from about 1920 onward.

60. Cannon, "Septic Abortions," pp. 163-64.

61. Scott, "Criminal Abortions," p. 78.

62. Cannon, "Septic Abortions," pp. 163-65.

63. Urquhart and Buckley, *Historical Statistics of Canada*, p. 40; Sam Shapiro and Edward C. Schlesinger, *Infant, Perinatal, Maternal, and Childhood Mortality in the United States* (Cambridge, Mass., 1968), pp. 143-49; Suzann Buckley, "Ladies or Midwives: Efforts to Reduce Infant and Maternal Mortality," in Linda Kealey, ed., *A Not Unreasonable Claim: Women and Reform in Canada, 1880s-1920s* (Toronto, 1979), pp. 131-50.

64. Edward Shorter, *A History of Women's Bodies* (New York, 1982), p. 98.

65. Canadian demographers and sociologists, while paying a good deal of attention to the decline in infant mortality, have virtually ignored shifts in maternal mortality. See, for example, Roderic Beaujot and Kevin McQuillan, *Growth and Dualism: The Demographic Development of Canadian Society* (Toronto, 1982); Carl F. Grindstaff, *Population and Society: A Sociological Perspective* (West Hanover, Mass., 1981); Warren E. Kalbach and Wayne McVey, *The Demographic Basis of Canadian Society* (Toronto, 1977); Johannes Overbeek, *Population and Canadian Society* (Toronto, 1980). One French-Canadian study actually appears to lament the fact that whereas before World War II the chance of survival of men between the ages of fifteen and thirty-five was better than that of women such is no longer the case. For this curious insistence on describing a decline in female mortality as really a case of "la surmortalité masculine," see Desmond Dufour and Yves Péron, *Vingts ans de mortalité du Quebec: les causes de décès, 1951-1971* (Montréal, 1979), pp. 58-59.

66. J.T. Phair and A.H. Sellers, "A Study of Maternal Deaths in the Province of Ontario," *Canadian Public Health Journal*, 25 (1934), pp. 563-79; see also F.W. Jackson, R.D. Defries, and A.H. Sellers, "A Five Year Study of Maternal Mortality in Manitoba, 1928-1932," *Canadian Public Health Journal*, 25 (1934), p. 97. On parity, see Linda G. Berry, "Age and Parity Influence on Maternal Mortality: United States, 1919-1969," *Demography*, 14 (1977), pp. 297-310; Steve Selvin and Joseph Garfinkel, "Paternal Age, Maternal Age and Birth Order and the Risk of Foetal Loss," *Human Biology*, 48 (1976), pp. 223-30.

67. On the relation of abortion deaths to maternal deaths in Britain in the 1930's, see Jane Lewis, *The Politics of Motherhood* (London, 1980), pp. 36-

38, 209-11. In the United States the Children's Bureau reported in the 1930's that a survey of 7,500 maternal deaths revealed one-fourth were abortion related; the New York Academy of Medicine set the figure at 17.5 per cent. See Helena Huntington Smith, "Wasting Women's Lives: The Frightful Toll of Abortion," *New Republic*, 28 March 1934, p. 178.

68.   Smith, "Wasting Women's Lives," p. 179.

69.   H.R.M. Johnson, "The Incidence of Unnatural Deaths Which Have Been Presumed to be Natural in Coroners' Autopsies," *Medicine, Science, and Law*, 9 (1969), p. 102, cited in Malcolm Potts, Peter Diggory, and John Peel, *Abortion* (Cambridge, 1977), pp. 24-25.

70.   Provincial Board of Health, Report of Vital Statistics, 1922-1946; Department of Health Services, Vital Statistics of the Province of B.C., 1947-1968.

71.   On the problems posed the collectors of statistics, see J.T. Marshall, *Vital Statistics in British Columbia* (Victoria, 1932). In September, 1922, the Vancouver General Hospital was advised by its solicitor that it was not legally bound to report abortions. See Vancouver City Archives, Vancouver General Hospital, MS 320, v.6.

72.   See Shorter, *A History of Women's Bodies*, pp. 139-76; Jo Oppenheimer, "Childbirth in Ontario: The Transition from Home to Hospital in the Early Twentieth Century," *Ontario History*, 75 (1983), pp. 36-60; Anne S. Lee, "Maternal Mortality in the United States," *Phylon*, 38 (1977), pp. 259-66. It is important to note that recent studies indicate that antibiotics were not in widespread use in Canada until the 1940's, antenatal care was limited, and home births were safer than hospital births. See C. Lesley Biggs, "The Response to Maternal Mortality in Ontario, 1920-1940" (M.Sc. thesis, University of Toronto, 1982); Biggs, "The Toronto Maternal Welfare Program, 1933-1947," paper delivered to the Canadian Society for the History of Medicine, 1983; Suzann Buckley, "From Prescriptions to Misconceptions: How to Reduce Maternal Mortality in Canada," unpublished paper.

73.   Potts, Diggory, and Peel, *Abortion* pp. 270-71; Shorter, *A History of Women's Bodies*, p. 195.

74.   McLaren and McLaren, "Discoveries and Dissimulations."

75.   W.D.S. Thomas, "Abortion Deaths in British Columbia, 1955-1968," *B.C. Medical Journal*, 12 (May, 1970), pp. 111-12. In a later study of 132 maternal deaths, Thomas found that sixty were due to direct obstetric causes and 27 per cent of these were abortion related. See J.L. Benedet, W.D.S. Thomas, and B. Ho Yuen, "An Analysis of Maternal Deaths in British Columbia, 1963 to 1970," *Canadian Medical Association Journal*, 110 (1974), pp. 783-87.

76.   *House of Commons Debates*, V, p. 4054; Victoria *Daily Colonist*, 23 January 1935, p. 8; Victoria *Daily Times*, 30 September 1937, p. 4; 27 February 1947, p. 7.

77.   In reporting that the seventh trial for abortion in two years was taking place in British Columbia, an editor of a Vancouver paper argued that

such tragedies resulted from lack of access to birth control. Women, he argued, were "driven to such extremes, not by any criminal intent, but by ignorance of scientific methods and the stupidity of our laws." Vancouver *Sun*, 28 August 1933, p. 4.

Chapter 3

1. M.W. to Marie Stopes, 25 September 1924, Stopes Papers, BM. Attempts were made by conservatives to prevent the entry into Canada of birth control material. "Our attention has been directed to certain books by a widely-known British authoress dealing with the subject of birth control. Attention has been given these and they have been submitted to the Departments of Government named above [Federal Departments of Customs and Post Offices], and they to have been barred admittance to and circulation in Canada." "Objectionable Books and Literature," *Annual Report of the Committee on Social Hygiene to the Social Service Council of Canada*, January, 1924 (Ottawa, 1924), p. 2.

2. G.B. to Dr. Ernest Matsner, 16 October 1936, Margaret Sanger Papers, Library of Congress, Vols. 17-18. Hereafter Sanger Papers, LC.

3. On Sanger, see Margaret Sanger, *An Autobiography* (New York, 1938); Gordon, *Woman's Body, Woman's Right*, pp. 213-30; Reed, *From Private Vice to Public Virtue*, pp. 67-106.

4. Margaret Sanger, *Family Limitation* (New York, n.d.).

5. On Stopes, see Keith Bryant, *Marie Stopes: A Biography* (London, 1962); Ruth Hall, *Passionate Pilgrim: The Life of Marie Stopes* (New York, 1977); Richard Allen Soloway, *Birth Control and the Population Question in England, 1877-1930* (Chapel Hill, 1981), pp. 208-33.

6. As advanced as she was, Stopes had some rather bizarre ideas. She believed that each woman's physiology was governed by a "fundamental pulse" that ordained that ten-day stretches of abstinence be followed by three or four days of "unions." She similarly opposed the use of the condom and coitus interruptus because these methods of birth control deprived the woman of the man's fluid. "The woman, too, loses the advantage (and I am convinced that it is difficult to overstate the physiological advantage) of the partial absorption of the man's secretion, which must take place through the large tract of internal epithelium with which they come in contact." *Married Love* (London, 1926 [18th ed.]), pp. 30ff, 71. See also Hall, *Dear Dr. Stopes*; Ellen M. Holtzman, "The Pursuit of Married Love: Women's Attitudes Towards Sexuality and Marriage in Great Britain, 1918-1939," *Journal of Social History*, 16 (1982), pp. 39-52.

7. Stopes declared the condom unaesthetic, the douche possibly harmful, and coitus interruptus unreliable and (for reasons noted above) hard on the woman. She preferred the cap (in particular, one called the "ProRace" cap) and quinine pessary. See Stopes, *Wise Parenthood* (London, 1926 [12th ed.]), p. 10.

8. See Marie Stopes, *"The First Five Thousand." Being the First Report of the First Birth Control Clinic in the British Empire* (London, 1925); Jane

Lewis, *The Politics of Motherhood* (London, 1980).

9.   See Ross Alfred Johnson, "No Compromise – No Political Trading: The Marxian Socialist Tradition in British Columbia" (Ph.D. thesis, University of British Columbia, 1975); Paul A. Philips, *No Greater Power: A Century of Labour in B.C.* (Vancouver, 1967); Martin Robin, *The Rush for Spoils: The Company Province, 1871-1933* (Toronto, 1972); Walter Young, "Ideology, Personality and the Origin of the CCF in British Columbia," *B.C. Studies*, 32 (1976-77), pp. 139-62. On women and socialism, see Linda Kealey, "Canadian Socialism and the Woman Question," *Labour/Le Travail*, 13 (1984), pp. 77-101.

10. See Anne Kennedy to Mrs. George Armstrong, 1 June 1923, American Birth Control League Papers, Houghton Library, Harvard University, Section 5362.110.1 (hereafter ABCL). On the political context of Sanger's activities, see Mari Jo Buhle, *Women and American Socialism, 1870-1920* (Urbana, 1981), pp. 268-78.

11. Sara Heppner to Anne Kennedy, 23 May 1923, ABCL.

12. Cora Hind to Anne Kennedy, 28 April 1923, ABCL.

13. Lillie A. Boynton to ABCL, 30 March 1923; Laura E. Jamieson to Margaret Sanger, 14 May 1923; Anne Kennedy to Laura E. Jamieson, 11, 27 June, 1923, ABCL. Isabel Ecclestone Mackay, a friend of Pauline Johnson, was a well-known novelist and poet; presumably her writings drew the attention of Margaret Sanger.

14. Mrs. Laura E. Jamieson graduated from the University of Toronto in 1908, organized the Vancouver Women's Branch of the International League for Peace and Freedom in 1921, sat as a juvenile court judge from 1927 to 1938, represented Vancouver Centre as a CCF MLA from 1939 to 1945 and 1952 to 1953, and was a Vancouver alderwoman from 1948 to 1950. Daisy Webster, *Growth of the N.D.P. in B.C.* (Vancouver, n.d.), pp. 48-49. Helena Gutteridge was appointed women's organizer by the Vancouver Trades and Labour Council in 1918 and sat as a Vancouver alderwoman in 1937. See Barbara Latham and Cathy Kess, eds., *In Her Own Right: Selected Essays on Women's History in British Columbia* (Victoria, 1980), p. 199.

15. *B.C. Federationist*, 19 June 1923, p. 6.

16. Laura E. Jamieson to Anne Kennedy, 4 July 1923, ABCL; *B.C. Federationist*, 6 July 1923, p. 1.

17. On Petersky, see Vancouver *Sun*, 17 February 1934, p. 2, and Margaret Sanger to Alexander Maitland Stephen, 1923, Alexander Maitland Stephen Papers, University of British Columbia Special Collections, folder 1-12; on Fewster, see his *My Garden Dreams* (Ottawa, 1926).

18. On Sanger's talk, see Vancouver *Province*, 4 July 1923, p. 12.

19. B.N. to Margaret Sanger (n.d.), ABCL, 110.8. It might be noted that a number of those who supported birth control and other feminist-related causes were attracted to theosophy, which provided a mystical defence of sexual equality. In the East such adherents included Flora MacDonald Denison, Blodwen Davies, and Alice Chown; in the West, Alexander

Maitland Stephen, Dr. Ernest Fewster, and Duncan MacNair. See Michele Lacomb, "Theosophy and the Canadian Idealist Tradition: A Preliminary Exploration," *Journal of Canadian Studies*, 17 (1983), pp. 100-20. See also Ramsay Cook, "Spiritualism, Science of the Earthly Paradise," *Canadian Historical Review*, 65 (1984), pp. 4-27.

20.   Alexander Maitland Stephen (1882-1942) taught at the Seymour School from 1918 to 1920, was involved with the Western Air Conditioning Corporation in the early 1920's, described his occupation as that of "writer" in the late 1920's, and taught at the B.C. School of Pharmacy in the 1930's. On Stephen, see his papers in UBC Special Collections and the Vancouver City Archives, Add. Mss. 56. On Stephen in the B.C. political world, see *The Canadian's Who's Who* (Toronto, 1936-1937), II, p. 1030; *New Frontier*, 2 (May, 1937), p. 1; Dorothy G. Steeves, *The Compassionate Rebel: Ernest Winch and the Growth of Socialism in Western Canada* (Vancouver, 1960), pp. 77, 114-15; Walter D. Young, "Ideology, Personality and the Origins of the CCF in B.C.," *B.C. Studies*, 32 (1976), pp. 139-62; Dorothy Livesay, *Right Hand, Left Hand* (Toronto, 1977), pp. 224-25.

21.   *B.C. Federationist*, 17 July 1923, p. 2.

22.   *Ibid.*, 16 May 1924, p. 2; 23 May 1924, p. 2; 30 May 1924, p. 2; 11 July 1924, p. 1; 18 July 1924, p. 1; 22 August 1924, p. 1; 13 March 1925, p. 1; 17 April 1925, p. 1.

23.   *Ibid.*, 27 February 1925, p. 4; 6 March 1925, pp. 1, 4.

24.   *Ibid.*, 3 September 1924, p. 2. T.A. Barnard, a Nanaimo bookseller and frequent contributor to the *B.C. Federationist*, was the CLP candidate in Comox in the provincial election of 1924.

25.   *Ibid.*, 15 August 1924, p. 2; 21 November 1924, p. 1; 28 November 1924, p. 1; 12 December 1924, p. 3; 23 January 1925, p. 1; 30 January 1925, p. 3; 6 February 1925, p. 1.

26.   Even the staid *Labour Statesman* provided some discussion of birth control, although this consisted mainly of reprints from other journals, such as the *Socialist Review*. See *Labour Statesman* on depopulation in France, 6 June 1924, p. 3; on eugenics, 11 July 1924, p. 2, and 21 November 1914, p. 2.

27.   Vancouver *Sun*, 12 August 1924, p. 6; *B.C. Federationist*, 8 August 1924, p. 1.

28.   *B.C. Federationist*, 26 December 1924, p. 1. The existence of the League in Vancouver was first noted in passing at the time of Kennedy's visit. See *B.C. Federationist*, 8 August 1924, p. 1. Soon after her visit to Vancouver, Sanger wrote to Stephen from Colorado to say that it was good to hear that "a definitive home" for the League had been established in Vancouver and that he should campaign for the repeal of the anti-birth control law by organizing mass meetings and bringing in visiting speakers. Sanger to Stephen, 1923, Stephen Papers, UBC Special Collections, folder 1-12.

29.   *B.C. Federationist*, 9 January 1925, p. 2.

30.   One difficulty in tracing the League's activities after 1925 is that the *B.C. Federationist*, which served as its mouthpiece, ceased publication in June

of that year. The *Western Clarion*, which on occasion also broached the issue, closed down in August of 1925. The *Labour Statesman*, controlled by the Vancouver Trades and Labour Council, attributed the *Western Clarion's* collapse to the overly intellectual nature of its discussions. It was certainly true that the narrowly labourist *Labour Statesman* would not devote the sort of attention to the subject of birth control (or women's issues in general) as did its recently departed rivals. The lively political discussions of the early 1920's were at an end.

31.   A.M. Stephen, "Activity in Canada," *International Aspects of Birth Control: Sixth International Neo-Malthusian and Birth Control Conference* (New York, 1925), I, pp. 133-36. Dr. Oswald Withrow, who participated at the New York conference, upon his return to Toronto inaugurated on May 5, 1925, the Ontario Birth Control League. The Ontario League initially attracted some attention but seems to have disappeared even before Withrow was sentenced in 1927 to seven years in prison for "attempting to procure an abortion." See *Toronto Daily Star*, 9 May 1925, p. 17; *Birth Control Review*, 9 (1925), p. 236; Dr. Oswald C.J. Withrow, *Poems from Prison* (Toronto, 1937).

32.   See G.B.C. to Sanger, 18 September 1923, ABCL; Mrs. R.B. to Sanger, July, 1935; Sanger to Mrs. R.B., 18 July 1935; Sanger to P.C., 23 August 1935, Sanger Papers, LC.

33.   See Ronald Grantham, "Some Aspects of the Socialist Movement in British Columbia, 1898-1933" (M.A. thesis, University of British Columbia, 1942), pp. 176ff.

34.   Lyle Telford to Stopes, 24 March 1932, Stopes Papers, BM.

35.   Lyle Telford to Stopes, 28 March 1932, Stopes Papers, BM. The next year a New Westminster doctor wrote Stopes to say that he, too, was establishing a birth control clinic, but no further information is available on this venture. See Dr. G.H.M. to Stopes, 13 October 1933, Stopes Papers, BM.

36.   See *Wrigley's B.C. Directory* under the appropriate years, names, and addresses.

37.   Edith How-Martyn to Sanger, 4 August 1936, Sanger Papers, LC; Vancouver *Sun*, 13 February 1936, p. 1.

38.   Vancouver *Sun*, 17 March 1936, p. 1; 3 December 1937, p. 14; Victoria *Daily Times*, 3 December 1937, p. 6.

39.   Victoria *Daily Times*, 20 November 1940, p. 12.

40.   R.R. to Stopes, 19 May 1921, Stopes Papers, BM.

41.   S.H. to Sanger, 9 September 1929, Sanger Papers, LC.

42.   J.B. to Sanger, 6 September 1934, *ibid.*

43.   See Vancouver City Directory under appropriate names. The CCF organ, the *Commonwealth*, carried advertisements for Margaret Brown's Feminine Hygiene Clinic in 1935 and for G. Duncan's sale of Margaret Sanger's *Family Limitation* in 1936.

44.   See A.L. to Sanger, 12 March 1928, ABCL, 110.8; A.G. to Sanger, 8

October 1928, ABCL, 110.3; R.B. to Sanger, July, 1935, Sanger Papers, LC.

45. On the response of English and American feminists to birth control, see McLaren, *Birth Control in Nineteenth Century England*, pp. 197-202; Gordon, *Woman's Body, Woman's Right*, pp. 95-116.

46. Dr. Helen MacMurchy, *Sterilization? Birth Control? A Book for Family Welfare and Safety* (Toronto, 1934), p. 88; see also Constance Lynd, "Race Suicide," *Woman's Century*, February, 1929, p. 49.

47. *Western Woman's Weekly*, 14 December 1918, p. 14.

48. MacMurchy, *Sterilization*, p. 149.

49. See, for example, B.O. Flower, "Prostitution Within the Marriage Bond," *Arena*, 13 (1895), p. 62.

50. Rev. Mabel McCoy Irwin, "Birth Control in Its Wider Aspects," *Woman's Century*, March, 1920, p. 23.

51. On Stockham, see Chapter One; Georgina Sackville, *Birth Control or Prevention of Conception* (Calgary, 1929); Sackville, *Unmarried Mothers and Illegitimate Children* (Calgary, 1929). See also the Sackville Papers in Public Archives of Alberta, file 77.259.

52. See McClung's articles in *Maclean's*, May, 1916, pp. 25-26; June, 1926, p. 28. See also Veronica Strong-Boag's introduction to Nellie McClung, *In Times Like These* (Toronto, 1972), p. viii.

53. Emily Murphy, "Companionate Marriage," *Chatelaine*, May, 1928, p. 56. See also her earlier article, "The Home: The Birthrate in Ontario," *National Home Monthly of Canada*, July, 1902, p. 12.

54. Carol Bacchi, "Race Regeneration and Social Purity: A Study of the Social Attitudes of Canada's English Speaking Suffragettes," *Histoire sociale/Social History*, 9 (1978), pp. 470-74; Veronica Strong-Boag, *The Parliament of Women: The National Council of Women of Canada, 1893-1924* (Ottawa, 1976), pp. 353-70.

55. Gillian Weiss, " 'As Women and Citizens': Clubwomen in Vancouver, 1910-1928" (Ph.D. thesis, University of British Columbia, 1983).

56. *Western Woman's Weekly*, 21 October 1922, p. 2.

57. Cited in Deborah Gorham, "Flora MacDonald Dennison: Canadian Feminist," in Linda Kealey, ed., *A Not Unreasonable Claim: Women and Reform in Canada* (Toronto, 1979), p. 66.

58. Edith Lang, "Moral Issues," *Woman's Century*, February, 1920, p. 52.

59. Cited in *New Generation*, March, 1930, p. 36. The *Western Producer*, thanks to the interest of Violet McNaughton, editor of the women's page, carried between January and November, 1927, a full discussion of the pros and cons of contraception.

60. *Winnipeg Free Press*, 31 March 1930, p. 1; see also, *Alberta Labour News*, 12 April 1930, p. 2.

61. *Winnipeg Free Press*, 8 June 1932, p. 4; see also, Rudolph Glanz, *The Jewish Women in America* (New York, 1976), I, pp. 102-03.

62. *Calgary Herald*, 21 January 1933, p. 25; see also, *Winnipeg Free Press*,

4 March 1933, p. 6; 20 January 1934, p. 14.

63. Emily Murphy, "Birth Control: Its Meaning," Vancouver *Sun*, 27 August 1932, p. 5; see also an unpublished manuscript by Murphy, "Mothers and Birth Control," in the City of Edmonton Archives.

Chapter 4

1. A.R. Kaufman to Alberta Department of Public Health, 9 September 1937, Sanger Papers, LC, vol. 18.

2. See, for example, Ian Bain, "The Development of Family Planning in Canada," *Canadian Journal of Public Health*, 5 (1964), pp. 334-40; Raymond Boutin, "The History of the Family Planning Movement in Canada," in Cenovia Addy, ed., *Family Planning and Social Work* (Ottawa, 1976), pp. 16-29. Kaufman's work is placed in an international context in Reed, *From Private Vice to Public Virtue*, part IV.

3. On birth control and the left in Britain, see McLaren, *Birth Control in Nineteenth Century England*; for America see Gordon, *Woman's Body, Woman's Right*; Buhle, *Women and American Socialism*; for France, see Angus McLaren, *Sexuality and Social Order: The Debate over the Fertility of Women and Workers in France, 1750-1920* (New York, 1983).

4. Wendy Mitchinson, "Historical Attitudes Towards Women and Childbirth," *Atlantis*, 4, 2 (1979), pp. 13-34.

5. On Kerr, see Rosanna Ledbetter, *A History of the Malthusian League* (Dayton, Ohio, 1976).

6. Hal D. Sears, *The Sex Radicals: Free Love in High Victorian America* (Lawrence, Kansas, 1977); see also the Canadian view of Harmon in the Winnipeg *Voice*, 12 May 1911, p. 3.

7. R.B. Kerr to the *Malthusian*, November, 1907, p. 84; December, 1917, pp. 98-99. The Malthusian League, with the *Malthusian* as its mouthpiece, was established in Britain by the Drysdale family following the sensational trial in 1877 of the secularists Charles Bradlaugh and Annie Besant for selling a birth control tract. Charles Watts, the publisher of the tract (Charles Knowlton's *Fruits of Philosophy*, which originally appeared in the United States in 1832), claimed to have been unaware of the book's contents, broke relations with Bradlaugh, and left for Toronto, where he edited *Secular Thought* in the late 1880's. See Ledbetter, *A History*, pp. 29-32; Toronto *Daily Globe*, 19, 22, 29 June 1877; Gregory S. Kealey, *Toronto Workers Respond to Industrial Capitalism, 1876-1892* (Toronto, 1980), pp. 400-01.

8. R.B. Kerr to the *Malthusian*, January, 1909, pp. 1-2; August, 1910, p. 67; December, 1910, pp. 103-04; July, 1912, p. 51; April, 1915, p. 29; June, 1917, p. 45.

9. *Ibid.*, December, 1908, p. 95; January, 1914, p. 6.

10. *Ibid.*, September, 1906, p. 65.

11. *Ibid.*, October, 1907, pp. 74-75.

12. Emma Goldman, *Living My Life* (Garden City, 1934), pp. 986-90; Richard Drinnan, *Rebel in Paradise: A Biography of Emma Goldman* (Berkeley, 1961), pp. 260-65.

13. Toronto *Star*, 27 April 1927, p. 28; also 28 April 1927, p. 17. Goldman had lectured on birth control since 1910 and helped introduce Margaret Sanger to the subject. The activities of both were reported in the Canadian press and the address of Sanger's American Birth Control League to which queries could be sent was prominently carried on the front page of the *One Big Union Bulletin*, 12 February 1925. Goldman's talk was chaired by Mrs. Alice Loeb, an active birth control propagandist who travelled to Germany to join the World League for Sexual Reform and offered her services in 1929 to prepare for Margaret Sanger's tour of Canada. See Alice Loeb to Sanger, 5 June 1929, Sanger Papers, LC, vol. 17.

14. None of the histories of the Canadian left deal extensively with attitudes toward population; for overviews, see D.J. Bercuson, *Fools and Wisemen: The Rise and Fall of the One Big Union* (Toronto, 1978); Gad Horowitz, *Canadian Labour in Politics* (Toronto, 1968); A.R. McCormack, *Reformers, Rebels, and Revolutionaries: The Western Canadian Radical Movement* (Toronto, 1977); Norman Penner, *The Canadian Left: A Critical Analysis* (Scarborough, 1977); Martin Robin, *Radical Politics and Canadian Labour* (Kingston, 1968); Walter D. Young, *The Anatomy of a Party: The National C.C.F., 1932-1961* (Toronto, 1969).

15. *B.C. Federationist*, 22 June 1912, p. 1.

16. *Western Clarion*, 13 August 1904, p. 1.

17. *One Big Union Bulletin*, 25 October 1923, p. 4; see also *Western Clarion*, May, 1918, pp. 7-8.

18. As bizarre as the idea of a "birth strike" might be, belief in its efficacy was not restricted to the left; the Vancouver *Daily World* reported (15 March 1919, p. 11) Dean Inge of England predicting that the policy of "race suicide" launched by the working classes would result in the creation of an "aristocracy of labour" that would use taxation to plunder the upper classes.

19. *One Big Union Bulletin*, 11 December 1924, p. 2.

20. *B.C. Federationist*, 22 November 1912, p. 5; *One Big Union Bulletin*, 30 March 1922, p. 2; 5 April 1923, p. 1; 3 May 1923, p. 4. For an anti-scouting poem, see Dawn Fraser, *Echoes from Labour's Wars: Industrial Cape Breton in the 1920s* (Toronto, 1976), pp. 35-37.

21. *Industrial Banner*, 2 July 1920, p. 3.

22. *One Big Union Bulletin*, 20 July 1922, p. 1.

23. *B.C. Federationist*, 27 December 1918, p. 2.

24. *One Big Union Bulletin*, 6 November 1924, p. 2.

25. *Ibid.*, 24 January 1931, p. 5.

26. Vancouver *Sun*, 13 February 1936, p. 1; also 17 March 1936, p. 1.

27. Victoria *Daily Times*, 3 December 1937, p. 6.

28. *Ibid.*, 20 November 1940, p. 12.

29. *One Big Union Bulletin*, 11 March 1926, p. 1.

30. See, for example, the *Western Clarion*, 27 September 1913, p. 1; 20 December 1913, p. 4; May, 1916, p. 8; June, 1917, p. 12.

31. *One Big Union Bulletin*, 6 November 1924, p. 2. For American women

socialists, see Neil K. Basen, "Kate Richard O'Hare: the 'First Lady' of American Socialism, 1901-1917," *Labour History*, 21 (1980), pp. 194-96.

32.   *One Big Union Bulletin*, 6 November 1924, p. 2.

33.   *Ibid.*, 25 June 1925, p. 2; see also Rose Henderson's article on 3 February 1917, p. 2.

34.   *Ibid.*, 16 April 1925, p. 2.

35.   *Ibid.*, 9 July 1925, p. 2.

36.   *B.C. Federationist*, 21 March 1919, p. 3. The more prominent role played by women and women's issues in the North American birth control debate as compared to the British was commented on by James D. Campbell of Winnipeg, who claimed that one reason he left England for Canada was his impatience with the male-dominated Malthusian League. Campbell to the *Malthusian*, August, 1923, p. 97.

37.   *House of Commons Debates*, 1 (1929), pp. 957-58. On economic conditions, see John Herd Thompson with Allen Seager, *Canada 1922-1939: Decades of Discord* (Toronto, 1985), pp. 138, 151.

38.   See, for example, the *One Big Union Bulletin*, 22 November 1919, p. 1; 30 July 1921, p. 4; 24 September 1921, p. 3.

39.   *Ibid.*, 13 November 1920, p. 2; see also Winnipeg *Voice*, 22 February 1918, p. 2.

40.   *Socialist Standard* article reprinted in *One Big Union Bulletin*, 21 August 1930, p. 4.

41.   *Ibid.*, 2 April 1931, p. 2. As part of the attack on the bogey of "over-population," the *One Big Union Bulletin* also reprinted Jonathan Swift's "A Modest Proposal," in which the sardonic suggestion is made that unwanted babies can always be stewed, roasted, baked, or boiled: 18 January 1923, p. 3.

42.   *Ibid.*, 28 May 1931, p. 2.

43.   *Canadian Tribune*, 27 April 1940, p. 2.

44.   *Industrial Worker* article reprinted in *One Big Union Bulletin*, 12 September 1929, p. 7.

45.   Irving Abella, *Nationalism, Communism, and Canadian Labour: The C.I.O. the Communist Party, and the Canadian Congress of Labour, 1935-1956* (Toronto, 1973); Ivan Avakumovic, *The Communist Party in Canada: A History* (Toronto, 1975).

46.   *Western Clarion*, 1 November 1920, p. 7; see also *United Farmers of Alberta*, 2 March 1931, p. 16.

47.   *One Big Union Bulletin*, 17 November 1927, p. 2. See also Richard Stites, *The Women's Liberation Movement in Russia: Feminism, Nihilism, and Bolshevism, 1860-1930* (Princeton, 1978), pp. 264, 355, 386-87; Gail Warshiovsky Lapidus, *Women in Soviet Society: Equality, Development and Social Change* (Berkeley, 1978), pp. 60-61, 112-13; Peter G. Filene, *Americans and the Soviet Experiment* (Cambridge, Mass., 1976), pp. 141-42.

48.   *C.C.F. News*, 15 October 1936, p. 4. On the threats posed by communism

to the Canadian family, see *Canadian Labour Press* supplement, "Communism and Your Home," 15 May 1936.

49.   The CPC youth paper, *Young Worker* (1924-1934), never mentioned birth control and only passing references to the issue were made in the party's senior publication, *The Worker* (1922-1936), which was replaced by the *Daily Clarion* (1936-1939). For a far fuller and more sympathetic analysis of the CPC, see Joan Sangster, "The Communist Party and the Woman Question, 1922-1929," *Labour/Le Travail*, 15 (1985), pp. 25-56; and Sangster, "Canadian Women in Radical Politics and Labour, 1920-1950" (Ph.D. thesis, McMaster University, 1984).

50.   Avakumovic, *Communist Party*, pp. 34, 74, 248.

51.   *Eighth Dominion Convention. Communist Party of Canada, 8-12 October, 1937*, p. 60.

52.   *Daily Clarion*, 1 August 1936, p. 3; 22 August 1936, p. 5; 29 August 1936, p. 4; 21 November 1936, p. 5; 11 December 1936, p. 3; 3 March 1937, p. 4; 23 March 1937, p. 3; 6 November 1937, p. 6; 13 November 1937, p. 4.

53.   A copy of the petition was sent by Edith How-Martyn to Margaret Sanger, 4 August 1936, Sanger Papers, LC, vol. 18. See also *Daily Clarion*, 29 August 1936, p. 4; Vancouver *Sun*, 13 February 1936, p. 1; *B.C. Workers News*, 15 March 1935, p. 1.

54.   *Eighth Convention*, p. 57.

55.   *Daily Clarion*, 4 July 1936, p. 8.

56.   *Ibid.*, 11 July 1936, p. 3; also 18 July 1936, p. 5; 19 October 1936, p. 3. On the latter date the *Clarion* published the photo of an American abortionist with the caption, "U.S.S.R. Abortion Law Solved All This."

57.   *Ibid.*, 3 October 1936, p. 5.

58.   For a comparison with events in the United States, see Robert Shaffer, "Women and the Communist Party, U.S.A.," *Socialist Review*, 9 (May-June, 1979), pp. 73-118.

59.   See Gene Homel, "Fading Beams of the Nineteenth Century: Radicalism and Early Socialism in Canada's 1890s," *Labour/Le Travailleur*, 5 (1970), pp. 7-32.

60.   Bercuson, *Fools*, p. 232.

61.   *B.C. Workers News*, 15 March 1935, p. 2.

62.   Kaufman to Sanger, 3 December 1935, Sanger Papers, LC, vol. 17.

63.   *B.C. Federationist*, 16 February 1914, p. 1.

64.   *One Big Union Bulletin*, 22 November 1928, p. 2.

Chapter 5

1.   E.M. Matsner, "The Trial of Dorothea Palmer," *Journal of Contraception*, 2 (1937), p. 80.

2.   See Dianne Dodd, "The Birth Control Movement on Trial, 1936-1937," *Histoire sociale/Social History*, 32 (1983), pp. 381-400; Gerald Storz and Murray Eaton, "Pro Bono Publico: The Eastview Birth Control Trial," *Atlantis*, 8 (1983), pp. 51-60.

3. A.H. Tyrer to Eva Dodge, Planned Parenthood Federation, 9 August 1944, Margaret Sanger Papers, Sophia Smith Collection, Smith College (hereafter Sanger/Smith).
4. Tyrer to Sanger, 22 March 1931, Sanger Papers, LC.
5. Tyrer to Stopes, 24 March 1931, Stopes Papers, BM.
6. Tyrer to Stopes, 10 April 1932, Stopes Papers, BM.
7. Alfred Henry Tyrer, *And A New Earth* (Toronto, 1941), p. xiv.
8. On Tyrer's life, see *ibid.*, and Tyrer to Stopes, 23 April 1931, Stopes Papers, BM.
9. *Some Facts About Birth Control* (Toronto, n.d.). A copy of this tract was enclosed in a letter, Tyrer to Stopes, 7 October 1932, Stopes Papers, BM. On its distribution, see also Tyrer to Stopes, 11 May 1932.
10. *Birth Control and Some of its Simplest Methods* (Toronto, n.d.). A copy of this tract was enclosed in a letter of Tyrer to Stopes, 23 April 1931, Stopes Papers, BM. Tyrer spent a good deal of time futilely attempting to interest Stopes and Sanger in a device that would assist in the insertion of a sponge and contraceptive jelly. For a diagram, see Tyrer to Stopes, 24 March 1931, Stopes Papers, BM.
11. Tyrer to Stopes, 11 November 1930, *ibid.*; see also Tyrer to Stopes, 26 December 1930.
12. Tyrer to Stopes, 11 November 1930, *ibid.*
13. Tyrer to Stopes, 24 March 1931, *ibid.*
14. Tyrer to Stopes, 26 December 1930, *ibid.*; Tyrer to Sanger, 4 February 1931, Sanger Papers, LC.
15. Those Americans from whom Tyrer attempted to obtain funds included John A. Kingsbury, George Bedborough, Dr. Karl Reiland, Robert Norwood, and Margaret Sanger's husband, Noah Slee. See Tyrer to Sanger, 19 March, 24 March, 3 April, 26 April 1931, Sanger Papers, LC.
16. Sanger to Tyrer, 21 March 1931, *ibid.*
17. Tyrer to Sanger, 3 April 1931; Sanger to Tyrer, 7 April 1931, *ibid.*
18. Tyrer to Sanger, 22 March 1931, *ibid.*
19. See Toronto *Mail and Empire*, 28 May 1931; Sanger to Skey, 1 June 1931, Tyrer to Sanger 7 July 1931, 18 July 1931, Sanger Papers, LC; Tyrer to Stopes, 17 July 1931, Stopes Papers, BM. Protestant interest in birth control was also manifested when Mary Willcox, secretary of the rector of Toronto's Church of the Ascension, wrote Sanger (7 April 1931, Sanger Papers, LC) to inquire about the activities of the Canadian Voluntary Parenthood League.
20. On the bureau's operation, see Tyrer to Eva Dodge, 9 August 1944, Sanger/Smith; Tyrer to Stopes, 10 April 1932, Stopes Papers, BM.; Dr. Rowena Hume to Sanger, 21 November 1932, Sanger Papers, LC. For a list of the doctors associated with the Canadian Birth Control League, see a pamphlet of the same name in the Clarence Gamble Papers, Countway Library (Boston, Mass.), G. 954 (hereafter Gamble Papers).
21. Tyrer, *New Earth*, p. 254.
22. Tyrer to Stopes, 29 November 1935, Stopes Papers, BM.

23. Tyrer, *New Earth*, p. 255.

24. *Ibid.*, p. 247; also Tyrer to Sanger, 24 November 1931, Sanger Papers, LC.

25. Stopes to Tyrer, 23 April 1931, Stopes Papers, BM.

26. Tyrer to Sanger, 8 February 1932, Sanger to Tyrer, February, 1932, Sanger Papers, LC. Tyrer had long been interested in eugenics. He approached the British Eugenics Society for help in 1930, unaware that a Canadian eugenics society was in the process of forming. See correspondence of 26 December 1930, 9 January 1931, Eugenics Society, Contemporary Medical Archives Centre, Wellcome Institute for the History of Medicine, D 52.

27. By 1943 nine printings of about 10,000 each had appeared. See Tyrer to Eva Dodge, 28 December 1943, 9 August 1944, Sanger/Smith. Tyrer also produced a sex education text for children, *Where Did We Come From, Mother Dear?* (Toronto, 1939). See also his pamphlet, *Your Child Needs Your Help* (Toronto, n.d.).

28. Tyrer, *Where Did We Come From*, p. 31.

29. *Ibid.*, p. 53.

30. Tyrer, *New Earth*, p. 243.

31. *Ibid.*, p. 249.

32. *Ibid.*, p. 253. See also Tyrer letter to the Toronto *Mail and Empire*, 3 December 1930.

33. Tyrer, *New Earth*, p. 244.

34. Tyrer to Stopes, 29 November 1935, Stopes Papers, BM. Tyrer was concerned that both Stopes and Sanger suspected he was interested in the "commercial side" of birth control, linked as he was to a manufacturer. Given his constant harping on money matters, it was hardly surprising that such suspicions should arise. See Tyrer to Sanger, 18 June 1933, Sanger Papers, LC; Tyrer to Stopes, 22 October 1935, Stopes Papers, BM.

35. Tyrer, *New Earth*, p. 249.

36. Tyrer to Stopes, 24 March 1931, Stopes Papers, BM.

37. For Hawkins's life, see her family album and the Birth Control Society of Hamilton Records, vol. II in the Birth Control Society of Hamilton Papers, Hamilton Public Library (hereafter BCSH).

38. Burgar to Stopes, 16 July 1929, Stopes Papers, BM.

39. Burgar to Stopes, 9 November 1929, *ibid*.

40. Burgar to Stopes, 17 March 1931, *ibid*. Lily Hendrie, honorary vice-president of the Hamilton Birth Control Clinic, visited Stopes. See Mrs. William Hendrie to Stopes, 1 January 1931, *ibid*.

41. Burgar to Stopes, 15 October 1931, *ibid*. On the hostility of the doctors, see their letter to Burgar, 30 April 1931, and Burgar to Hawkins, 14 May 1931, BCSH.

42. Tyrer reported Hawkins's activities in a letter of 24 November 1931, Sanger Papers, LC. Sanger congratulated Hawkins on her clinic, 30 March 1932, *ibid*.

43. See the pamphlet *A Short History of the Birth Control Society of Hamilton* and the society's Annual General Meeting Report of 15 January 1934, BCSH.

44. Hawkins to Stopes, 6 February 1932, Stopes Papers, BM; Hawkins to Janet Whitemarch of the American Birth Control League, 13 November 1935, Sanger/Smith.

45. Hawkins to Stopes, 2 December 1931, Stopes Papers, BM; Stopes to Hawkins, 15 January 1932, BCSH. Although Hawkins warned Sanger of the "anti-American feeling" in Canada, Sanger in 1933 did make a successful lecture tour of Ontario. See Hawkins to Sanger, 21 November 1932, Sanger to Hawkins, 6 December 1932, Sanger Papers, LC.

46. See the letters from women in Calgary, Saskatoon, and Winnipeg in Record Book, BCSH.

47. On Bagshaw, see her file in the papers of the BCSH. On the visits to New York, see Marjorie A. Prevost, assistant director, Birth Control Clinical Research Bureau, to Hawkins, 25 November 1931, BCSH. See also Marjorie Wild, *Elizabeth Bagshaw* (Toronto, 1982).

48. Gladys Gaylord to Hawkins, 25 March 1932, BCSH.

49. Hawkins to Sanger, 21 November 1932, Sanger Papers, LC.

50. Hawkins to Stopes, 24 March 1932, Stopes Papers, BM.

51. Entry of 11 November 1935, Record Book, BCSH; Hawkins to Janet Whitemarch, 13 November 1935, Sanger/Smith.

52. On Archbishop J.T. McNally's attack, see the Hamilton *Spectator*, 11 October 1933, 24 January 1934; for references to socialist opposition see Annual General Meeting, 15 January 1934, BCSH.

53. Brandt to Hawkins, 12 September 1934, BCSH.

54. See the pamphlet *An Outline of the Work and Aims of the Birth Control Society of Hamilton* in BCSH.

55. Birth Control Society, *Progress Report: June 1935* (Hamilton, n.d.), p. 5, BCSH.

56. *Ibid.*, p. 3.

57. *Ibid.*, p. 2. A 1934 report noted that of 946 patients, sixty became pregnant after and sixteen were pregnant before visiting the clinic. Presumably the latter were seeking abortions. See report of 9 October 1934, Record Book, BCSH.

58. See Hawkins to Stopes, March, 1932, 8 January 1936, Stopes Papers, BM.

59. The clinic initially cost $1,600 a year to run.

60. Patients on relief who received free contraceptives were expected to make eventual restitution.

61. *Progress Report: June 1935*, p. 1.

62. See 1933, 1934, 1935 Record Books, BCSH.

63. Soloway, *Birth Control and the Population Question in England, 1877-1930*, p. 277; Reed, *From Private Vice to Public Virtue*, p. 211.

64. See Herc Munro, "'The Eccentric World of Alvin Ratz Kaufman," *The Executive* (April, 1962); *Toronto Saturday Night*, 17 October 1936; W.V.

Utley, *A History of Kitchener* (Waterloo, 1937), pp. 278, 282, 285, 287, 410.

65. Kaufman to Abraham Stone, 20 May 1937, Sanger/Smith.

66. PIB Bulletin #1, Birth Control Activities and Procedures, 15 June 1933. Updated versions were produced 15 December 1933, 15 September 1934, 1 November 1940. Parents' Information Bureau Papers, University of Waterloo; hereafter PIB Papers.

67. J.B.S. Haldane, *Heredity and Politics* (New York, 1938), p. 107. Kaufman eventually distributed a two-page tract entitled *Technique of Vasectomy* (Kitchener, n.d.).

68. On Weber, see Dorothea Palmer Papers, University of Waterloo, Box 3, file 20 (hereafter Palmer Papers). Weber might have worked in Chicago with Dr. Irving F. Stein. See Clarence Gamble to Kaufman, 21 May 1935, Gamble Papers, G. 955.

69. See Marjorie Prevost to Mary Hawkins, 25 November 1931, BCSH. Kaufman also wrote to England for advice; see Kaufman to Marie Stopes, 17 October 1932, Stopes Papers, BM.

70. Kaufman to Clarence Gamble, 29 May 1935, Gamble Papers, G. 955. To instruct doctors on the fitting of diaphragms, Kaufman circulated *General Procedure and Technique of Contraception* (Kitchener, n.d.).

71. Kaufman to Clarence Gamble, 21 April 1937, Gamble Papers, G. 958.

72. Kaufman to Clarence Gamble, 12 July 1934, Gamble Papers, G. 954.

73. Kaufman to Clarence Gamble, 29 May 1935, Gamble Papers, G. 955. On Gamble, see Reed, *From Private Vice to Public Virtue*, pp. 255-81; Doone and Greer Williams, *Every Child a Wanted Child: Clarence James Gamble, M.D. and His Work in the Birth Control Movement* (Cambridge Mass., 1978).

74. Kaufman to Clarence Gamble, 29 May 1935, Gamble Papers, G. 955; see also Kaufman to Randolph Cautley, 20 May 1935, Gamble Papers, G. 955.

75. PIB #15, Instructions to Social Service Workers, 1 September 1934, Sanger/Smith.

76. *Birth Control Methods* (Kitchener, n.d.), pp. 10-11; also *Birth Control and Some of its Simplest Methods* (Kitchener, n.d.).

77. The "Parents' Clinic" was established at Windsor on May 1, 1934, with Gladys A. Brandt as director. In one year it had only 161 patients while the PIB received applications from 608 women from the same area. Shortly thereafter the clinic was abandoned by Kaufman and taken over by the Essex County Maternal League under the direction of Mrs. Grace Joyce. The Toronto clinic was begun in February, 1933, with Mrs. Norman R. Beal as its director and Dr. Margaret Batt as its medical adviser. See Mrs. Mary Beal to Sanger, 4 May 1934, Sanger Papers, LC.

78. Kaufman to Eric Matsner, 6 May 1937, Sanger/Smith; Kaufman to Clarence Gamble, 26 April 1937, Gamble Papers, G. 958.

79. Kaufman to Clarence Gamble, 21 July 1937, Gamble Papers, G. 958.

80. Kaufman to Gilbert Colgate, 17 February 1938; Kaufman to Abraham

Stone, 14 February 1938, Sanger/Smith.

81. Kaufman to Mary Hawkins, 27 April 1933, included in a letter sent by Mary Hawkins to Marie Stopes, 30 April 1933, Stopes Papers, BM.

82. Kaufman later compared his methods to those of Sears-Roebuck; see Kaufman to Florence Rose, 16 January 1936, Sanger Papers, LC.

83. See PIB #15, Instructions to Social Service Workers.

84. Kaufman to Gamble, 12 July 1934, Gamble Papers, G. 954.

85. PIB, Procedure in Establishing Birth Control Activities, 21 June 1933.

86. Kaufman to Sanger, 17 January 1942, Sanger/Smith.

87. On one worker's activities, see Sara Diamond's interview of Vivian Dowding, Simon Fraser University Reserve Library, 2405 B., and Mary F. Bishop, "Vivian Dowding: Birth Control Advocate, 1892- ," in Latham and Pazdro, eds., *Not Just Pin Money*, pp. 327-35.

88. Kaufman to Sanger, 17 January 1942, Sanger/Smith.

89. See PIB #15.

90. Kaufman to Gamble, 12 August 1937, Gamble Papers, G. 958.

91. Kaufman to Eric Matsner, 31 October 1935, Sanger/Smith.

92. Because he was a rubber manufacturer it was widely believed that Kaufman produced his own contraceptives. He did have diaphragms made in Kitchener but relied mainly on established firms such as W.J. Ingram and Bell of Toronto, Gynae Research Laboratories, Holland-Rantos, and Durex of New York for supplies. See Kaufman to Stopes, 1935, Stopes Papers, BM.

93. Kaufman to Edith How-Martyn, 5 April 1935, Sanger Papers, LC.

94. See Sanger to Kaufman, 23 July 1941, Sanger/Smith.

95. Kaufman to Sanger, 17 January 1942, Sanger/Smith. See also Kaufman to Gamble, 12 July 1934, Gamble Papers, G. 954.

96. Kaufman to Sanger, 2 April 1937, Sanger Papers, LC.

97. Soloway, *Birth Control*, p. 277.

98. Attempts were made to have the Toronto Board of Control or Federated Community Services take over the clinic. When these failed the Toronto League for Race Betterment assumed responsibility. See Kaufman to Mrs. A. Pyke, 12 July 1938, Gamble Papers, G. 959; Gladys Brandt to Sanger, 23 March 1936 and 30 November 1937, Sanger Papers, LC; *The Birth Control Bulletin* (Toronto, Toronto League for Race Betterment, May, 1937), Vol. 1, no. 1.

99. Kaufman to Mrs. A. Pyke, 12 July 1938, Gamble Papers, G. 959; Kaufman to C.M. Smith, 10 April 1940, Gamble Papers, G. 961.

100. Lucy Ingram Morgan, "An Analysis of 2126 Cases Registered at the Toronto Birth Control Clinic Between October 3, 1933 and December 20, 1934," p. 64, Gamble Papers, G. 956.

101. Sanger Papers, LC.

102. A.R. Kaufman, "The Parents' Information Bureau of Canada," *Journal of Contraception*, 3 (1938), pp. 54-55; Morgan, "An Analysis." On the preparation of Morgan's report, see Kaufman to Lucy Ingram Morgan, 13 April, 5 October, 19 November, 22 December 1938, Gamble Papers, G. 959.

103. PIB #15.
104. Reed, *From Private Vice to Public Virtue*, pp. 311ff.
105. Kaufman to C.S. Curtis, 27 June 1933, Gamble Papers, G. 954.
106. Kaufman to Gamble, 12 March 1936, Gamble Papers, G. 957.
107. PIB #1, 15 September 1934.
108. Kaufman to Eric Matsner, 6 May 1937, Sanger/Smith; Kaufman to Gamble, 17 August 1936, Gamble Papers, G. 957.
109. Morgan, "An Analysis," p. 66.
110. "Clinic Reports," *Journal of Contraception*, 8 (1943), p. 119.
111. What follows is drawn mainly from the Palmer Papers.
112. See Bill Stephenson, "The Great Birth Control Trial," *Maclean's*, 23 November 1957, pp. 22-23, 76-80; Gerald Stortz, "Of Tactics and Prophylactics," *Canadian Lawyer* (March, 1982), pp. 4-6; Stortz and Eaton, "Pro Bono Publico"; Dodd, "The Birth Control Movement on Trial."
113. Chief Manion's testimony, Palmer Papers, Box 3, file 19.
114. Claris Edwin Silcox, "Eastview and the Public Good," *Canadian Forum*, 17 (May, 1937), p. 47.
115. PIB #1.
116. Kaufman to Sanger, 17 January 1942, Sanger/Smith.
117. See the Dun and Bradstreet report on Palmer in Palmer Papers, Box 6, file 46. Palmer was involved with a man whom she married once his divorce was completed.
118. Mary Hawkins to Sanger, September, 1936, Sanger Papers, LC.
119. Dorothea Palmer to F.W. Wegenast, 26 June 1937, Palmer Papers, Box 6, file 46.
120. Kaufman to Gamble, 1 October 1936, Gamble Papers, G. 957.
121. Mercier's chief witnesses were Dr. Joseph de Haitre, Dr. Léon Gérin-Lajoie, and Dr. Ernest Couture. To demonstrate that some Protestants were also opposed to birth control, Mercier also called Canon Arthur Walley and Dr. Richard Cargill. Neither provided convincing evidence. See Palmer Papers, Box 6, file 19, Box 4, files 25-27.
122. *Ibid.*, Box 3, file 19. See also Kaufman to Gamble, 26 October 1936, Gamble Papers, G. 957.
123. Wegenast called Professor H.R. Kemp of the University of Toronto to provide evidence of the economic hardship of unrestricted fertility and J.W. Buckley of the Toronto District Labour Council to demonstrate labour's concern for access to birth control information. See Palmer Papers, Box 6, files 22, 24.
124. *Ibid.*, files 20, 23, 24.
125. *Ibid.*, file 23.
126. *Ibid.*, files 20-24.
127. *Ibid.*, files 23-24.
128. Kaufman to Abraham Stone, 20 May 1937, Sanger/Smith.
129. Palmer Papers, Box 6, file 35; R. vs. Palmer (1937) *Ontario Weekly Notes*, 371, p. 270.
130. E.R. Norman, *Church and Society in England, 1770-1970* (Oxford, 1976), p. 270.

131. Soloway, *Birth Control*; Norman, *Church and Society*, pp. 333-47, 412.
132. *Toronto Globe*, 3 June 1932. It was reported that married Anglicans who purchased contraceptives from druggists would have to sign for them "in a book like poisons." Victoria *Daily Colonist*, 29 September 1934, B.C. Provincial Secretary, Public Health Branch Clipping File.
133. *Toronto Empire*, 24 February 1934, p. 1; C.F. Brown, "The Churches and the Stork," *The Survey* (1931), pp. 418-20. In Vancouver the Reverend J. Buchanan Tonkin of the First Unitarian Church defended birth control in the late 1920's. See Vancouver *Sun*, 17 March 1928, p. 5.
134. United Church of Canada, *Report of Commission on Voluntary Parenthood and Sterilization* (Ottawa, 1936); see also Hugh Dobson Papers, United Church of Canada Archives, file 15.
135. "Birth Control Progress," *Saturday Night*, 17 October 1936, pp. 11, 14; *Birth Control Review* (November, 1936); *Birth Control Notes*, 1 June 1937, pp. 4, 5.
136. Silcox, "Eastview," p. 49.
137. Gladys Brandt to Stopes, 29 September 1937, Stopes Papers, BM.
138. *Toronto Star*, 28 April 1927, p. 17. In 1924 Dr. Hastings provided a report of a meeting of the British Eugenics Education Society, held in Toronto, which supported birth control; see *Health Bulletin* (Department of Public Health, Toronto), August, 1924, p. 107.
139. See letters to Stopes for 1 September 1921, 16 December 1922, 8 September 1924, 20 February 1925, Stopes Papers, BM.
140. A.D.L. to Sanger, 12 March 1928, Sanger Papers, Houghton Library, 110.8.
141. Sanger to A.L.G., 8 October 1928, Sanger Papers, Houghton Library, 110.8.
142. *Toronto Star*, 28 April 1927, p. 17.
143. Reed, *From Private Vice to Public Virtue*, pp. 143-97; Soloway, *Birth Control*.
144. *Canadian Medical Association Journal*, 37 (1937), p. 496. On March 25, 1937, Dr. Cyril B. Romer, president of the Greater Vancouver Health League, declared it was the doctor's duty to provide birth control information. The Vancouver General Hospital was the first in the country to provide birth control information by allowing Henry M. Grant of the San Francisco Family Relations Bureau to open a "sex education institute" in its auditorium. *Canadian Medical Association Journal*, 37 (1937), p. 206. See also D.N. Trimble, "Contraception," *University of Toronto Medical Journal* (April, 1937), pp. 234-40.
145. Kaufman to Guy Birch, 26 February 1941, Gamble Papers, G. 961.
146. Kaufman to Gamble, 21 July 1937, Gamble Papers, G. 958.

Chapter 6
1. Cited in Pierre Berton, *The Dionne Years: A Thirties Melodrama* (Toronto, 1978), pp. 263-64.
2. *New York Times*, 29 August 1935, p. 17.
3. Kaufman to Edith How-Martyn, 18 October 1935, Sanger Papers, LC.
4. Kaufman to Eric M. Matsner, 17 December 1937, Sanger/Smith. See also Kaufman to Miss Rose, 16 June 1936, Sanger Papers, LC. Sanger sent

a correspondent in Lachine the names of eight doctors in Quebec who would provide contraceptive information; six were in Montreal, one in Lachine, and one in Huntington. Their names suggest they were all anglophones. See Sanger to P.M., 25 August 1935, Sanger Papers, LC.

5. A.H. Tyrer, *To the Protestant Ministers of Canada* (Toronto, 1938), p. 6.

6. The following discussion is based on R.P. Beaujot, "Canada's Population: Growth and Dualism," *Population Bulletin*, 33, 2 (1978); T.R. Balakrishnan *et al., Patterns of Fertility in Canada* (Ottawa, 1979).

7. The baby boom was fueled in part by a surge of post-war pro-natalism. During the war the government in effect had supported birth control by distributing condoms to servicemen, but it swung around after the armistice to support the notion that women were to return to their "normal role" of bearing and raising children. See E. Wuorio, "Baby Boom," *Maclean's*, 1 July 1943, pp. 12, 60; E.L. Chicanot, "We Can Build a Population as Well as Import It," *Saturday Night*, 3 June 1944, p. 5; Dr. Ruth MacLachan, "A Note to Brides: Don't Delay Parenthood," *Chatelaine* (May, 1946), pp. 29, 44; Ruth Roach Pierson, "The Double Bind of the Double Standard: V.D. Control and the CWAC in World War II," *Canadian Historical Review*, 62 (1981), pp. 44-45, and Pierson, *Canadian Women and the Second World War*, CHA Booklet No. 37 (Ottawa, 1983), pp. 13, 21; Genevieve Auger and Raymonde Lamothe, *De la Poêle à frire à la ligne de fue* (Montréal, 1981), p. 34; Denise Riley, *War in the Nursery: Theories of the Child and Mother* (London, 1983). It is also likely that post-war prosperity in Canada, as in the United States, led to a decline in "vigilance" by birth control users. See Richard A. Easterlin, *Birth and Fortune: The Impact of Numbers on Personal Welfare* (New York, 1980), p. 57.

8. Carl F. Grindstaff, "The Baby Bust: Changes in Fertility Patterns in Canada," *Canadian Studies in Population*, 2 (1975), pp. 15-22.

9. See Colette Carisse, *Planification des naissances en milieu Canadian-français* (Montréal, 1964); Leroy O. Stone and A.J. Siggner, *The Population of Canada* (Ottawa, 1974); Balakrishnan, *Patterns of Fertility*, pp. 73-78, 83.

10. See Jacques Henripin, "From Acceptance of Nature to Control: The Demography of French Canadians," *Canadian Journal of Economics and Political Science*, 23 (1957), pp. 10-19; Henripin, *Trends and Factors*.

11. The following discussion draws heavily on Marie Lavigne, "Réflexions féministes autour de la fertilité des Québécoises," in Nadia Fahmy-Eid and Micheline Dumont, *Maîtresse de maison, Maîtresse d'école: femmes, familles et éducation dans l'histoire du Québec* (Montréal, 1983), pp. 318-38.

12. See Marta Danylewycz, "Changing Relationships: Nuns and Feminists in Montreal, 1890-1925," *Histoire sociale/Social History*, 28 (1981), p. 413; Micheline Dumont, "Vocation religieuse et condition féminine," in Marie Lavigne and Yolande Pinard, *Travailleuses et féministes: les femmes dans la société québécoise* (Montréal, 1983), pp. 271-92.

13. For a lament on the decline of the large family, see Abbe Albert Tessier, "Onze enfants, mais c'est immoral," *Relations*, 3 (1943), pp. 296-97.

14. On fertility differentials, see M. Lamontagne and J.C. Falardeau, "Life Cycle of French Canadian Urban Families," *Canadian Journal of Economics and Political Science*, 13 (1947), p. 235; on infant mortality, see Dr. Joseph Gauvreau, "La mortalité infantile," *La Semaine social du Canada* (Montréal, 1924), pp. 162-75.

15. Lavigne, "Réflexions," 327.

16. Archives de l'archevêché de Saint-Boniface. On early references to herbal abortifacients, see R.L. Seguin, *La vie libertaire en Nouvelle France* (Ottawa, 1972), p. 279; on extended lactation, see Jacques Henripin, *La Population canadienne au début du 18e siècle: nuptialité, fécondité, mortalité infantile* (Paris, 1954), pp. 86-87; on abortion, see Andrée Lévesque, "Deviant Anonymous: Single Mothers at the Hôpital de la Miséricorde in Montreal, 1929-1939," *Historical Papers* (1984), p. 182.

17. Tamara Hareven and Randolph Langenbach, *Amoskeag* (New York, 1978), p. 256; Horace Miner, *St. Denis: A French Canadian Parish* (Chicago, 1963), pp. 169, 269. See also the articles of Bettina Bradbury: "The Family Economy and Work in an Industrializing City: Montreal in the 1870s," *Historical Papers* (1979), pp. 85-86; "Pigs, Cows and Boarders: Non-Wage Forms of Survival Among Montreal Families, 1861-91," *Labour/Le Travail*, 14 (1984), pp. 9-46; "Women and Wage Labour in a Period of Transition: Montreal, 1861-1881," *Histoire sociale/Social History*, 27 (1984), pp. 115-31.

18. Errol Bouchette, "La population française du Canada," *Revue canadienne*, 1 (1905), pp. 362-83; P. Louis Lalonde, "La revanche des berceaux," *Action française*, 2 (1918), pp. 98-108; Michael Behiels, "L'Association catholique de la jeunesse canadienne-française and the Quest for a Moral Regeneration, 1903-1914," *Journal of Canadian Studies*, 13 (1978), pp. 27-41; M. Lavigne, Y. Pinard, and J. Stoddart, "La Fédération nationale St-Jean Baptiste et les revendications féministes au début du XXe siècle," *Revue d'histoire de l'Amérique française*, 29 (1975), 353-73; Susan Mann Trofimenkoff, "Henri Bourassa and 'the Woman Question,'" *Journal of Canadian Studies*, 10 (1975), pp. 3-11; Trofimenkoff, *Action française: French Canadian Nationalism in the Twenties*, pp. 80-82.

19. On the question of whether the church really could control morality, see J.P. Wallot, "Religion and French Canadian Mores in the Early Nineteenth Century," *Canadian Historical Review*, 52 (1971), pp. 51-94. On Catholics taking up moral crusades launched by Protestants, see James Mohr, *Abortion in America: The Origins and Evolution of National Policy* (New York, 1978).

20. R.P. Martin, "La dépopulation," *Semaine sociale du Canada* (Montréal, 1924), p. 140. See also *L'Action française*, 10 (1923), p. 144.

21. Dr. Gaston Lapierre, "Les campagnes internationales actuelles d'eugénisme," *Revue trimestrielle canadienne*, 21 (1935), p. 356.

22. Andrée Lévesque, "Mères ou malades: les Québécoises de l'entre-guerres vues par les médecines," *Revue d'histoire de l'Amérique française*, 38 (1984), p. 30. See also Lapierre, "Les campagnes," p. 362.

23. L. Ferland, "Le prix d'une vie," *Canada française*, 25 (1938), p. 927.

24. J.C. McGee, "Niveau de vie versus famille," *Culture*, 10 (1949), pp. 412-16; 11 (1950), pp. 85-85, 177-81.

25. Hervé Blais, *Les tendances eugénistes au Canada* (Montréal, 1942); Blais, "L'Eugénisme au Canada," *Culture*, 2 (1941), pp. 324-37; Jacques Rousseau, *L'Hérédité et l'homme* (Montréal, 1945), pp. 196-212.

26. Lapierre, "Les campagnes," p. 360.

27. Blais, *Les tendances*, p. 120. See also *Catholic Register*, 3 November 1938, p. 4.

28. M.C. Forest, "Que faut-il penser de l'eugénisme?" *Revue dominicaine*, 36 (1930), p. 364.

29. P. Louis Marie Lalonde, *L'Hérédité: Manuel de génétique* (La Trappe, 1936), p. 417; see also R.P.C. Chaput and Dr. P. Dumas, *La méthode Ogino-Knaus* (Montréal, 1935). The rhythm method, based on the discoveries of Ogino and Knaus, was so unreliable that an unexpected child was referred to by some in Quebec as "un petit Ogino." See *Magazine Maclean*, 5 (December, 1965), p. 67.

30. The SERENA movement was begun by Gilles and Rita Breault, who trained other couples in the "symptothermal method." See Marie-Paule Doyle, "Serena Canada: Twenty Years of Family Planning in Action," in C. Addy, ed., *Family Planning and Social Work in Canada* (Ottawa, 1977) pp. 30-39.

31. Virginia Thompson, "Some Religious Views on Family Planning," in Ben Schlesinger, ed., *Family Planning in Canada: A Source Book* (Toronto, 1974). On the attempts of the Church to hold on to its female parishioners, see Le collectif Clio, *L'Histoire des femmes au Québec depuis quatre siècles* (Montréal, 1982), pp. 400-04; on reforms in Quebec in divorce and civil marriage complementing birth control, see Susan Mann Trofimenkoff, *The Dream of a Nation: A Social and Intellectual History of Quebec* (Toronto, 1982), p. 318.

32. *Relations*, 26 (1966), pp. 325-27; 28 (1968), pp. 309-11. On the liberal Catholic stance, see also Norman St. John Stevas, *The Agonizing Choice* (London, 1971), pp. 322-25.

33. On a comparison with other countries, see Marilyn Jane Field, *The Comparative Politics of Birth Control: Determinants of Policy Variations and Change in Developed Nations* (New York, 1983).

34. On the prosecution of Harold Fine, see the Toronto *Globe and Mail*, 26 April 1961, p. 4; 28 April 1961, p. 6.

35. *A Short History of Planned Parenthood of Toronto* (Toronto, n.d.).

36. The IPPF was created in Stockholm in 1953 as a continuation of Margaret Sanger's efforts to co-ordinate international efforts in the family planning field. See Beryl Suitters, *Be Brave and Angry: Chronicles of the International Planned Parenthood Federation* (London, 1973). On the Cadburys, see the Toronto *Daily Star*, 14 July 1973, p. 93.

37. See Kaufman to George Cadbury, 5 May 1953, 18 March 1957, Barbara

Cadbury Library, Planned Parenthood of Toronto.

38. Barbara Cadbury, "Birth Control as Social Policy," *Canadian Welfare* (January, 1968), pp. 12-17.

39. *International Planned Parenthood Federation Reports*, 7 (1964), p. 24.

40. See C. Tietze *et al.*, "The Teaching of Fertility Regulation in Medical Schools," *Canadian Medical Association Journal*, 94 (1966), pp. 717-22; C.W. Schwenger, "Population and Family Planning in Public Health," *Canadian Journal of Public Health*, 59 (July, 1968), pp. 278-79.

41. *House of Commons Debates*, 11 (1951), pp. 1869-78, 1888-92.

42. *Financial Post*, 18 February 1961, pp. 1, 7, 8; 11 May 1963, p. 36; 1 June 1963, p. 28. Canadian women were first informed about the new contraceptive by Gerald Angelin, "The Pill That Could Shake the World," *Chatelaine* (October, 1953), pp. 16-17, 99.

43. *Canadian Journal of Public Health*, 59 (1968), p. 257; Edward Shorter, "Twenty-Five Years on the Pill," *Weekend Magazine*, 18 August 1979, pp. 14-16.

44. See Jacques Henripin and Nicole Marcil-Gratton, "L'Avortement, la contraception et la fécondité au Québec et au Canada," in J.J. Levy and A. Dupras, eds., *La Sexualité au Québec* (Montréal, 1981), p. 302.

45. See, for example, C.G. Darwin, *The Next Million Years* (London, 1952); Fairfield Osborn, ed., *Our Crowded Planet: Essays on the Pressures of Population* (New York, 1962); J.B. McGeachy, "H Bomb Warfare or Birth Control: Choice for an Overgrown Race," *Financial Post*, 16 June 1965, p. 7.

46. Field, *Comparative Politics*, p. 207.

47. *Maclean's*, 4 March 1964, p. 4; 21 March 1964, pp. 11, 36; 2 May 1966, p. 2.

48. Toronto *Globe and Mail*, 12 October 1936, p. 17.

49. Radwanski, *Trudeau*, pp. 90-95; Walter Stewart, *Shrug: Trudeau in Power* (Toronto, 1971), p. 12.

50. Jeffrey Weeks, *Sex, Politics and Society: The Regulation of Sexuality Since 1800* (London, 1981), pp. 249-59.

51. Cited in Suitters, *Be Angry*, p. 387. In 1978 the Family Planning Division of the National Department of Health and Welfare was dismantled by the Liberal government as an economy measure.

52. See R.M. Salas, *International Population Assistance: The First Decade* (New York, 1979).

53. The first public call for reform of the abortion law was by Joan Finnigan, "Should Canada Change its Abortion Law?" *Chatelaine* (August, 1959), pp. 17, 103-05. See also R.S. Rodgers, *Sex and Law in Canada* (Ottawa, 1962), p. 66; Wendell W. Watters, *Compulsory Parenthood: The Truth About Abortion* (Toronto, 1976).

54. *Canadian Medical Association Journal*, 97 (1967), p. 1233.

55. Eleanor Wright Pelrine, *Abortion in Canada* (Toronto, 1972), p. 32.

56. Beaujot, "Canada's Population," p. 8.

57. Henripin and Marcil-Gratton, "L'Avortement," p. 302.

58. "Abortion," *New Canadian Encyclopedia*.

59. See *Chatelaine*, 43 (June, 1970), p. 4; 43 (September, 1970), p. 1; 43 (October, 1970), pp. 34-35, 80; 44 (March, 1971), pp. 23, 62-63; Pelrine, *Abortion*, p. 105.

60. Eleanor Wright Pelrine, *Morgentaler: The Doctor Who Couldn't Turn Away* (Toronto, 1975); Catherine Germain and Sylvie Dupont, *Henry Morgentaler: un entretien* (Montréal, 1976).

61. Robin F. Badgley, *Report on the Operation of the Abortion Law* (Ottawa, 1977); Larry D. Collins, "The Politics of Abortion," *Atlantis*, 7 (1982), pp. 2-20; Mary F. Bishop, "The Politics of Abortion: Trends in Canadian Fertility Policy by Larry Collins – revisited," *Atlantis*, 8 (1983), pp. 105-18.

62. Surveys carried out in 1985 indicated that 53 per cent of Canadians were pro-choice and only 4 to 16 per cent were strongly opposed to abortion. A majority was not in favour of free-standing clinics but simply wanted better access made available to hospitals. Toronto *Globe and Mail*, 15 June 1985, p. 1. See also Ann Collins, *The Big Evasion: Abortion, The Issue that Won't Go Away* (Toronto, 1985); Kathleen McDonnell, *Not an Easy Choice: A Feminist Re-examines Abortion* (Toronto, 1984).

Conclusion

1. See an account of similarly contradictory trends in America in Mary P. Ryan, "Reproduction in American History," *Journal of Interdisciplinary History*, 10 (1979), pp. 319-32.

2. For Sanger, see Gordon, *Woman's Body, Woman's Right*; for Stopes, see Hall, *Passionate Pilgrim: The Life of Marie Stopes*.

3. As the Badgley report notes, there are marked regional disparities in access to abortion. According to one representative of a city agency who reported to the Badgley committee, "It is impossible for one hospital in a province to handle the total number of requests. A great number of women in our province are forced to seek abortions in the United States. This is costly and excludes the women under a certain income." Robin F. Badgely, *Report on the Operation of the Abortion Law* (Ottawa, 1977), p. 160.

4. Anne Oakley, *Subject Women* (Oxford, 1981), p. 65.

5. Lorna Marsden, "Family Planning and Women's Rights in Canada," in Benjamin Schlesinger, ed., *Family Planning in Canada: A Source Book*, (Toronto, 1974), p. 87. For the argument that what is needed is not a better contraceptive but a better relationship between men and women, see Diane Kinnon, "The Birth Control Gap," *Healthsharing* (Spring, 1985), pp. 15-18.

6. M. Fitzgerald, C. Guberman, and M. Wolfe, eds., *Still Ain't Satisfied: Canadian Feminism Today* (Toronto, 1982). Even earlier Canadian feminists launched themselves into the campaign for freer access to birth control information. *The Birth Control Handbook* produced by Donna Cherniak

and Allan Feingold at McGill in 1968 had been distributed to 50,000 readers by 1969. See *Women Unite!* (Toronto, 1972), pp. 109-13, 121-24.

7. Canadian Advisory Council on the Status of Women, *Ten Years Later* (Ottawa, 1979.).

8. For the definition of reproductive technologies as "all forms of biomedical interventions and 'help' a woman may encounter when she considers having – or not having – a child," see R. Arditti, R.D. Klein, and S. Minden, eds., *Test Tube Women* (London, 1984), p. 1.

9. J. Hanmer and P. Allen, "Reproductive Engineering: The Final Solution?" *Feminist Studies*, 2 (1982), p. 72.

10. A. Côté, "Fécondation in Vitrio: Du devoir conjugale à l'immaculée conception," *La Vie en Rose*, 22 (December, 1984-January, 1985), p. 18.

11. Kathleen McDonnell, "Claim No Easy Victories: The Fight for Reproductive Rights," in Fitzgerald *et al.*, eds., *Still Ain't Satisfied*, p. 40. The agenda for future struggles over reproduction are spelled out in Connie Clements, "A Case for Lay Abortion," *Healthsharing* (Winter, 1983), pp. 9-14; Thomas Schapiro, *Population Control Politics* (Philadelphia, 1985).

Index

THE CANADIAN
SOCIAL HISTORY SERIES

Terry Copp,
*The Anatomy of Poverty: The Condition of the Working Class
in Montreal 1897-1929,* 1974.

Gregory S. Kealey, Peter Warrian, Editors,
Essays in Canadian Working Class History, 1976.

Alison Prentice,
*The School Promoters: Education and Social Class
in Mid-Nineteenth Century Upper Canada,* 1977.

Susan Mann Trofimenkoff and Alison Prentice, Editors,
*The Neglected Majority:
Essays in Canadian Women's History,* 1977.

John Herd Thompson,
The Harvests of War: The Prairie West, 1914-1918, 1978.

Donald Avery,
*"Dangerous Foreigners": European Immigrant Workers
and Labour Radicalism in Canada, 1896-1932,* 1979.

Joy Parr, Editor,
Childhood and Family in Canadian History, 1982.

Howard Palmer,
*Patterns of Prejudice:
A History of Nativism in Alberta,* 1982.

Tom Traves, Editor,
Essays in Canadian Business History, 1984.

Alison Prentice and Susan Mann Trofimenkoff, Editors,
*The Neglected Majority:
Essays in Canadian Women's History,* Volume 2, 1985.

Ruth Roach Pierson,
*"They're Still Women After All":
The Second World War and Canadian Womanhood,* 1986.

Bryan D. Palmer, Editor,
*The Character of Class Struggle: Essays in Canadian Working-
Class History, 1850-1985,* 1986

Angus McLaren and Arlene Tigar McLaren,
*The Bedroom and the State:
The Changing Practices and Politics of Contraception and
Abortion in Canada, 1880-1980,* 1986.